American Indian Leaders

AMERICAN INDIAN LEADERS

Studies in Diversity

Edited by
R. DAVID EDMUNDS

UNIVERSITY OF NEBRASKA PRESS
LINCOLN AND LONDON

For Jeri, my wife and my friend

First Bison Book printing: 1980
Most recent printing indicated by first digit below:
1   2   3   4   5   6   7   8   9   10

Library of Congress Cataloging in Publication Data
Main entry under title:

American Indian leaders.

Includes index.
1. Indians of North America—Biography. I. Edmunds, Russell David,
1939–
E89.A48   970.004'97   [B]   80–431
ISBN 0–8032–1800–1
ISBN 0–8032–6705–3 pbk.

Contents

Introduction   vii

Old Briton   1
R. David Edmunds

Joseph Brant   21
James O'Donnell

Alexander McGillivray   41
Michael D. Green

Red Bird   64
Martin Zanger

John Ross   88
Gary E. Moulton

Satanta   107
Donald Worcester

Washakie   131
Peter M. Wright

Sitting Bull   152
Herbert T. Hoover

Quanah Parker   175
William T. Hagan

Dennis Bushyhead   192
H. Craig Miner

Carlos Montezuma   206
Peter Iverson

Peter MacDonald   222
Peter Iverson

The Contributors   243

Index   245

A section of photographs follows p. 114.

Introduction

R. DAVID EDMUNDS

THROUGHOUT history, Indian leaders and their methods of leadership have both perplexed and fascinated other Americans. When the first Europeans arrived on the eastern shore of what is now the United States, they encountered Indian people indigenous to the region and immediately sought out tribal leaders through whom problems in Indian-white relations could be mediated. But the colonists arrived in the New World burdened with the cultural baggage of the old World. A product of the Renaissance, the colonists were citizens of newly emerging nation-states, and they assumed that Native American political institutions reflected a similar pattern of centralized power, kings or princes, and royal lineages. Therefore, they referred to "Indian nations," Indian potentates (*King* Phillip is a good example), and Indian "princesses" such as Pocahontas.

Native American peoples of the eastern seaboard, however, were not organized into nation-states. Most tribes were loose confederations of people speaking the same language, sharing a similar way of life, belonging to common clans, and tracing their origin back to an identical beginning. Most tribes were scattered among several villages and the political ties between these settlements were usually tenuous. Only rarely did tribal leaders emerge who represented the entire tribe. More often, each village or group of villages was led by village leaders who attempted to defend the interests of their particular community. Therefore, part of a tribe could go to war while another part remained at peace. Treaties or agreements signed by leaders from some villages were often ignored or opposed by residents of others. Such a loose political structure bewildered Europeans and created confusion in relationships between the two races.

Among most tribes of the East Coast there was also a divison of leadership based on function. The village chiefs (sometimes called peace chiefs) generally were older men with long experience as tribal counselors. They guided the village members during their everyday existence. Village chiefs gave advice to tribal members, mediated minor disputes, and often represented their people in negotiations with other friendly tribes. Their position of leadership was not based upon any formal statute, but, like that of patriarchs of the Old Testament, rested upon the respect and compliance of their followers. Village chiefs were frequently the leaders of clans, extended family units comprising much of the population of a particular village.

In contrast, war chiefs were leading warriors who traditionally exercised authority only during periods of intertribal warfare. Often younger men, war chiefs were leaders whose past success on the warpath had earned them the respect and confidence of their peers. Other warriors joined with them because they were successful; they inflicted maximum losses on their enemies while suffering minimum losses among their followers. Some tribes had warrior societies, organizations of young men dedicated to defending the tribe from its enemies. Among tribes with such societies, war chiefs often occupied positions of prominence in these associations. During periods of peace, however, a war chief held no more authority than any other respected warrior in the tribe.

In comparison to European political leaders, both peace and war chiefs exercised only limited control over their followers. Unlike that of Old World sovereigns who held a mortal power over their people, a peace chief's authority was limited primarily to persuasion and his ability to reflect the attitudes and values of his tribesmen. He led because he epitomized the will of his people. If a significant number of the people in his village disagreed with him, they turned to another leader and his power diminished. Most Indian villages were rife with factionalism, a problem that greatly limited the influence of any particular peace chief. He could not force those tribesmen who disagreed with him to accept his decisions. If the factionalism became too intense, villages split and opposing factions formed new villages. Similarly, war chiefs did not "command" the tribesmen in their war parties. They led only because their followers had confidence in them. If the war chief insisted upon policies opposed by individual warriors, those individuals were free to leave the war party and return to their homes.

As the white frontier spread west across the continent, the role of the war chiefs increased. Because many of the tribes were forced to fight for their lands, military leaders exercised a growing influence among their people. The war chiefs had formerly led their tribe only during periods of war, but since the Indians now saw themselves as continually threatened by white men, they regularly turned to their war chiefs for advice and counsel. Although many village chiefs opposed this changing pattern of leadership, they seemed powerless to stop it.

Because the war chiefs played such leading roles in the confrontations with whites, they are the leaders who emerge from the pages of history. It is ironic that both white historians and the general public have been more interested in those leaders who opposed American policy than in many other Indians who tried to maintain friendly relations with the frontiersmen.

Such warriors are the subject of Alvin M. Josephy's fine volume *The Patriot Chiefs: A Chronicle of American Indian Resistance*. Originally published in 1961, the book has become one of the most frequently adopted texts in Indian history and Native American studies courses. Written in a clear, straightforward style, the volume contains nine chapters focusing on such leaders as King Phillip, Pontiac, Tecumseh, and Crazy Horse. Josephy is generally sympathetic to his subjects and portrays their resistance to white culture as a logical, patriotic struggle of Indian people against oppression. But as Josephy states in the foreword to his volume, "there were many other leaders of heroic stature" who also "were, in a way, patriots too, in that they recognized the inevitabilities of historic situations and tried peacefully to find paths of security for their peoples." It is leaders such as these, as well as others, who will be discussed in the pages of this book.

Upon close examination, Indian leadership has manifested itself in a wide variety of patterns. Some chiefs, like the subjects of Josephy's essays, have violently resisted any compromise with the European or American invaders. Two chapters in this volume focus upon such men. Donald Worcester's essay on Satanta and Herbert T. Hoover's depiction of Sitting Bull both describe Indian leaders dedicated to maintaining their people's traditional way of life. Like their fathers before them, both Satanta and Sitting Bull preferred to range across the plains, following the buffalo herds. When they saw that their way of life was threatened, both men struck back in the time-honored manner of warriors. Ultimately they were defeated, imprisoned, and their tribes confined to reservations. But they remained leaders of their people. After his return to Standing Rock, Sitting Bull continued to oppose the acculturation programs of the government. He eventually turned to the messianic promises of the Ghost Dance, hoping for a religious deliverance for the Sioux. His adherence to his ideals eventually cost the Hunkpapa his life. Satanta's shackles were more formal. In order to leave jail and rejoin his family, he acquiesced in part to the white man's demands. But after he was unjustly returned to prison he sought freedom in the only manner remaining to him: suicide. Both men's reputations have continued to grow since their death and they have now become symbols of the plains tribes' fight to retain their homeland.

Other Indian leaders provide interesting case studies in red diplomacy. Realizing that various European powers were contesting among themselves for control of the North American continent, some chiefs attempted to ally their people with one or more of the European powers, hoping that such an alliance would prove to their tribe's advantage. During the colonial period, Old Briton of the Miamis epitomized this pattern of Indian leadership. Aware of his people's dependence on European trade goods, the Miami leader withdrew from the French confederacy and sought closer economic and military ties with the British colonies. He anticipated that his association with the British would both increase the flow of trade goods to his village and give the Miamis a measure of political freedom denied them under the French. Unfortunately, Old Briton relied too heavily on British promises; and when the French sent a military force against his village, he paid the ultimate price for his miscalculation.

Like Old Briton, the Mohawk leader Thayendenegea, or Joseph Brant, also allied himself and his people with the British during a colonial war, the American Revolution. Once again the British were unable to protect their Indian allies, and the Mohawk lands were overrun and occupied by the colonists. But in

Brant's case, the British at least provided a refuge for him and his people, establishing the Grand River Reserve in Ontario. James O'Donnell's article also illustrates that Brant fits another picture of Indian leadership that began to emerge in the late eighteenth and early nineteenth centuries: tribal leaders who have the rudiments of a formal European education. Brant's familiarity with European ideas facilitated his acculturation toward the image of a British gentleman and shaped his later life at his estate on the Grand River in Canada.

A formal education at boarding schools in Charleston, South Carolina, enabled another Indian diplomat, Alexander McGillivray, to protect his people's interests in the decade following the American Revolution. As Michael Green demonstrates, McGillivray shrewdly used his knowledge of both American and European politics to ally his Creek kinsmen first with Spain, then with the United States, in a desperate attempt to safeguard their homeland. Like Old Briton, McGillivray understood his tribesmen's dependence on trade goods, and like Joseph Brant he eventually adopted many tenets of European culture, but he was more successful than either of them in his attempts to manipulate American and Spanish officials to the Creeks' advantage. In addition, McGillivray represented a pattern of Native American leadership that was particularly important in Indian-white relations in the South. He was of mixed-blood lineage, and although his actions proved beneficial to his people, they also were financially rewarding to himself.

Mixed-blood leaders have played a critical role in Indian-white relations within the region comprising the modern state of Oklahoma. Gary Moulton's chapter outlining the career of John Ross indicates that this acculturated Cherokee leader spent his life working within the white man's system to protect his people and their property. Although only one-eighth Cherokee by blood, Ross fought doggedly to keep the Cherokees from being removed from their homes in Georgia and Tennessee to present-day Oklahoma. Although Ross's efforts failed, he continued to serve the tribe as "principal chief" during the post-removal and Civil War period. Tragically, Ross's career illustrates one of the major problems plaguing Indian leadership in the nineteenth century: factionalism. The existence of factions within many of the tribes impeded efforts by tribal leaders to unify their people. Non-Indians also took advantage of the factionalism, often profiting at the Indians' expense. Unfortunately, such factionalization continues to impede modern Native American politics.

Dennis Bushyhead, another acculturated mixed-blood leader, also had difficulty in unifying the Cherokee Nation. Like John Ross, Bushyhead was determined to defend the sovereignty of his tribe from state and federal encroachment. A product of the "Gilded Age," Bushyhead appreciated the great political influence held by large corporations during the 1880s and decided that the Cherokees' only chance for survival lay in developing a partnership with the business community. If major railroad or mining companies were granted special privileges in the Cherokee Nation, perhaps they would use their political influence to assist the tribe in defending its special status against the United States. Craig Miner discusses this unique approach to tribal leadership and shows that Bushyhead, like McGillivray, sometimes profited from his political leadership of the tribe.

William T. Hagan's essay on Quanah Parker destroys one myth associated with the famous Comanche chief, but illustrates that Parker exemplifies another pattern of Indian leadership quite common throughout the reservation period. Although local legends in southwestern Oklahoma and northern Texas still champion Quanah Parker as the foremost Comanche war chief, Hagan points out that Parker, born in 1849, was too young to serve as a leader of war parties during the prereservation days. Rather, during the reservation period, Parker rapidly rose to a position of leadership. Since older, more traditional chiefs either died or abdicated their power, federal agents chose to work through Parker in dealing with the tribe. His subsequent control of annuities and grazing leases enabled the young mixed-blood to attain a position of prominence among his people. Like McGillivray, Bushyhead, and others, Parker used his political influence for personal gain. Local myth aside, cooperation, rather than resistance, was the key to Quanah Parker's success.

Cooperation with federal authorities also contributed to the ascendancy of Washakie, the most influential leader among the Wind River Shoshones. Although Washakie rose to prominence as a typical war chief, his decision to ally his people with the white man against their Indian enemies proved beneficial for both Washakie and his tribe. As Peter Wright indicates, the Shoshones needed the assistance of federal troops to defend their homeland from the more numerous Sioux, Cheyennes, and Arapahoes. Working with government officials, Washakie safeguarded Shoshone interests and finally secured a reservation in the most desirable part of the Shoshone homeland. Washakie's career represents one of the few instances in which traditional, non-acculturated leaders have been successful in cooperating fully with the federal government, both before and during the reservation period.

In contrast, Carlos Montezuma seemed to cooperate with almost no one. Peter Iverson's chapter on Montezuma illustrates that Montezuma, like many other acculturated Indian leaders at the turn of the century, was torn between an adherence to white values and a loyalty to his people. In many ways Montezuma exemplified what white reformers wanted Indians to be: educated, urbane, and progressive. But the Yavapai leader was drawn back to the tribal communities. Concerned over substandard economic and health conditions on the reservations, he blamed the Bureau of Indian Affairs and lashed out at the government through his newspaper, *Wassaja*. Although Montezuma's leadership reflects Native American attempts to develop a pan-Indian movement, it also indicates the uncertainty and confusion prevalent both in Indian policy and among the Indian communities during the first decades of the twentieth century.

As Iverson's second essay points out, the Navajo Peter MacDonald epitomizes the dynamic leadership needed by Native Americans in the late twentieth century. Like a number of other successful Indian leaders, MacDonald is a product of two cultures, having grown up within the Navajo community but educated at a major university. Yet like leaders from the past, MacDonald used his ability to acquire services from the government as a base for his rise to power within the tribe. Today, the problems facing MacDonald and the Navajo Nation are typical of the issues facing other reservation communities, for example, how to provide for economic opportunity on the reservations without disrupting the traditional ways of the people. The vast supplies of coal and uranium on the Navajo Reservation will continue to be much in demand. MacDonald and other tribal leaders are determined that such resources will be developed only under Navajo control. The outcome of this modern Indian-white confrontation still remains uncertain.

Finally, Martin Zanger's discussion of the Winnebago chief Red Bird and the Winnebago uprising of 1827 illustrates that one of the most common patterns of historic Indian leadership may result as much from white attitudes as from any action on the part of the Native Americans. As Zanger illustrates, Red Bird was a local Winnebago leader from western Wisconsin. Although he played only a minor part in the uprising, he surrendered to white authorities. Yet both government officials and white historians have exaggerated his role in the affair, depicting him as the originator of a widespread conspiracy. After his capture he was described in "noble savage" terms by his white captors, who sought to inflate their own importance by increasing the prestige of their foe. In retrospect, other historically famous Indian leaders may have benefited (or suffered) from similar aggrandizement.

Of course there are many other patterns of Indian leadership. Some Native Americans exercised considerable influence within their particular village or tribe, but since their endeavors were abstruse or were focused upon domestic concerns, they remain relatively unknown to the outside world. The formidable controls exercised by Iroquois women partially fit this pattern of Indian leadership. Other Native Americans, such as the Shawnee Prophet or Wovoka, held great sway as religious leaders, and they too exercised a powerful influence over their people. But the varieties of Indian political leadership within the realm of Indian-white relations remains so broad that it was decided to limit this volume to that type of leadership. And even within this framework there are many more leaders who made intriguing and significant contributions. It is hoped that the essays in this book will be of value to students of American Indian history as well as to lay readers interested in the history of the United States.

Old Briton

R. David Edmunds

THE MIDDLE YEARS of the eighteenth century were traumatic times for the Indian people of the Great Lakes and Ohio Valley. For over seven decades many of the tribesmen had maintained a close relationship with the government of New France. Jesuit priests from Montreal had entered their villages, founding missions and converting souls to Christianity. Meanwhile, French traders and explorers had traversed the west, establishing trading centers and military posts along major waterways. Unfortunately for the Indians, however, the rapid spread of the fur trade soon broke down the self-sufficiency of the tribes. Responding to the demand for fur, Indian hunters spent their efforts trapping beaver and muskrat, bartering the pelts for powder, lead, and other merchandise available from French traders. Originally, such commodities had been luxury items, but by the mid-1700s they had become necessities. Enmeshed in the fur trade, the tribesmen needed the products of European technology to provide for their families.

Yet the French often could not supply their red allies with adequate amounts of such provisions. New France was forced to import almost all her trade goods, and both French traders and military posts in the west suffered a perennial shortage of trade merchandise. Although military officers were generous with their gifts and French traders gave their Indian customers liberal credit, the Frenchmen frequently did not have enough lead and powder to meet the tribesmen's demands. Moreover, even during periods of relative abundance, French goods remained expensive. Since French officials leased many of the western trading posts to the highest bidder, the traders attempted to

1

recoup the cost of the lease by charging higher prices for their merchandise.

In contrast, British trade goods, when they were available to the western tribes, were much less expensive. Although British merchants were also forced to import part of their merchandise, by the mid-1700s some goods destined for the Indian trade were being inexpensively produced in the colonies. In addition, several groups of British traders continually vied for the western trade, and the competition kept the prices down.[1]

For the western tribesmen, the problem was not the cost of British goods, but gaining access to them. Realizing they could not compete economically with the British, French officials relied on their greater military power in the west. French agents warned British traders to remain east of the Appalachians, and French military posts in Michigan and Indiana sent out patrols to guard such waterways as Lake Erie and the Ohio River. Meanwhile, tribes particularly loyal to New France, especially the Potawatomis, Ottawas, and Chippewas, assisted the French in turning back British traders and in keeping the other Indians within the French alliance.

Not all the western tribes were happy with the French trade monopoly. During the early 1740s part of the Hurons had abandoned their villages near Detroit and moved to the Sandusky Bay region to gain better access to British traders. The discontent spread to other tribes. Along the upper Wabash, Miami warriors complained bitterly about the shortage of French trade goods and met secretly, seeking opportunities to trade their furs to the British.[2]

Among the Miami malcontents, La Demoiselle, a prominent chief of the Piankashaw band, emerged as the most outspoken critic of the French trading system. Although La Demoiselle's village was located in northwestern Indiana, near modern Fort Wayne, the old chief had lived earlier along the lower Wabash and had traveled extensively on the Ohio, where he frequently met British traders. Thoroughly convinced of the superiority of British merchandise, he had always encouraged trade with the British and was much disliked by the French. Indeed, the old chief's affinity for the British was so well known that his friends had christened him "Old Briton," and he answered as often to that nickname as to "La Demoiselle."

Angered by the inability of the French to provide his people with adequate goods, Old Briton hoped to withdraw the Miamis from the French alliance. Once the ties with the French were broken, he believed that British traders would flock into the Ohio Valley, providing his people with inexpensive merchandise and making the Miami villages important centers of commerce in the west. The chief also argued that a break with New France would be politically advantageous. No longer subservient to French Indian policy, the Miamis could ostensibly ally themselves with the British. Since British political control over tribes in the west always had been minimal, the Miamis would actually achieve an independence of action they had been denied under the French. Perhaps his people could emerge at the fulcrum of power in the Ohio Valley, holding the balance between the British and the French and manipulating both sides to their own advantage. Regardless of the outcome, the Miamis were suffering under the French, and almost any type of British alliance was better than starvation.

The major problem facing Old Briton was how to effect the break with New France. The Miami chief realized that any attempt to lead part of his tribesmen away from the French toward closer ties with the British would be strenuously opposed by both New France and pro-French Indians. In fact, many of his kinsmen still remained loyal to New France, and other Miami chiefs jealous of his growing influence would use their authority to either stop or limit such a defection. As it turned out, dissident Hurons eventually provided the catalyst for Miami action.

At Sandusky, Nicolas, a pro-British Huron chief, actively plotted against the French. Influenced by both the Senecas and British traders, Nicolas hoped to bring all the western tribes into a general plan to attack the French forts. Early in 1747 Huron and Seneca messengers arrived in the Miami villages urging Old Briton and his followers to attack Fort Miamis, a French post at the headwaters of the Maumee River. They informed the Miamis that Nicolas intended to attack Detroit, that the Chippewas would fall upon Michilimackinac, and that other tribes had also agreed to rise up against their French allies. Believing that such a general uprising would ensure success, Old Briton readily agreed to join the conspiracy. Such a large-scale revolt might deny the Miamis a

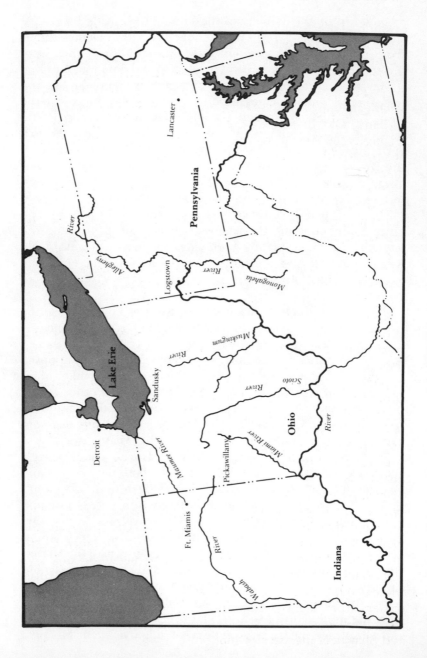

position of dominance in the fur trade, but it certainly would give them access to British traders.

But the Huron plot failed. French officers at Detroit learned of the conspiracy and thwarted Nicolas's attempts to capture their post. The Chippewas killed a few French traders in northern Michigan but made no attempt to assault Michilimackinac. In Indiana, Old Briton and his followers attacked Fort Miamis, seizing eight French soldiers and burning part of the stockade, but the Miami leader was reluctant to kill his prisoners. Aware that Nicolas had failed, he evidently feared that he and his followers might be singled out for French retribution. Moreover, with the failure of the general uprising, many Miamis remained reluctant to break with New France and interceded on the captives' behalf, urging Old Briton to release them.

Although new messengers arrived from the Hurons urging Old Briton to continue the attacks on the French, the old chief learned that Nicolas had abandoned his village at Sandusky and had sought sanctuary in eastern Ohio. Miamis returning from Lake Erie informed him that the Chippewas had sued for peace and that the French garrison at Detroit had been reinforced with fresh troops from Canada. The uprising obviously had failed, but the disarray in the west now provided the Miami leader with an opportunity to at least withdraw from the French system and seek closer ties with the British. During the autumn of 1747 he led all the Miamis who would follow away from their villages along the Wabash and Maumee to a new town, Pickawillany, at the juncture of the Great Miami River and Loramie's Creek, in western Ohio.[3]

Pickawillany occupied a site well chosen for Old Briton's purposes. He believed the village was removed far enough from French posts to make it generally inaccessible to French military power. Any major French expedition against the town could be intercepted by Miami scouts who would warn Old Briton and his men of the enemy's approach. Yet the site was sufficiently close to the western Indians that tribesmen from Michigan, Indiana, and Illinois might easily venture there to barter their fur for British trade goods. Moreover, the new village was readily accessible to traders from Pennsylvania and Virginia, merchants who had already established small trading centers among the Delawares and Shawnees in eastern Ohio.

Eager to develop ties with the British, Old Briton got in touch with Shawnee and Seneca tribesmen during the winter of 1747–48 and asked them to intercede with the British in the Miamis' behalf. He boasted that with adequate trade goods he could easily detach large numbers of the western Indians from the French alliance, and that at least a dozen villages were only awaiting his message before leaving the French and joining him at Pickawillany. In reply, the Senecas asked Old Briton to wait until the following spring, when they would escort the old chief and his counselors to Pennsylvania. Meanwhile, both the Senecas and the Shawnees met with colonial officials, advising them of Old Briton's requests and making preliminary arrangements for the meeting.[4]

The Miami request struck a responsive chord among traders and political officials in Pennsylvania. Frontier merchants such as George Croghan and Christopher Gist had earlier been active among the Shawnees and dissident Hurons, but the chance to establish a trading post among the Miamis in western Ohio offered promise of spectacular profits. They urged Governor James Hamilton to appoint commissioners to meet with the Miamis and to conclude a formal treaty with the tribe. Envisioning an opportunity to weaken the French alliance and to expand British political control in the Ohio Valley, Hamilton informed the Senecas that he would welcome the Miamis in Philadelphia.

In June 1748, the Senecas and Shawnees told Hamilton that they soon would escort the Miami delegation to Pennsylvania. Although Old Briton had chosen to remain at Pickawillany, he had sent three tribesmen, including his son Assapausa, to meet with the officials. Held at Lancaster, the council began on July 19 and lasted for five days. Since the Miamis spoke no English, their speeches were translated by Andrew Montour, a mixed-blood Oneida employed by the British Indian Service.

At first Assapausa and his companions spoke with the British treaty commissioners, convincing them that Old Briton and his followers were "really and sincerely come off from the French and heartily in the British interest." Boasting that they represented all the Miamis (even those still loyal to New France), the Miami spokesmen presented the commissioners with wampum, a calumet, and thirty beaver pelts designed to catch the attention of the traders in attendance. They also assured the commissioners that several other western tribes could be detached from the French and that Old Briton was eager to initiate such activity.

Impressed by the Miamis' sincerity, the commissioners admitted Old Briton and his people into the realm of British "Friendship and Alliance." They assured the Miami delegates that the Miamis were now "our own Flesh and Blood, and what hurts them will equally hurt us." They promised the Miamis that if their tribe would have no further association with the French, the British would "exercise unfeigned affection" toward them and would "give [them] assistance on all occasions." After concluding the proceedings with a banquet and other forms of "handsome Entertainment," the Miami delegates and British commissioners signed a formal treaty on July 23, 1748. The Miamis then traded several bales of beaver pelts they had brought with them and on the following day left for Ohio.[5]

At Pickawillany, Old Briton received the news of the treaty with elation. The British promises of "assistance on all occasions" seemed to assure the Miamis that their new allies would send aid if the French attempted to force them to return to their former homes in the Wabash and Maumee valleys. Moreover, economic ties with the British colonies developed rapidly as British traders followed the Miami delegates back to Ohio. Other Miamis ventured east, carrying pelts to British posts in New York and Pennsylvania. Meanwhile, Old Briton made plans to entice other Indians to his village, sending runners to several tribes in Indiana and Illinois.[6]

Old Briton's flight to Pickawillany and the resulting British treaty caused much concern among French officials in Canada. Envisioning the new village as a direct threat to French control of the Ohio Valley, the Marquis de la Galissonière, acting governor general of New France, made plans to drive the recalcitrant Miamis back from Ohio. During the spring of 1748 he assembled a force of French soldiers and pro-French Indians at La Chine, a village near Montreal on the St. Lawrence River. Hoping to rid Ohio of both Old Briton and the British influence, La Galissonière ordered Pierre-Joseph Celoron, the commander of the force, to go to Pennsylvania and float down the Ohio. Celoron was instructed to post lead plates on the river bank claiming the region for France and to force all British traders back into Pennsylvania. La Galissonière also told Celoron to ascend the Great Miami to Pickawillany, where he was to arrest Old Briton and lead the Miamis back to their former homes.[7]

Celoron and 265 men left La Chine on June 15, 1749. Paddling their canoes up the St. Lawrence, they reached the eastern end of Lake Erie and then portaged across to the headwaters of the Allegheny. They then floated down the Allegheny to its junction with the Monongahela and turned west, following the broad Ohio as it carried them back toward New France.

Celoron's party had been treated coolly by Iroquois tribesmen along the Allegheny, but the French commander hoped that his expedition would overawe the Algonquians along the Ohio and force them to cut their ties with the British colonies. He was sorely mistaken. On August 8 he arrived at Logstown, a large mixed village of Shawnees, Delawares, Mohicans, and a few Iroquois located about eighteen miles downstream from the junction of the Allegheny and Monongahela. Although the tribesmen permitted the French to come ashore, several British traders remained in the village and Celoron received information that the Indians planned to attack his encampment. By keeping his men constantly at arms he forestalled the attack, but three days of conferences with the Indians produced little of value for New France. The British traders promised to withdraw east of the Appalachians and the assembled tribesmen agreed to visit the governor general in Canada, but Celoron had little faith that either promise would be honored. Commenting that Logstown was an evil place "seduced by the alluremants of cheap merchandise furnished by the English," the French officer and his party left the village on August 11, floating down the Ohio toward the west.[8]

During the four days the French party remained in their village, the Indians at Logstown learned of Celoron's intention of surprising Old Briton and dispatched messengers overland to Pickawillany. Forewarned, the Miami chief mustered his supporters, and when Celoron arrived on September 13 he found the villagers at Pickawillany well armed with British muskets and ready for any emergency. Celoron's forces outnumbered the Miamis, but the French commander evidently feared to risk a military confrontation against such a dangerous and well-prepared enemy. Although he ordered the two remaining British traders to leave the village, Celoron decided to negotiate with Old Briton.

Aware that the French were reluctant to use their military superiority, Old Briton agreed to the negotiation. He realized that his warriors were too few to successfully drive the French expedition from their village, but if the French could be coaxed away with false promises, the wily old chief was willing to try. On September 17 he met with Celoron in council, accepted French gifts, and listened attentively as the French commander advised him that the "bones of his ancestors," buried along the Wabash, called him back to his village. Celoron promised Old Briton that all his past transgressions would be forgotten if he would lead his people back into Indiana. He warned the Miami that if he remained at Pickawillany, his people would starve. His expedition, Celoron said, had already intimidated British traders "whom I have notified to retire from off my territories; and if they come back there again they will have reason to be sorry for it."[9]

On the following day, Old Briton gave his formal reply. He informed the French commander that the Miamis at Pickawillany were delighted to see the French and thanked Celoron "for the kind words which you have addressed to us." Old Briton admitted that his people missed "the bones of our forefathers," and acknowledged they were grateful that Celoron had asked them to return to their former home. Assuring the officer that he had "none other but good answers to give you," the chief promised to return to Indiana, but informed the Frenchman that since "the season is too far advanced," the move could not take place until the following spring. Winter was approaching and their old wigwams in Indiana had been burned. The Miamis would be forced to remain at Pickawillany, but they would spend the winter months "correcting our faults . . . and reflecting seriously upon what you have told us." When spring arrived, they would return to Indiana.[10]

Old Briton's speech had a sobering impact on Celoron. Since

wigwams could be constructed with little difficulty, he knew that the Miami chief was simply procrastinating. Still, the Frenchman had been outmaneuvered and was forced to accept the Indian's explanation. Grasping at straws, Celoron tried to persuade Old Briton to accompany the French expedition back to Fort Miamis to make preparations for his people's arrival in the spring, but the Miami wisely declined. Realizing that the conference had reached an impasse, Celoron prepared to leave the village. But before he departed he again spoke to the Miamis, warning them to "be faithful then to your promise." Their French father had been tolerant in the past, but if they persisted in their folly, they would suffer. Celoron assured Old Briton he should "fear the resentment of a father, who has only too much reason to be angry with you, and who has offered you the means of regaining his favor." On September 20, 1749, the French expedition left Pickawillany.[11]

Celoron's failure to force the Miamis to abandon Pickawillany was a great moral victory for Old Briton. The French had sent an army to chase the Miamis home, but he, Old Briton, had stood up to the French officer and refused to surrender his people. Of course he had promised to return to Indiana in the spring, but both the French and the Miamis knew that such an agreement was no more than a charade, a means for the French to temporarily save face and avoid bloodshed. Celoron's threat to stop British traders was meaningless. The French expedition had hardly left Pickawillany before Old Briton dispatched messengers to the British merchants still active among the Shawnees informing them he had refused the French demands and asking them to return to his village.

Encouraged by the old Miami's stubbornness, George Croghan led a large party of British traders to Pickawillany in November 1749, establishing a major British trading center in western Ohio. Old Briton welcomed the merchants into his village and smiled approvingly as the white men unloaded pack horses laden with muskets, powder, lead, bolts of cloth, hardware, foodstuffs, and other necessities. Miami warriors even assisted the traders in erecting several log storehouses and a small stockade. No longer would his people fear the "starving time," the late winter months when the French had always been short of provisions. Now his village would become the most important trading center in the west and Old Briton would be honored over all the other Miami leaders.[12]

Urged on by the British traders, Old Briton spent the winter of 1749–50 attempting to entice other tribesmen to his village. Messengers were sent as far west as Illinois vividly describing the wealth in trade goods available in the Miami village. Other runners sped to the Weas, Piankashaws, Kickapoos, Mascoutens, and Potawatomis. Although the Potawatomis generally refused Old Briton's overtures, the other tribes responded and in the spring sent warriors laden with furs to Pickawillany to trade for British merchandise. The Weas and Piankashaws were particularly susceptible to Old Briton's offers. Both tribes had recently become alienated from the French. During the winter the Piankashaws had suffered from an epidemic, which they assumed was of French origin. Meanwhile, several Wea chiefs had visited Canada, where they believed they had been ignored by French officials. Angered over the alleged insult, the Wea chief Le Comte accepted Old Briton's invitation in May 1750 and led more than three hundred Weas and Piankashaws to Pickawillany.[13]

At first, the French seemed powerless to limit the growing influence of the dissident Miami chief. La Pied Froid and other loyal Miami chiefs assured Celoron that French prestige among the tribes had suffered immeasurably when his expedition had failed to bring Old Briton back from Pickawillany. They also told him that the old chief now laughed at the French and boasted he would never return to Indiana. In late November 1749, officials at Detroit sent a messenger to Pickawillany demanding that Old Briton order Croghan away from the village, but the old chief treated the messenger contemptuously and the man fled back to Michigan thankful to escape with his life. Although pro-French Potawatomis were dispatched to Ohio to intercept British traders bound for Pickawillany, they achieved little success. Finally, during the summer of 1750, French officials attempted to bribe Old Briton into returning. They provided Jean Coeur with an ample supply of trade goods and ordered him to go to Pickawillany to distribute the merchandise as gifts. Old Briton accepted the trade goods, but he refused to return to New France.[14]

The French attempts to bribe the Miamis played into Old Briton's hands. The chief readily informed visiting British traders of the French efforts, describing in detail the attempts to bring him back to Indiana and exaggerating the amount of goods given as presents by Coeur. In the fall of 1750 the traders carried news of the generosity of the French back to Pennsylvania, where it was viewed with alarm. After only two years Pickawillany had already become an important center for Pennsylvania's Indian trade, and colonial officials were anxious to safeguard the Miami chief's loyalty. Commenting, "I am really of the opinion that since so large an addition is made to the Trade of the Province by their Means," Governor James Hamilton persuaded the Pennsylvania assembly to counter the French gifts with bribes of their own. In late November he dispatched George Croghan and several other traders with British presents for the Miamis at Pickawillany.[15]

Croghan arrived in the Miami village on February 17, 1751. Old Briton welcomed the British party and accepted the gifts of trade goods sent by the Pennsylvania assembly. Pleased with his new importance, the old Miami boasted that Pickawillany had become one of the largest villages in Ohio. He also informed Croghan that several villages of Weas and Piankashaws from the lower Wabash now sought closer ties with the British colonies and were sending emissaries to Pickawillany. Encouraged that the British trade network seemed to be expanding, Croghan spent the next few days enlarging and repairing his stockade and storehouse.

The Weas and Piankashaws arrived on February 21 and Old Briton immediately presented them to Croghan and the other traders. Envisioning their villages on the lower Wabash as future bases for an expanding British trade, Croghan presented the newcomers with gifts from his private warehouse. He also offered them a political alliance with the British colonies. The Wea and Piankashaw delegates were eager to trade with the British, but they were surprised at the offer of such formal political ties. Undecided over their reply, they asked for several days to consider the new proposition.

Before the Weas and Piankashaws could reach a decision, their deliberations were interrupted by Miami scouts who reported they had discovered a small party of Ottawas en route for

Pickawillany. Old Briton at first believed the Ottawas were the vanguard of a large French expedition sent against his village. Mustering his warriors, he prepared to defend the village, when other scouts returned, informing him that the Ottawas were alone and only wished to meet with the Miamis. Angered that the disruption might have frightened the visiting Weas and Piankashaws, Old Briton agreed to meet with the Ottawas, but he used the conference to belittle the French and their allies. Standing in stony silence, he watched as the Ottawas entered Pickawillany, carrying a French flag and small gifts of tobacco and brandy. The Ottawas pleaded with the Miamis to return to the French, warning Old Briton that his "French father" had become impatient and "would send for them no more." If the Miamis remained in Ohio, the French and their allies would attack Pickawillany.[16]

To dramatize his reply, Old Briton first presented the Ottawa emissaries with belts of black wampum, symbolic of war. He then chided them for being servants of the French, reminding them that they too had quarreled with the government in Montreal. Vowing never to return to the Wabash, the old chief declared, "We have been taken by the Hand by our Brothers the English, and by the six Nations, and the Delawares, Shannoahs and Wyendotts . . . and as you threaten us with War in the Spring, We tell You if You are angry, We are ready to receive You, and resolve to die here before We will go to You." Seeing that their misson had failed, the Ottawas ended the conference and left Pickawillany.[17]

Encouraged by Old Briton's determination, the Weas and Piankashaws accepted Croghan's offer and signed a treaty of friendship and alliance with the colony of Pennsylvania. They also agreed to accompany the Miamis to an intertribal council, sponsored by the British, to be held at Logstown later in the spring. But in May 1751, when the British and their allies assembled at Logstown, Old Briton and his tribesmen were absent. The Miami chief feared that the French and Ottawas might carry out their threat to attack Pickawillany and he was reluctant to leave his village undefended.[18]

Old Briton's apprehensions were justified. Angered over his continued intransigence, French officials made plans to mount another military expedition against Pickawillany. During the summer of 1751 a small party of French and Indians left Canada for Detroit, where they planned to enlist the aid of other loyal tribesmen, and then march across Ohio to the Miami village. After capturing Old Briton, the French soldiers intended to erect a new military post at Pickawillany.

Fortunately for the Miamis, the plan failed. At Detroit, Celoron attempted to recruit Potawatomi and Ottawa warriors to participate in the expedition, but his efforts proved unsuccessful. Local Ottawas and Potawatomis assured him that they would join in the attack, but they believed that the French were sending a substantial force from Canada. When the French party arrived in Detroit, it numbered only fifty men, and the Ottawas and Potawatomis refused to accompany the expedition. Aware of the large population at Pickawillany, the Detroit tribesmen warned the Sieur de Bellestre, commander of the Canadian party, that his force was much too small to attack Pickawillany. If the French would send more soldiers, the Detroit warriors would assist them. If not, they would wait until a larger expedition could be organized.[19]

Undaunted by the Ottawa and Potawatomi refusals, Bellestre decided to attack Pickawillany on his own. Only eighteen members of the original party would accompany him, but late in the summer he left Detroit for the Miami village. Meanwhile, other Indians from Detroit had informed Old Briton of the refusal of the Potawatomis and Ottawas to accompany the expedition. Evidently believing that the campaign had been abandoned, Old Briton and most of his followers left Pickawillany on their autumn hunt, leaving the village practically deserted. When Bellestre arrived at Pickawillany, the few remaining tribesmen took refuge in the British stockade. The French raiders managed to capture two British traders and to kill an old Miami warrior and his wife, whom they surprised in a cornfield, but there were too few of them to attack the palisade. Disgusted over his lost opportunity, Bellestre returned to Canada.[20]

The French raid against Pickawillany infuriated Old Briton, who now redoubled his efforts against the French. In January 1752, he invited warriors from many tribes to Pickawillany and he urged them to take up the hatchet against New France. To emphasize his commitment, Old Briton ordered three captured French soldiers to be ceremoniously killed and a fourth had his ears cut off before he was sent to the governor of Canada as a warning. Meanwhile, warriors from Pickawillany sped through the forests, attacking French traders and fomenting revolt among the western tribes. On the Wabash, the Piankashaws ambushed French travelers, killing nine traders and two slaves. Wea warriors refused repeated French demands that they report to French posts and fled to the Ohio River, where they conducted British merchants toward the Illinois country. The Shawnees agreed to join the Miamis in a general war against Canada, while farther to the west, on the prairies of Illinois, the Illinois Confederacy, Osages, and other tribes met in council to discuss withdrawing from the French alliance. Even the St. Joseph Potawatomis, the most faithful of the western tribes, were rumored to be wavering in their loyalty to New France.[21]

Fearing the complete collapse of their western alliance, French officials made plans for another expedition against Old Briton's village. In the spring of 1752 they enlisted the assistance of Charles Langlade, a mixed-blood Ottawa from Michilimackinac who held great influence among the northern tribes. Langlade may have accompanied the Ottawas delegation humiliated by Old Briton in February 1751, for he harbored a deep resentment toward the old Miami and was anxious to participate in the planned attack. In May 1752 he led a large war party of Ottawas and Chippewas south down the shores of Lake Huron. Intending to recruit additional warriors in the Detroit region, he planned to move quickly and strike Pickawillany before Old Briton could be warned.

Ironically, while Langlade was en route for Detroit, French officials at Montreal decided to cancel the expedition. Afraid that Langlade also might fail, Governor Duquense feared that another French defeat might spark an open rebellion among the disaffected western tribes. Rather than risk an attack on Pickawillany, he preferred to concentrate all his efforts on preventing British traders from entering Ohio. If the supply of British trade goods could be cut off, there would be no reason for the Miamis to remain at Pickawillany.[22]

Unaware of the change in plans, Langlade passed through De-

troit, where additional Ottawa and Potawatomi warriors swelled
his ranks to about 240 men. Meanwhile, British agents at Oswego
informed Governor Hamilton that the French planned another
attack on Old Briton, but the governor discounted the intelligence as just another rumor. Even if he had wished to rush
assistance to the Miamis, his hands were tied. His Quaker-
dominated assembly had grown reluctant to become enbroiled in
conflicts in Ohio and had even rejected the Wea and Piankashaw
treaty negotiated by Croghan during March 1751. Although they
were eager for an expanded western trade, the Quakers wanted
no part of the frontier warfare.[23]

   At Pickawillany, Old Briton made no preparations to meet the
new threat to his village. Because his conspiracy had spread to all
the surrounding tribes, he expected his neighbors to warn him if
the French planned another expedition. Moreover, the old chief
probably believed that the French could no longer muster
enough warriors to mount a serious attack. Mistakenly secure in
the British alliance, he relied upon assistance from the
Pennsylvanians and the Iroquois if such an attack did come. He
did not protest in mid-June 1752 when most of the warriors from
Pickawillany left the village to hunt along the Ohio. Unaware of
Langlade's raiders, the old Miami believed Pickawillany was safe
from attack, and he, Old Briton, had finally achieved a position of
preeminence among the western Indians.

   He was sorely mistaken. At midmorning on June 21, Langlade's raiders struck Pickawillany so suddenly that many Miami
women were captured in their cornfields. Surprised by the on-
slaught, Old Briton fled to the British stockade, where he tried to
rally the few warriors and British traders left to defend the
village. Meanwhile, Langlade's warriors spread through
Pickawillany, disarming isolated Miami warriors and seizing
Miami and British property. Within the palisade, Old Briton
found he commanded a force of only twenty fighting men,
including a handful of British traders. Throughout the morning
they defended themselves, firing at the French Indians who now
surrounded their stronghold. But the outlook was grim. The
attackers outnumbered them more than ten to one. Moreover,
Langlade held another trump card: he had captured many of the
defenders' families.[24]

Late in the afternoon Langlade called a ceasefire and offered to return his Miami prisoners and to withdraw from the village if Old Briton would leave the stockade and surrender all the British traders. Reluctantly Old Briton agreed. Several of the Miamis and one of the traders in the stockade had already been wounded. The defenders had no water, and among Langlade's Miami prisoners were Old Briton's wife and young son.[25]

Both Old Briton and Langlade violated the terms of the surrender. Although he surrendered five traders, Old Briton hid two others in the stockade. Langlade's breach of promise was much more serious. When Old Briton and his companions emerged from the palisade, Langlade's warriors seized the wounded British trader, stabbed him to death, then cut out his heart and ate it. Old Briton suffered a similar fate. Langlade greatly resented the old Miami's humiliation of the Ottawas. Moreover, he believed that Old Briton was the leading British troublemaker in the west. Determined to make an example of his enemy, Langlade ordered his execution. To add to the drama, after Old Briton's death, the French-allied Indians threw his body into a kettle of water, boiled it, then ate his remains before his trembling tribesmen.[26]

With Old Briton's death, the conspiracy sponsored by the Miamis collapsed. Most of the Miamis at Pickawillany returned to the Wabash and Old Briton's village was deserted. British aspirations received at least a temporary setback and French military power again asserted itself through the Maumee and Wabash valleys. Yet Old Briton's brief bid for power illustrates several facets of Indian-white relations during the colonial period. Most important was the Indians' heavy reliance on European trade goods. It is significant that the periods of greatest Indian unrest in the west coincide with those times when the French were plagued with a shortage of trade merchandise. Also significant is the role played by traders in British political intrigues among the Indians of the Ohio Valley. It is not surprising that merchants such as George Croghan—men with trade goods—emerged as both economic and political mediators between the Indians and the British colonies. Moreover, Old Briton also used the promise of plentiful, inexpensive trade goods as the primary lure to attract other tribesmen to Pickawillany.

Like other Indian leaders who both preceded and followed him, Old Briton attempted to strike a middle ground between two colonial powers. By breaking with the French and allying his people with the British, he hoped to achieve a degree of independence impossible within the political structure of New France. Since Pickawillany was located far to the west, Old Briton hoped that he could act without British restrictions, yet rely on the British alliance for protection. Meanwhile, his personal stature would be enhanced and his people would enjoy the benefits of British trade goods.

But Old Briton put too much stock in British promises. Pennsylvania was eager to extend its western Indian trade and was willing to promise "assistance on all occasions," but colonial officials lacked both the will and the means to honor such guarantees. Old Briton's village was outside the effective realm of British military power and the colonists were unwilling to spend either the money or effort needed to ensure the Miamis' safety. Like Tecumseh and those warriors refused refuge at Fort Miamie after the Battle of Fallen Timbers, Old Briton learned that the British were generous with their promises, but miserly with their military assistance if much risk was involved.

NOTES

1. For a discussion of the British and French trade policies, see Bert Anson, *The Miami Indians* (Norman: University of Oklahoma Press, 1970), p. 42, and W. Neil Franklin, "Pennsylvania-Virginia Rivalry for the Indian Trade of the Ohio Valley," *Mississippi Valley Historical Review* 20 (March 1934): 463–80.

2. "Memorandum of What Has Taken Place . . . in Detroit, 1738–41," *Michigan Pioneer and Historical Collections,* vol. 34 (Lansing, Mich.: Wynkoop, Hallenbeck, and Crawford Co., 1905), pp. 195–202. Also see Charles A. Hanna, *The Wilderness Trail,* vol. 2 (New York: G. P. Putnam's Sons, 1911), p. 165.

3. Events surrounding the Huron revolt are described in "Journal of Occurrences in Canada, 1747–48," *Documents Relative to the Colonial History of the State of New York,* ed. Edward B. O'Callaghan, 15 vols. (Albany, N.Y.: Weed and Parsons, 1853–87), 10:137–45, and in R.

David Edmunds, *The Potawatomis: Keepers of the Fire* (Norman: University of Oklahoma Press, 1978), pp. 42–44.

4. "At the Court House at Lancaster, Wednesday, July 20, 1748," *Minutes of the Provincial Council of Pennsylvania,* vol. 5 (Harrisburg, Pa.: Theo. Finn and Co., 1851), pp. 307–10.

5. The minutes of the treaty negotiations at Lancaster can be found in ibid., pp. 307–19.

6. Return of the western tribes who traded at Oswego, August 1749, *Documents Relative to the Colonial History of New York,* 6:538; Report of John Lindsay, June 25, 1751, in *The Papers of Sir William Johnson,* ed. Alexander Flick et al., 13 vols. (Albany, N.Y., 1921–62), 9:82.

7. Excellent accounts of Celoron's expedition, including Celoron's journal and the journal of Father Bonnecamps, a priest accompanying the French party, can be found in *Ohio Archaeological and Historical Publications,* vol. 29 (Columbus: Ohio Archaeological and Historical Society, 1920), pp. 331–450. Succeeding citations of Celoron's journal refer to this source.

8. Celoron's journal, pp. 352–59.

9. Ibid., pp. 373–74.

10. Ibid., 374–75.

11. Ibid., pp. 375–76.

12. Nicholas Wainwright, *George Croghan: Wilderness Diplomat* (Chapel Hill: University of North Carolina Press, 1959), pp. 30–31.

13. Reports to Raymond, May 1750, *Collections of the Illinois State Historical Library,* 34 vols. (Springfield: The Library), 29:194–200; Reports to Raymond, April–March 1750, ibid., pp. 174–75; Raymond to La Jonquière, May 22, 1750, ibid., pp. 207–8.

14. Celoron's journal, p. 377; Governor Hamilton to the Assembly, August 8, 1750, *Minutes of the Provincial Council of Pennsylvania,* 5:454–55; Henry Clinton to Hamilton, September 3, 1750, ibid., p. 462.

15. Message from Governor Hamilton to the Assembly, August 8, 1750, *Minutes of the Provincial Council of Pennsylvania,* 5:454–55.

16. William Darlington, ed., *Christopher Gist's Journals* (Pittsburgh: J. R. Weldin and Co., 1893), pp. 50–52.

17. Ibid., pp. 52–53.

18. Minutes of the Provincial Council, May 7, 1751, *Minutes of the Provincial Council of Pennsylvania,* 5:522–24.

19. Baron de Longueuil to the French Minister, April 21, 1752, *Collections of the State Historical Society of Wisconsin,* 25 vols. (Madison: The Society, 1854–), 18:107.

20. La Jonquière to Rouille, October 29, 1751, *Collections of the Illinois State Historical Library,* 29:420–21; French Minister to Duquense, May 15, 1752, *Collections of the State Historical Society of Wisconsin,* 18:119.

21. Martin Kellogg to William Johnson, April 13, 1752, *Minutes of the Provincial Council of Pennsylvania,* 5:574; La Jonquière to the French Minister, September 25, 1751, *Collections of the State Historical Society of*

Wisconsin, 18:82; Longueuil to the French Minister, April 21, 1752, ibid., pp. 108–13.

22. Lawrence Henry Gipson, *The British Empire before the American Revolution,* 15 vols. (New York: Alfred A. Knopf, 1939–70), 4:219–20.

23. John Mills to Hamilton, April 27, 1752, *Minutes of the Provincial Council of Pennsylvania,* 5:573–74. For a discussion of the Quakers' reluctance to support their western allies, see Robert L. D. Davison, *War Comes to Quaker Pennsylvania, 1682–1756* (New York: Columbia University Press, 1957).

24. Alfred T. Goodman, ed., *Journal of Captain William Trent* (Cincinnati: Robert Clarke Co., 1871), pp. 86–87.

25. Ibid.

26. Ibid., pp. 87–88.

Joseph Brant

JAMES O'DONNELL

DURING THE War for American Independence, one of the British partisans best known and most hated by the colonials was the Mohawk warrior Joseph Brant. Romanticized at length by succeeding generations of historians, Brant's image was so shaped by filiopietistic American writers that one nineteenth-century work characterized him "as the most ferocious being ever produced by human nature."[1] Of course writers on the British side had an entirely different impression of Brant. Daniel Claus, his friend, biographer, and fellow officer in the British Indian department, wrote that he "allways knew him the most sober quiet and good natured Indian I ever was acquainted with." Brant's teacher, the Reverend Mr. Eleazar Wheelock, described him as "of a sprightly genius, a manly and genteel disposition, of a modest courteous, [and] benevolent temper."[2]

Hyperboles like those labeling Joseph Brant as the most ferocious being ever produced by human nature notwithstanding, his charisma and leadership qualities were such that they attracted much attention during his lifetime and were expanded by later biographers. His biography has been attempted in brief and at length, the most voluminous such work being the two-volume study done in the nineteenth century by William L. Stone, *Thayendenegea: The Life of Joseph Brant*.[3] Other treatments of Brant's life are based on Stone's early work. The most recent surveys touching on Brant's life are Barbara Graymont's *The Iroquois in the American Revolution* and William T. Hagan's *Longhouse Diplomacy and Frontier Warfare*.[4]

Despite all the attention Joseph Brant has received, he remains a rather elusive personality, in part because of the colorful accounts of his revolutionary career and in part because of the long shadows cast by the company in which he moved.

Thayendenegea, as his proper Mohawk name goes, was born about 1742, the son of Aroghyiadecker (Nickus Brant), a prominent leader on the New York frontier during the mid-eighteenth century. His grandfather Sagayeeanquarashtow was one of the four Indian "kings" who had visited Queen Anne's court early in the century. Joseph Brant's older sister, Molly, moreover, was for many years the loyal consort of Sir William Johnson, the British Indian superintendent north of the Ohio from 1755 to 1774, and an influential woman to her tribesmen. So powerful was her voice behind the scenes in Iroquois councils that some observers believed her capable of influencing decisions in a major way. Major Tench Tilghman, an American observer at negotiations with the Iroquois in 1776, claimed that Molly Brant and the other Iroquois women were the deus ex machina of tribal politics. Tilghman wryly observed that "women govern the Politics of Savages as well as the refined part of the world."[5]

Whatever Molly Brant's influence and however she used it in her younger brother's behalf, Joseph Brant's own intelligence brought him to the attention of William Johnson. Because Sir William believed that the Indians ought to be converted to Christianity, there were Anglican missionaries and teachers in the Mohawk town of Canojohare when Joseph Brant was a child. From these instructors the young Brant learned the fluent use of written Mohawk.[6] When he was in his late teens, two eastern Indians, David Fowler and Samson Occum, visited the Mohawk country on a recruiting mission for Moor's Charity School in Lebanon, Connecticut. Under the guidance of the Reverend Mr. Eleazar Wheelock, the school was open to white and Indian youths, in particular whites who wished to become missionaries and Indians who might return to their peoples as teachers. Fowler and Occum enlisted Sir William Johnson's aid (despite the non-Anglican nature of the school) in persuading three young Mohawks—Joseph Brant, Negyes, and Center—to accompany them back to Connecticut.[7]

On their arrival in Lebanon on August 1, 1761, Negyes, Center and Joseph were so suspicious of their surroundings that they kept their horses ready at all times to flee back to the Mohawk country. Wheelock described Negyes and Center as being little better than naked and unable to speak a word of English. While

Wheelock's judgment may have been an example of self-serving ethnocentrism, he was, nevertheless, impressed with Joseph Brant: "The other being of a family of distinction among them, was considerably cloathed, Indian-fashion, and could speak a few words of English."[8]

Of the three young men undertaking the trauma of attendance at boarding school far from home, only Brant succeeded. Center became ill and Negyes was dissatisfied, so they returned to the Mohawk country on October 23, 1761. Joseph Brant, however, remained behind at Wheelock's request to help teach Mohawk to Samuel Kirkland, a young charity scholar studying at Moor's School. Wheelock wanted Kirkland to visit the Mohawk country to recruit more students. Brant and Kirkland left Lebanon on November 4, 1761, on a brief visit to the Iroquois country; and by the time of their return on November 24, they had recruited two more young Mohawks.[9]

Over the next two years Joseph Brant attended several terms at Wheelock's institution in order to improve his written Mohawk and to learn spoken and written English. He also continued to instruct Samuel Kirkland, but the young minister had great difficulty in mastering Mohawk.[10] Meanwhile, Joseph Brant cultivated his skill as an interpreter. When Ralph Wheelock visited Brant's home in March 1768, he conferred with an Onondaga sachem, later reporting, "By Joseph Brant's help I was able to discourse with him, and delivered to him my discourse to his nation."[11]

However well Joseph Brant progressed as a student at Moor's, he remained a Mohawk, a fact that neither he nor his European companions ever forgot. In 1763 he returned home to the Mohawk country, reportedly at the request of his older sister, Molly.[12] Some traditional accounts suggest that Molly was upset because her brother had to do women's work in the garden. Although she may have been disturbed about manual labor at the school, she probably was fearful of what might happen to him if he remained in the eastern settlements after the anticipated Indian war erupted on the western frontier. Molly wanted Joseph safe in the Indian country, beyond the reach of vengeful colonists. Molly's husband, Sir William Johnson, had learned in 1761 that Pontiac and the Ottawas at Detroit were upset over

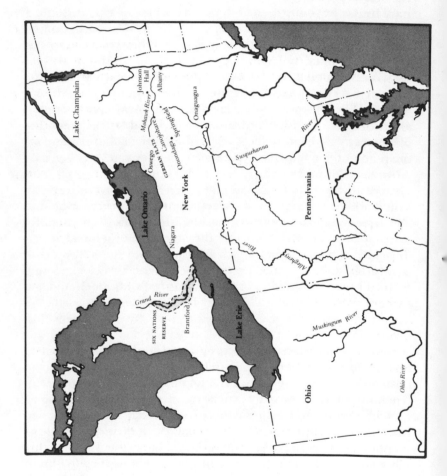

British Indian policy. Johnson had warned General Jeffrey Amherst that a tightfisted Indian policy would result in frontier warfare, but the Indian-hating Amherst proceeded with his plans for financial cutbacks. Not surprisingly, in 1763–64 Pontiac led the western tribesmen in an uprising, a rebellion precipitated in part by Amherst's policies.

Although Joseph Brant never returned to Wheelock's school, he retained the literary abilities he had acquired there as well as his fundamental belief in the necessity of education for his people. Because of his skill at translation, he continued to aid the missionaries from time to time and soon was regarded by Sir William Johnson and others as perhaps the most able translator in the northern Indian department. Daniel Claus believed that Brant provided more accurate translations of native speeches than any of the other interpreters in the department's employ. Moreover, Brant's service to the British was more significant than that of other interpreters because as a respected Mohawk he could attend meetings of the tribal council such as those held at Onondaga, take notes on the discussions, and then put them in writing for the use of the British officials. It was, for example, his report from Onondaga which informed Guy Johnson of the critical discussions there in late 1774 and early 1775.[13]

In the years between the end of Pontiac's Rebellion and the American Revolution, while serving as Johnson's interpreter, Brant married Margaret, daughter of the Oneida leader Skenandon. Then at Margaret's death he married her sister Susanna, who cared for him and his young children until her death. Joseph Brant's third wife was Catherine Croghan, the Mohawk daughter of George Croghan, a member of the British Indian department and a confidant of Sir William Johnson.[14]

When Sir William Johnson died in the summer of 1774, he was succeeded as superintendent of northern Indian affairs by his nephew and son-in-law, Guy Johnson, who was immediately dependent on Joseph Brant's diplomatic and literary skills. When the Iroquois council met at Onondaga in the fall of 1774, Joseph Brant was there in his capacity both as a Mohawk and as interpreter-secretary for Guy Johnson. During the course of the tribal deliberations in late October, November, and December of 1774, Brant took notes on the discussions and forwarded them to

Guy Johnson. Both Brant and Johnson were concerned that the Iroquois people might be influenced by the colonial point of view in the disagreement then beginning between Great Britain and her colonies.

Since Joseph Brant and the Mohawks lived in such close proximity to the colonists, it became dangerous for anyone with known Loyalist sympathies to remain at Canojohare. Brant's role as aide to Guy Johnson necessitated his constant attendance wherever the superintendent was located. In the summer of 1775, as tempers rose over the question of loyalty to the king, Johnson and Brant found it necessary to leave the Mohawk Valley for the relative safety of the British post at Niagara. There Johnson and Brant ran afoul of the usual politics born of civilian-military rivalries. The military commandant at Niagara and his superiors in Canada were inclined to dominate Indian affairs in their own way. Guy Johnson, on the other hand, thought that his imperial commission gave him undisputed power equal to that formerly held by his uncle. Already frustrated by the demands of his office, Johnson decided that the only way to clarify his position was by a trip to England. He persuaded Joseph Brant to accompany him, since he could benefit from Brant's charisma and Brant at the same time could satisfy his curiosity about the British Isles. Because of the bitter accusations by the Americans against the British government and its officials, Joseph Brant may have wished to visit England in order to obtain an "official" explanation of the growing dispute. Regardless of the reasons, the motivation for the trip must have been compelling, for both Johnson and Brant chose to be absent from their posts at an extremely critical time in the colonies.[15]

For more than six months during late 1775 and early 1776, Joseph Brant, Guy Johnson, and their companions, John of the Lower Mohawk Town and Captain Gilbert Tice of the rangers were wined and dined by the leading dignitaries in England. Johnson sat for a portrait with Benjamin West (in which Brant probably is the native figure in the background), and Brant was painted by George Romney. Brant, moreover, reportedly sought out opinions on both sides of the question pertaining to the American war. On the basis of the answers he received, he concluded (according to an extremely pro-British source) that all the Americans wanted was domination of the country and that they intended to obtain the mastery of the Indians and then take their liberty. Only the power of the Crown protected the Mohawks and other tribesmen from the greed of the Americans.[16]

In June 1776, Johnson, Brant, and their companions boarded a packet for America. As they reached American waters, they were attacked by an American privateer of superior force; Brant and John the Mohawk climbed into the ship's rigging with the new rifles that they had been given in England and proceeded to pick off officers on the deck of the American vessel. Because of this interruption in their voyage and damage to their vessel, the travelers did not reach New York until July 29, 1776. General Howe was about to begin his campaign against Washington and the colonists at New York, and Joseph Brant volunteered his services and remained with Howe until after New York was occupied by the British.

With New York captured, both Brant and Guy Johnson were anxious to return to their posts in the Mohawk country. General Howe had not succeeded in taking Albany, but Brant was confident that they could move through the back country. Guy Johnson, however, was horrified at the thought of possible capture and unhappy over Howe's apparent lack of concern for both the Iroquois and their agents. Johnson kept pressing the general for specific instructions and detailed promises of support, neither of which the general would give. When it became clear that Guy Johnson was reluctant to risk his life in the forests, Brant, John, and Tice disguised themselves as colonists, traveled at night, and took the long route to the Mohawk country via the Susquehanna River. Guy Johnson was left behind to fret in New York, where he would stay for another three years of ineffectual service before finally making his way back to the Iroquois country.[17]

When Joseph Brant reached the lands of his people in the fall of 1776, he found that there was much unrest. The pressure from the colonists had driven most Loyalists away from their homes, and the pro-British Iroquois were drifting toward Niagara, the closest British stronghold. Although plans were already underway to recruit forest soldiers to assist General John Burgoyne in the campaign of 1777, Brant found that his association with General Howe and Guy Johnson was resented by the officials at Niagara. Jealousy and envy, "the monsters of all discord and mischief," had led those in charge at Niagara to deny Brant encouragement and supplies. Brant was not to be given anything from the king's stores; he had to obtain whatever ammunition or other supplies he needed on his own credit.[18]

Given the discord between the military, the Indian department, and tribal leaders, any accomplishments by the Iroquois were major feats. Since members of the "faithful Mohawks" had left their homeland to take up residence under the protection of the British garrison, Brant was able to recruit thirty Mohawks at Niagara in January 1777. He took this small party into the Six Nations country and encamped there in case they were needed to repel American invaders.

With the coming of spring, Brant and his followers traveled to Onaguaga in search of additional recruits. The British campaign plans for 1777 included an invasion southward from Lake Champlain and eastward via the Mohawk River valley, and Brant sought to lead Iroquois warriors on a series of preliminary raids through the Mohawk Valley. There was a moment of high drama on June 27 when Brant with about one hundred warriors confronted some four hundred American militiamen under General Nicholas Herkimer. Believing that discretion was the better course, Brant chose to parley with the general about the abusive treatment the natives had received from the Americans. Although this conference resulted in little concrete achievement, it was evidence of Brant's stature and diplomatic skill in avoiding what might have been a disastrous engagement.[19]

As General Burgoyne's ill-fated expedition made its way tediously southward, Joseph Brant was among those Iroquois leaders who led warriors to the general's assistance. Brant and his party remained only a brief time, however, before they returned to their base of operations at Onaguaga. From that village during late 1777 and most of 1778, Brant led several parties of warriors and rangers in raids against American settlements in the Mohawk Valley. By mid-July 1778 the forest soldiers had attacked Springfield, near Otsego Lake, and in September they raided as far eastward as German Flats.[20]

During late 1778 and early 1779, there were numerous substantiated reports that General Washington had given orders for a major invasion of Iroquoiania. The country was to be laid waste and the power of the Iroquois broken forever. Brant was alarmed; there were no British forces close enough to assist the Iroquois and not enough warriors to turn back a major invasion.

Joseph Brant decided, therefore, a twofold course of action. First he exercised his diplomatic skill by going to Montreal to confer with General Frederick Haldimand, the British military commander in Canada. Haldimand was impressed by Brant and sympathetic to his overtures. He assured the chief that if the Iroquois homelands were destroyed, the British would aid in their restoration. It is unlikely that the general fully appreciated the extent of what he was promising, given the substantial nature of Iroquois houses and farms. But Brant interpreted Haldimand's promise as a British pledge of faith to the Iroquois wherever they might live after the war. When the conference ended, Brant returned to Niagara and thence to the Iroquois country, where he joined in the futile attempt to turn back the Americans.[21]

In late summer 1779, General John Sullivan's army swept through the Iroquois country, burning towns and destroying cornfields. Unable to hold back the enemy, most of the pro-British Iroquois fled north to Niagara, where they huddled around the fort, dependent on the British garrison for food and other necessities. Food was a major problem, since the garrison could barely feed itself, much less thousands of hungry visitors. Matters were made worse by crop failures on the farms near Niagara and near the British post at Detroit.

Given all these difficulties, Joseph Brant was greatly relieved to learn late in 1779 that Guy Johnson was finally returning to the Iroquois country. To his great dismay, however, he found that Johnson was a changed person. Indeed, Guy Johnson's behavior after his return to Niagara was a puzzle to all who observed him. He no longer was a tolerant administrator and willing listener; Molly Brant reported that his temper had grown so violent that he was emotionally unstable. From the records of the government auditors, moreover, we know that Johnson entered into collusion with merchants at Niagara to profit at government expense—150 rifles were debited against government accounts when the entry should have been 50, and 1,156 kettles were charged to the king when the number should have been 156.[22]

By 1780 the two men who had worked together for so long, who had crossed and recrossed the Atlantic together, and who had served as comrades-in-arms had come to a parting of the ways. Daniel Claus, a brother-in-law of Guy Johnson and friend and admirer of Brant, tried to uncover the nature of the dispute between Brant and Johnson but to no avail: "Unless Joseph has greatly altered of late since I saw him last I am almost persuaded he is not the aggressor; for I allways knew him the most sober quiet and good natured Indian I ever was acquainted with, and most heartily and sincerely disposed to serve Government to my knowledge he was opposed and envied for so doing from his first arrival from England in the Six Nation country in the spring of 1777."[23]

In the spring of 1780, partly as a result of the growing rift with Johnson, Brant made plans for a journey to the Ohio country. To be sure, he was not going there just to escape unpleasantness among the Iroquois; he was going there to see if he could rally the native peoples of the northwest to the king's cause. Since the Ohio country was under constant harassment from the adjoining colonial frontier, the northwestern tribes were tempted to abandon their support of the British. Brant hoped that if he could rally the western Indians, their example might also help stiffen the resistance of the southern tribes, who had been intimidated by the crushing defeat of the Cherokees in 1776.[24]

The Iroquois had conferred with the northwestern tribes earlier in the war. Western chiefs such as Sasterassee of the Hurons had journeyed from Detroit to Niagara to meet with Iroquois leaders and had received Six Nations war belts admonishing the western peoples to strike the Americans. A year later a delegation of Iroquois had crossed Lake Erie to Detroit, again urging the Michigan and Ohio tribes to remain faithful to their British father.[25]

Intent on strengthening the ties between the Iroquois and the western nations, Brant traveled in 1781 to Ohio, where he joined with Simon Girty to lead a large war party of Tories and western tribesmen against American shipping on the Ohio River. In August, Brant and his followers attacked a flotilla of canoes and longboats carrying supplies from Virginia to George Rogers Clark in Kentucky. Firing from ambush, the Indians killed thirty-seven Americans, including their commander, Colonel Alexander Lochery, and captured fourteen boats full of provisions.[22]

Brant's victory over the Long Knives raised the morale of the Ohio Indians. During the previous year they had suffered much at the hands of Clark and his Kentucky militia. In 1780 Clark's forces had penetrated the Shawnee country in central Ohio, destroying Shawnee towns such as Chillicothe and Pickaway. Although the Kentuckians complained loudly about Indian "savagery," Brant learned that the frontiersmen were also guilty of needless violence. Shawnee warriors reported that the Kentuckians had slaughtered their women and children, killing one woman by "ripping open her belly." Other militiamen had dug up Shawnee graves, stealing the burial gifts and then scalping the corpses. In addition, the Indians complained, the Americans had advanced upon their villages flying white flags of truce, which were discarded when the tribesmen came within firing range.[27]

Following his victory on the Ohio, Brant rode to Detroit, where the British needed his assistance in maintaining the loyalty of other northwestern tribes. By late 1781 several of the tribes near Detroit suffered from food shortages and had lost many warriors to the Long Knives. Captain Pipe, the Delaware chief who had led his people away from the Muskingum River to new towns near Detroit, was particularly vocal in his complaints to the British. Brant was present on November 9 when Captain Pipe delivered a speech laced with bitterness. Especially significant was the old Delaware's use of sarcasm when he referred to the British as "our father." Denouncing the British, Captain Pipe harangued:

> *Father*! I have said *Father*, tho indeed I am ignorant of the cause for so calling him. . . . Some time ago You put a War hatchet into my hands, saying; take this Weapon, and try it on the heads of my Enemies, the Long Knifes. . . . *Father*! Many lives have been lost on your account! Nations have suffered and been weakened! Children have lost Parents, brothers, and relatives. Wives have lost Husbands. . . .

While you, *Father*! are setting me on Your Enemy . . . I may per-
chance happen to look back, . . . and what shall I see? I shall probably
see my *Father* shaking hands with the Long Knifes. And while doing
this he may be laughing at my folly in having obeyed him.[28]

Brant spent the winter of 1781–82 at Detroit using all his influence to keep the neighboring tribes loyal to the British. He assured Captain Pipe and other leaders that their British father
would never abandon his red children. During February 1782,
six Oneidas from New York arrived to assist Brant in his efforts,
but in the months that followed, disquieting rumors reached
Detroit from the east. Messengers informed Brant and his friends
that the Americans had defeated General Charles Cornwallis and
that those Iroquois remaining in New York were preparing to
make peace with the Long Knives. At first the Mohawk leader
refused to believe the reports, but in March 1782 he sailed from
Detroit for Niagara, hoping to use his influence against such
peace overtures if the rumors proved true.[29]

To Brant's chagrin, when he reached Oswego he learned that
the British had already signed a truce with the Americans; no
further military activity was to take place. Although disappointed
by the cease-fire, he remained loyal to the Crown. Therefore,
when British Indian agents asked him to carry official news of the
armistice to the western tribes, he reluctantly agreed. One
hopeful piece of information awaiting Brant in Oswego was
that Guy Johnson had been dismissed from the Indian superintendency in favor of Sir John Johnson, Sir William's son and
heir. Returning from England, John Johnson assumed the office
during the summer of 1782, then made plans to visit Detroit and
other British posts in the west. In August 1782, Brant accompanied the new superintendent back to Detroit, where the Mohawk leader again met with the western Indians.

Although he was unhappy over the armistice, Brant attempted
to placate the western tribesmen and keep them allied with the
British. He pointed out that the Iroquois decision to enter the
conflict had been based on the realization that neutrality might
have split their league. He also spoke at some length about the
close ties between his people and the Crown. When Sir John
Johnson had asked them to lay down their hatchets, the Iroquois
had complied, he explained: "The War not being of our own

making, we readily agreed to what Sir John had recommended to us, altho, we the Six Nations are never hasty in our resolve when matters of war are concerned, and altho, we have laid the hatchet aside, should they give us just cause to use it, we shall nevertheless be able to take it up in defence of our rights. We mean to take care that we give no cause of rupture on our Parts. Brothers and Nephews, We desire you to pay attention to this, and to do the same thing that we have resolved."[30]

After urging the western tribes to follow Sir John Johnson's advice to release all prisoners as a sign of good faith in the peace, Brant then proposed a covenant between the western tribes and the Iroquois: "Brothers and Nephews, you the Hurons, Delawares, Shawnees, Mingoes, Ottawas, Chippewas, Poutawattamis, Creeks, and Cherokees, We the Six Nations with this Belt, bind your hearts and minds with ours, that there may be never hereafter a separation between us, let there be Peace or War, it should never disunite us, for our interests are alike nor should any thing ever be done but by the voice of the whole, as we make but one with you."[31]

Following the close of the council at Detroit, Brant and his companions met with Alexander McKee, a British Indian agent at Sandusky, and then returned to Niagara. From the Iroquois refugee camps at Niagara, Brant wrote General Haldimand in Canada, asking him to honor his pledges of assistance to the Iroquois, made at Montreal in 1779. Brant requested that the Iroquois be given permanent refuge in Canada, for if they had sided with the Americans, they would not have been driven from their homes. The long list of items seized by the Americans during the war included a wide variety of things, from Molly Brant's fancy dresses to the sheep and cattle of ordinary tribesmen, although it did not include the lands and crops that had been seized or destroyed.[32]

Fortunately for the Iroquois, General Haldimand was favorably impressed with Joseph Brant and with the argument he presented. Haldimand agreed that the Mohawks and their Iroquois allies had sacrificed much by serving the British. During the winter of 1782–83, therefore, Brant and Haldimand considered the possibilities for a new Iroquois homeland. By March 1783, the two men agreed on what they believed most of the Mohawks would accept—new lands along the Grand River, just north of Lake Erie, in Canada. Brant, furthermore, was commissioned by Haldimand as "Captain of the Northern Confederate Indians."[33]

Haldimand's principal motive in commissioning Brant may have been to reward him for his wartime services, but the primary effect of the commission proved significant. Brant assumed the position of chief spokesman and negotiator for all the pro-British Iroquois. Final approval concerning the choice of lands, therefore, would be made by Brant, who was familiar with the region along the Grant River.

Meanwhile, General Haldimand took steps to clear title to the territory. Shortly after his spring meetings with Brant, he sent out a party of surveyors to the Grand River. Once the area had been surveyed, he had to satisfy the territorial claims of the Mississaugas, a Canadian tribe that claimed the region. At a meeting in May of 1784, the Mississaugas sold their claims to the area with a plea to "Captain Brant": "We hope you will keep your young men in good Order, as we shall be in one neighborhood, and hope to live in friendship with each other as Brethren ought to do." With the completion of this cession (funded by the British), General Haldimand issued a proclamation granting the Grand River lands to the Mohawks and their allies.[34]

The first of the Mohawk families began moving to the Grand River lands in late 1784 and early 1785, with Joseph Brant as their acknowledged leader. In this capacity, Brant was to find both praise and condemnation. Much of the praise would come from European and American visitors who saw in his life the model that they thought all Indians should follow. Brant was also generally accepted by most of his people, but there were a few persistent and vocal opponents who questioned his attempts to attract settlers, for he had encouraged a number of white farmers and merchants to move into the area and take up lands which the Mohawks were not using.[35]

Why was Brant urging these non-Indian peoples to settle in the midst of his people? One historian of the Grand River Mohawk settlement has suggested that he did it to provide productive models for the native people to observe. Given the frame houses and prosperous farms that these Iroquois had abandoned in New York, however, it seems a specious and ethnocentric argument.[36]

It may be more appropriate and useful to suggest a reason based on the life-style which Brant followed in the postwar years. While he was very much his own person, his role model seems to have been his brother-in-law, William Johnson. Throughout his entire young adulthood, Brant had seen and experienced the comfort and influence that Johnson enjoyed at his gracious estate in the Mohawk Valley. A description of the way Brant was living in the 1790s is illuminating:

> Captain Brant . . . received us with much politeness and hospitality. Here we found two young married ladies, with their husbands, on a visit to the family, both of them very fair complexioned and well looking women. But when Mrs. Brant appeared superbly dressed in the Indian fashion, the elegance of her person, grandeur of her looks and deportment, her large mild black eyes, symmetry and harmony of her expressive features, though much darker in the complexion, so far surpassed them, as not to admit of the smallest comparison between the Indian and the fair European ladies; I could not in her presence so much as look at them without marking the difference. Her blanket was made up of silk, and the finest English cloth, bordered with a narrow stripe of embroidered lace, her sort of jacket and scanty petticoat of the same stuff, which came down only to her knees; her gaiters or leggans of the finest scarlet, fitted close as a stocking, which showed to advantage her stout but remarkably well formed limbs; her mogazines ornamented with silk ribbons and beads.
>
> . . . .
>
> Tea was on the table when we came in, served up in the handsomest China plate and every other furniture in proportion. After tea was over, we were entertained with the music of an elegant hand organ, on which a young Indian gentleman and Mr. Clinch played alternately. Supper was served up in the same genteel stile. Our beverage, rum, brandy, Port and Maderia wines. Captain Brant made several apologies for his not being able to sit up with us so long as he wished, being a little out of order, and we being fatigued after our journey went timeously to rest; our beds, sheets, and English blankets, equally fine and comfortable.
>
> . . . .
>
> Dinner was just going on the table in the same elegant stile as the preceding night, when I returned to Captain Brant's house, the servants dressed in their best apparel. Two slaves attended the table,

the one in scarlet, the other in coloured clothes, with silver buckles in their shoes, and ruffles, and every other part of their apparel in proportion.[37]

There seem to have been two other facets of William Johnson's successful career that Brant wished to emulate: land agent and patron of the church. Indeed, the allotting of lands by Brant in his somewhat baronial manner was questioned from time to time by other Mohawks, but his close ties to the British government and position within the tribal power structure usually allowed him to prevail. Nevertheless, questions about his right to grant lands and the profits he may have enjoyed continued to arise. His leadership role was strained also by his assumption that General Haldimand's 1784 proclamation granting Candadian lands to the "Mohawk Nation" had the Iroquois Confederacy as a sovereign community. This was especially troublesome because it was largely on this basis that many of Joseph Brant's actions were taken. He even went so far as to argue that disposing of excess land was a necessity for Mohawk survival. To Governor John Graves Simcoe of Upper Canada, Brant "stated the impracticability of the Indians supporting themselves by their hunting, of the Indians themselves they could not provide for their old men and children by their farms, and that he conceived the leasing of them to be the only mode by which they could maintain themselves and their families." When he pushed too far and awakened his critics, Brant used his connections within the traditional Iroquois matriarchy—"the mothers and aunts"—to silence the opposition. Since his sister was the brilliant and powerful Molly Brant, Joseph well understood the most effective manner to play the politics of the Iroquois council.[38]

Brant had long desired to see the Iroquois converted to Christianity (as had Sir William Johnson), and he maintained that interest after moving to Canada. Soon after locating on the Grand River lands, he collaborated with his old friend from the Indian Department, Daniel Claus, in preparing a new edition of the Mohawk Prayer Book. Printed in 1786, the new volume contained not only the Mohawk Prayer Book in both Mohawk and English but also Joseph Brant's translation of the Anglican Book of Common Prayer and the Gospel of Mark. In the late 1780s a church was constructed in the Grand River settlement.

When the former missionary at Canojohare, the Reverend Mr.
John Stuart, visited in 1788, he brought some of the silver com-
munion plates which once had been in the Mohawk church in
Fort Hunter in New York. Stuart found "that the Mohawk Village
is pleasantly situated on a small but deep River—the Church
about 60 feet in length & 45 in breadth,—built with squared logs
and boarded on the outside and painted—with a handsome
steeple & bell, a pulpit, reading-desk, & Communion-table, with
convenient pews." Stuart could also have observed that Joseph
Brant's major difficulty in his role as patron of the church was his
desire to have a local clergyman whom he knew and whom he
could dominate. According to one writer, Stuart believed that the
Mohawks were "afraid of the restraint which the continued residence of a Clergyman would necessarily lay them under."
Because of Brant's central influence in this as in all questions of
authority, the number of white missionaries at Grand River
remained low.[39]

Brant continued to reside on the Grand River lands until his
death after the turn of the century. Loyal to the British cause, he
attempted to assist the Crown in negotiating between the Ohio
tribes and the United States during the border wars of the 1790s.
But in this endeavor he failed. Although he was able to retain his
preeminence among the Canadian Iroquois, the western tribes
no longer heeded his counsel. He died on his estate, near Brant-
ford, Ontario, on November 24, 1807.

Like many others of his generation of Native American leaders,
Joseph Brant was a man caught between two worlds. Born and
instructed in traditional Iroquois ways, he also received an education from English teachers. Afterwards he could function in
either society, yet the whites would never admit him freely to their
society save as a curiosity, and he was no longer an Iroquois in the
purest sense. While he was his own person, his model seems to
have been his brother-in-law, Sir William Johnson. Brant knew
the magnificent style in which Johnson lived and he understood
that Johnson had used his position to dominate landholdings and
politics in the Mohawk Valley. Thus to the traditional role of
sachem (which Brant played whether or not it was ever given to
him), he added that of baronial landlord, treating the Grand
River reserve as if it belonged to him. Such an observation is not

necessarily negative—he had come out of the American Revolution as the best-known and most powerful individual in the Six Nations. He may also have acquired a certain sense of mission from his revolutionary experiences which led him to conclude that his style of leadership was the only one that would enable his people to survive and avoid a repetition of their earlier tragedies.

NOTES

1. Carlo Botta, *History of the War of Independence of the United States of America*, trans. George Alexander Otis, 2 vols. (Philadelphia: J. Maxwell, 1821), 2:553.

2. Daniel Claus, Anecdotes of Joseph Brant [manuscript materials about Brant], Public Archives of Canada, Ottawa, Military Group m.g. 19, vols. 1, 2; Eleazar Wheelock, quoted in James T. Flexner, *Mohawk Baronet, Sir William Johnson of New York* (New York: Harper Bros., 1959), p. 292.

3. William L. Stone, *The Life of Joseph Brant—Thayendanegea* (New York: G. Dearborn and Co., 1838).

4. For biographical data on Joseph Brant, see ibid.; L. A. Wood, *The War Chief of the Six Nations* (Toronto: Glascow, Brook and Co., 1920); Harvey Chalmers and E. B. Monture, *Joseph Brant; Mohawk* (East Lansing: Michigan State University Press, 1955); Barbara Graymont, *The Iroquois in the American Revolution* (Syracuse, N.Y.: Syracuse University Press, 1972); William T. Hagan, *Longhouse Diplomacy and Frontier Warfare* (Albany: New York State American Revolution Bicentennial Commission, 1976); and Charles M. Johnson, *The Valley of the Six Nations* (Toronto: Champlain Society, 1964).

5. Entry for August 1775, Diary of Tench Tilghman, Library of Congress, Washington, D.C.

6. Flexner, *Mohawk Baronet*, 292.

7. Eleazar Wheelock, *A Plain and Faithful Narrative of the Original Design, Rise, Progress, and Present State on the Indian Charity-School at Lebanon, Connecticut* (Boston: R. S. Draper, 1763), passim.

8. Ibid., p. 40.

9. Ibid., pp. 41–42.

10. Samuel Kirkland to Eleazar Wheelock, May 22, 1767, in *A Continuation of the Narrative of the Indian Charity School* . . . (London: J. and W. Oliver, 1769), p. 17.

11. Journal of Ralph Wheelock in ibid., Appendix, p. 45.

12. See Flexner, *Mohawk Baronet*, and Hagan, *Longhouse Diplomacy*.

13. Claus, Anecdotes of Brant; Joseph Brant's notes, enclosed in Guy Johnson to Thomas Gage, December 14, 1774, Thomas Gage Papers, William L. Clements Library, University of Michigan, Ann Arbor.

14. Graymont, *The Iroquois*, p. 53. Also see the Brant genealogical data in Jean Johnston, "Ancestry and Descendants of Molly Brant," *Ontario History* 18 (June 1971): 86–92.

15. Guy Johnson, Extract of Activities, July 17 to October, 1775, Germain Papers, William L. Clements Library; Flexner, *Mohawk Baronet,* p. 186; Claus, Anecdotes of Brant.

16. Claus, Anecdotes of Brant.

17. "A Review of the Northern Indian Department by Guy Johnson, October 3, 1776," British Headquarters Papers, no. 280 (microfilm), Institute of Early American History and Culture, Williamsburg, Virginia; Claus, Anecdotes of Brant.

18. Claus, Anecdotes of Brant.

19. Hagan, *Longhouse Diplomacy,* p. 20; Graymont, The Iroquois, pp. 116–17.

20. Graymont, *The Iroquois,* pp. 174–79.

21. Ibid., pp. 180–90.

22. Audited Accounts [Financial accounts], Niagara, 1780–82, Public Archives of Canada.

23. Daniel Claus to Frederick Haldimand, April 19, 1781, Claus Papers, vol. 3, Public Archives of Canada.

24. James H. O'Donnell III, *Southern Indians in the American Revolution* (Knoxville: University of Tennessee Press, 1973), pp. 34–53.

25. A. S. DePeyster to Thomas Brown, April 5, 1780, British Headquarters Papers, no. 2672 (microfilm), Institute of Early American History and Culture; DePeyster to Alexander McKee, June 22, 1780, ibid.

26. Hagan, *Longhouse Diplomacy,* pp. 46–48.

27. John Macomb to Daniel Claus, September 14, 1781, Claus Papers, vol. 3, Public Archives of Canada; William Homan to Captain Bird, August 15, 1780, British Museum Additional MSS, no. 21781 (photostat), Institute of Early American History and Culture; Alexander McKee to DePeyster, August 22, 1780, ibid.

28. John Heckewelder, who was present, wrote: "I never heard an Indian speech delivered with more force, clearness, good sense, and so to the purpose as this." Heckewelder expressed doubt that Baubien, the interpreter, actually reported the true meaning of everything Captain Pipe said. See "Remarks on Captain Pipe's Spirited Speech to the Commandant at Detroit on the 9th Day of November, 1781," Collections of the American Philosophical Society, Philadelphia.

29. DePeyster to McKee, February 6, 1782, Claus Papers, vol. 3, Public Archives of Canada; DePeyster to McKee, April 3, 1782, ibid.

30. Journal of the Council at Detroit, 1782, American Philosophical Society.

31. Ibid.

32. William Potts to McKee, October 8, 1781, American Philosophical Society; Brant to Haldimand, May 21, 1783, in Johnson, *Valley of the Six Nations,* pp. 38–40. Also see note 36, below.

33. Johnson, *Valley of the Six Nations,* p. xxxv.

34. Brant to Haldimand, March, 1783, in ibid., pp. 50–51.

35. Johnson, *Valley of the Six Nations,* p. xliii.

36. For the argument that Brant wanted European models for the Iroquois farmers, see ibid. Detailed inventories of household goods and claims for losses suffered by the Oneidas tend to negate such a hypothesis. See the lists in the Pickering Papers, Massachusetts Historical Society, Boston.

37. Patrick Campbell, "A Visit with Joseph Brant on the Grand River, 1792," from Campbell's *Travels in the Interior Inhabited Parts of North America in the Years 1791 and 1792,* reprinted in part in Johnson, *Valley of the Six Nations,* pp. 59–61.

38. Johnson, *Valley of the Six Nations,* pp. xliv, xlviii, 76.

39. Ibid., pp. lxxiv, lxxx, 238. Although Stuart's analysis had an element of truth in it, Brant was painfully aware of the political and social turmoil that a clergyman could cause if he was so inclined. His example in this case was the Reverend Mr. Samuel Kirkland, with whom Brant had been a student at Wheelock's school. The best source for Kirkland's activities is the Kirkland Papers in the Hamilton College Library, Clinton, New York.

Alexander McGillivray

Michael D. Green

ALEXANDER MCGILLIVRAY is probably the best-known Creek in the history of the Creek Confederacy. Though never the subject of a full-length biography, he has been explained, described, analyzed, and dissected in countless biographical sketches.[1] A prodigious correspondent, he wrote many letters during his public career (1777–93) which long have been a major source for students of the history of United States–Spanish relations in the Southeast. Fascinated by McGillivray, historians writing in the nineteenth century often compared him to European statesmen well known to their readers; thus we have one scholar calling him "the Talleyrand of Alabama" and another "the Machiavelli of these early times." Willis Brewer, an early student of Alabama history, claimed that McGillivray had "the controlling mind in Alabama." Other writers, recognizing his mixed parentage—McGillivray's father was a Scots trader, his mother the daughter of the marriage of a native woman and a French army officer—simply called him a "half-breed," sometimes coupling it with a ludicrous attempt to identify various of his character traits as Scottish, French, or Indian. One author, boggled by his conception of the mix, decided the result was bound to be explosive. Another, perhaps swayed by his understanding of McGillivray's deeds, described the mixed-blood as "the most felicitous compound of the kind ever seen." McGillivray's contemporaries were less scientific in their characterizations, but they also portrayed the Creek leader in colorful terms. Appellations like *dicatator, emperor,* and *king of kings* dot the correspondence of United States and Spanish functionaries who thought they knew him. The Creeks, who really did know him, called him *Isti atcagagi*

41

thlucco, Great Beloved Man, a title conveying respect for both McGillivray and his policies.[2]

Born probably in 1759, Alexander McGillivray was raised in a culturally mixed setting at his father's trading plantation at Little Tallassee, an Upper Creek town on the banks of the Coosa River just north of present Montgomery, Alabama. In 1773 the elder McGillivray sent his already literate fourteen-year-old son to Charleston for a more formal education. His academic career cut short by the Revolution, the young McGillivray returned to Little Tallassee in 1777 and accepted a commission as assistant commissary in the British Indian service. He held the post until the end of the war.[3]

McGillivray's task during the war years was to build and maintain cordial relations between England and the Upper Creeks and to organize a military alliance if such an arrangement was possible. It was a heavy responsibility for a young man, but one for which he was advantageously suited by his birth into the Wind clan of the Creek Nation.

The Creeks had a strong and extraordinarily complex clan system. At various times there may have been as many as fifty distinct clans, but seven to ten were clearly larger and more prominent than the rest. Of this small number, the Wind clan, which supplied a heavy proportion of the highest-ranking officials in the civil governments, was the most prestigious. Almost all the towns in the Confederacy had Wind people, and because of their special political responsibilities many members of the clan occupied positions of leadership in the councils. McGillivray therefore had clan kinsmen in influential positions throughout the Nation, bound by clan obligations and encouraged by clan loyalties to be receptive to him and his ideas. In addition, his uncle, the Koasati leader Red Shoes, was one of the half-dozen most powerful headmen in the Confederacy. Any young man gained valuable advantages from a high-placed uncle.[4]

McGillivray's royal commission gave him entry into national government where his kinsmen gave him their attention; what he did with it depended on his own talents. Viewed from the perspective of the Creek headmen, McGillivray's most apparent attribute was his literacy. Creeks able to read and write English

were rare and the National Council's need for capable and trust-
worthy interpreters was growing rapidly. Moreover, McGillivray
could do more than simply make English words intelligible. His
educational experience enabled him to translate the wishes,
policies, and cultural peculiarities of the Creeks' English-speak-
ing neighbors. The young assistant commissary in the service of
King George thus became much more than his official position
would suggest. In addition to his obvious diplomatic duties,
McGillivray became an adviser, a man whose insights and ideas
reflected his multicultural experience.[5]

The Creeks gave McGillivray a mixed reception. There were
elements of Creek society that were predisposed to be receptive,
but there were other groups equally prepared to oppose him.
Riddled with factionalism based on local interests, competing
loyalties, and conflicting ambition, the Creek Confederacy was a
coalition of groups only loosely committed to political agreement.
Its origins lay in an ancient alliance of formerly independent
tribes speaking many different languages and tracing their
several pasts through quite separate and distinct histories. Some
of the Creek towns had entered the alliance voluntarily, others
were the survivors of conquered enemies, but all defined
themselves in particularistic terms. They were not Creeks; they
were Cowetas, Cussetas, Tuckabatchees, Alabamas, Koasatis, and
so forth. McGillivray was a Koasati, one of the original founding
allies of the Confederacy.[6]

This multinational heritage encouraged town particularism
within the Confederacy and fostered a complex set of concentric
loyalties which became progressively weaker as one passed beyond the borders of any given town into the larger context of
its regional neighborhood. There were two concentrations of
Creek people. One group, the Lower Creeks, lived in the Chattahoochee and Flint river valleys of southwestern Georgia, southeastern Alabama, and northern Florida. Separated by several
hundred miles of dense forest, the Upper Creeks resided farther to the west, on the upper reaches of the Alabama and the
lower courses of its two main tributaries, the Coosa and
Tallapoosa rivers, in central and eastern Alabama. The only
reasonably accurate census of the Creeks, taken in 1832, revealed
about 7,400 Lower Creeks in ten towns and something over

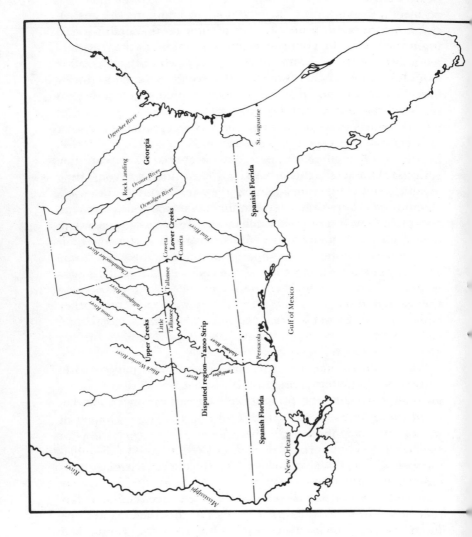

14,000 Upper Creeks in forty-two towns. The Creek population in the late eighteenth century is unknown, but the proportions were roughly the same.[7]

Divided into this bipartite regional organization, the Confederacy maintained peace between the member towns and provided some shelter for foreign refugees. The name *Creek* was the late-seventeenth-century invention of the Charles Town traders, and there is little evidence to suggest that there was much of a sense of national identity before the mid-nineteenth century. Although representatives from the various towns met periodically during the eighteenth century, there was no supreme leader or national capital, and it is clear that the National Council of the Creek Confederacy was never intended to be a European-style policy-making government with administrative power. There was no parliamentary machinery for accommodating differences of opinion. Frequently paralyzed by heated factional disputes, the council could do nothing unless all the members agreed on a course of action. During the American Revolution, contention between pro-British and pro-American factions frustrated McGillivray's efforts to create a united pro-British policy in the National Council. Despite his labors, the Nation officially maintained a position of neutrality. Many towns, on the other hand, exercised their ancient prerogative to act independently. Since most of them more or less supported the British, McGillivray saw all the action he cared for.[8]

Whatever McGillivray's motivation may have been when he entered the British service in 1777, it is quite clear that by 1783 his self-identity was Creek, his loyalties were to the Creeks, and his future was inextricably tied to the Nation. He had emerged during the war years as a war leader of some repute, as a respected adviser, interpreter, and spokesman for the National Council, and as a man mature beyond his years who had gifts no other Creek possessed.

McGillivray's talents were put to the full test in the decade following 1783. At the Treaty of Paris, Great Britain transferred the trans-Appalachian West to the United States and returned Florida to Spain. Both actions were potentially catastrophic for the Creeks since the transfer of territories placed the Creek homelands at the mercy of their enemies. The new state of

Georgia, bordering the Creeks on the east, had a reputation for aggression. Spain's policies were uncertain, and the future of the Creek Nation was seriously threatened. This crisis thrust McGillivray into diplomatic view and propelled him into a position of major leadership within the Creek Nation.[9]

McGillivray's response was clear. The Creeks were "a free Nation," he argued, and Great Britan had "no right to give up a Country she never could call her own." Asserting that Creek political independence and territorial integrity were legally un-impaired, McGillivray intended to gain recognition for the Creeks as a sovereign nation.[10] The difficulty in realizing this goal, he recognized, lay in the claims of the United States that it had a treaty right to "divide our territories into countries and . . . settle on our lands as though they were theirs." Creek protests that "we . . . have done no act to lose our independence, and nat-ural rights in favor of the Said King of Great Britain that invests him with the power to cede our properties" made little impression on the newly independent North American states.[11] Feeling betrayed and vulnerable, McGillivray decided to seek the needed political and territorial guarantees through separate treaties with both the United States and Spain. The Creeks could then better defend themselves from their neighbors. Georgia revealed her purpose immediately. Claiming an exclusive right to treat with the Creeks, she forced a small number of headmen who had led the pro-American faction during the recent war to sign a treaty of peace in November 1783 which relinquished Creek lands to Georgia. The state demanded a three-million-acre tract on the eastern border of the Nation as compensation for damage allegedly done during the war by pro-British warriors. Far from providing the recognition of rights the Creeks desired, the Treaty of Augusta was a clear indication that Georgia, a grasping neighbor held in check in recent decades only by the power of the British government, was now embarking on an unrestrained career of territorial expansion at the expense of the Creeks.[12]

Having no faith in the ability of the United States, that "dis-tracted Republic," to influence Georgia's Indian policy, McGilliv-ray turned to the Spanish.[13] He asked for "his Majestys most Gracious Protection" for the Creek people and their property "as is by them claimed and now held in actual possession," meaning all their lands, whether in the United States or Florida, and ignoring the cession made at Augusta. "It would be good Policy in the crown of Spain to Grant us our Desires," McGillivray instructed, because the Creeks could be "Very dangerous Neighbours." They did not like the Americans, but their final decision would depend on which community, Georgia or Florida, supplied their goods. Georgia had begun a massive campaign to dominate the Creek trade, McGillivray warned, but a connection with Spain would better suit his "political opinions." McGillivray lay the choice before the Spanish. Accede to the Creeks' demands and they would "Gain & Secure a powerfull barrier in these parts against the ambitious and encroaching Americans." Refuse and "the Americans will very Shortly engross the Indian trade & of consequence gain the Indians to their Interest, & who will make the worst use of their influence." Aside from guaranteeing Creek territory, Spain had to permit the establishment of a trade in West Florida like that the Creeks once enjoyed with the English. A "plentiful Supply of Goods" would seal the friendship, "for Indians will attach themselves to & Serve them best who Supply their Necessities."[14]

A shrewd diplomat, McGillivray became a power broker between the Spanish and Americans. The Creeks, with a potential army of 3,500 to 6,000 warriors, outnumbered the combined military forces of the United States and Spanish Florida. Whichever side enjoyed their alliance gained a substantial degree of security. But to threaten war and dangle peace in the name of recognition and respect was a policy which the Creeks could successfully pursue only if they exercised an unprecedented political and military unity and discipline. McGillivray's reading of history and his wartime experience in the National Council convinced him that a strong Creek state with a consistent policy that could be enforced internally provided the best basis for Creek survival. Such a goal could not be quickly or easily realized, he knew, because of the traditions of town autonomy within the Confederacy and factionalism within the Council. McGillivray thus had to play for time, and an alliance with Spain offered the best way to buy the time he needed.

On June 1, 1784, McGillivray and several Creek headmen signed the Treaty of Pensacola with Spain. It gave the Creeks much of what they wanted, including a guarantee of Creek lands within Florida and a pledge of support for their protection. The treaty also authorized the development of a trade that soon blossomed into the establishment in Pensacola of Panton, Leslie and Company, a Loyalist refugee firm based in St. Augustine which hoped to capitalize on McGillivray's silent partnership. Shortly after the treaty ceremonies, Governor Estevan Miro of Louisiana appointed McGillivray Spanish commissary among the Creeks.[15]

The Treaty of Pensacola, McGillivray's first major public act as a Creek leader, was also the first step in his program to create what he called an atmosphere in which "we May be . . . Kept Independent of the American States. So that we Shall be enabled to continue our resistance with effect. & to preserve our Lands, any cessions of Which we are determined never to Consent to."[16] Consistent support from Spain was vital to the success of his policy. Spanish aid came in many forms, including diplomatic mediation with the United States Congress and the pledge of large amounts of guns and powder so the Creeks could defend themselves, as the commandant of Pensacola facetiously put it, "from the Bears and other fierce Animals."[17]

With the immediate future secure, McGillivray was free to turn his attention to the task of reforming Creek government. The initial problems, as he saw them, were to impose a degree of political discipline upon the fractious Confederacy and to exercise some direction over the actions of the National Council. The Creek government was not and never had been "democratic." The councils made the decisions and there were individuals who clearly dominated the proceedings. Still, what McGillivray had in mind involved a demonstration of personal leadership and a degree of individual authority that was quite without parallel in Creek history. But McGillivray did not seek power egotistically. His fears were for the survival of the Creek Nation and he sought and used power in the hope of assuring an independent future for his people.

McGillivray's plans for Creek government verged on the revolutionary, but he frequently used traditional means to achieve his highly nontraditional ends. He worked through the National Council. It is clear that most of the micos (kings) did as he asked most of the time, but he was careful not to tamper outwardly with the council form. His pose in public was as adviser and spokesman to the micos in council, never as a mico himself. His title, Isti atcagagi thlucco (Great Beloved Man), is a demonstration of this decision. The attachment of *thlucco* ("big" or "great") is unique to McGillivray, but the Creek Nation was full of beloved men. Every town council had several, usually distinguished by age but always notable for their good advice, who sat on the sidelines of government offering suggestions and clearing away obfuscation. Their wisdom was highly respected and their voices were strong and clear. No particular clan dominated the ranks of the beloved men. In Little Tallassee the micos were generally Beavers, the henihas (second men) were usually Winds. As a Wind, McGillivray could not properly be a mico, but he could become a heniha if he became adept in his old age in the rituals of government and religion. A young man should not be a heniha, but a young man wise beyond his years might be a beloved man. McGillivray was politically astute enough to be satisfied with such a title.[18]

Titles are useless without talent, however, and McGillivray faced problems in enforcing his will on the micos who sat with him in the National Council. One influential faction would not do his bidding. Led by two prominent headmen, Hoboithle Mico (Tame King) of the Upper Town of Tallassee, and Eneah Mico (Fat King) of Cusseta, an important Lower Town, this anti-McGillivray coterie of Creek leaders followed their own interests and consistently sabotaged the centralist purpose of the Great Beloved Man.[19]

There were many origins for the conflict between McGillivray and these opponents. In part, the actions of the two micos can be explained by their leadership of the pro-American faction during the Revolution. They and McGillivray, as British commissary, were at constant loggerheads during the war, and their pre-1783 animosity continued after that conflict. Parallel to and perhaps underlying this difference in Revolutionary ideology was a clan rivalry. The details, including Hoboithle Mico's clan, are unknown, but an American spy reported from the Creek Nation in 1790 that Hoboithle Mico, "with his clan, pronounced McGillivray a boy and an usurper" and acted in ways that were "derogatory to his family clan and consequence." This suggests that a feud of much deeper significance than recent politics or future goals separated the two men and kept the council divided.[20]

In addition, Hoboithle Mico and Eneah Mico were civil leaders in their own towns. The Creeks had a dualistic governmental structure. The civil councils of micos, henihas, and beloved men ruled in time of peace, settling disputes between townsmen, supervising the distribution of agricultural land, overseeing the location and construction of new houses, managing the many ceremonies, and conducting relations with other towns and nations. Though vitally important to the well-being of the people, these were not crisis tasks, and the civil councils governed with a relaxed air. In time of war the civil councils stepped aside in favor of government by the warriors, who ruled for the duration of the crisis with powers which resembled those of a mild martial law. When the Revolutionary War ended, the warriors should have handed authority back to the civil leaders. This transition did not occur during the McGillivray years, partly because a state of emergency continued to exist in the form of threats from all sides, but also because the war leaders of the Upper Towns, the core of the pro-British faction, were the main source of support for McGillivray. Indeed, there is evidence to suggest that McGillivray encouraged the warriors to continue in power. Many micos were victims of this change in political form and, jealous of their loss of influence, joined together in their opposition to McGillivray.[21]

The extent to which persuasion entered into McGillivray's efforts to counter his opposition is unknown, but it seems likely that he devoted a large amount of time and attention to the task of talking his enemies into supporting him. His ill success is readily measured by his use of force or the threat of force to bring the factions into line. There were times when the Great Beloved Man more closely resembled a modern strongman than an imaginative and selfless patriot.

The war councils were the most readily available and the most easily used enforcement mechanism at McGillivray's disposal. Creeks were conditioned to tolerate vigorous war leadership. As long as the Great Beloved Man could command the loyalty of the warriors and convince the townspeople that a continued state of national emergency justified their retention of local governmental authority, he could be reasonably confident that his support would not shrink. But no leader can hold his following through the influence of others, no matter how well placed they are. There had to be something positive in the lives of the people, more tangible than promises of a stable and secure future, that could be directly attributed to McGillivray. To meet this obligation he provided trade.

Every town had a Panton, Leslie and Company trader who did business on a license issued by McGillivray, subject to a body of regulations which McGillivray, as a Creek headman, helped to write, and which McGillivray, as Spanish commissary, enforced. In his Spanish capacity McGillivray also distributed the king's presents, largely given in the form of enormous quantities of guns, powder, lead, and flints. But what he gave he could also withhold. Towns loyal to McGillivray's opponents found it hard to get traders, and munitions from the king went only to those who carried a "ticket" signed by the Great Beloved Man. Headmen aligned with McGillivray's opponents had trouble arming their hunters and warriors. While McGillivray's largesse, direct and indirect, was an important source of power, the threat of its discontinuation was even more important. By exercising that threat McGillivray introduced a new element of compulsion into Creek politics.[22]

But the Great Beloved Man went beyond the subtle threat of force. He maintained a squad of political hit men recruited from his clan kinsmen and paid with "frequent and profuse presents." The ostensible purpose of his "constables" was to guard McGillivray against the frequent attempts on his life by Georgians. But it is reported that "on some occasions" they also "acted as executioners." On at least five occasions McGillivray engaged in politics of assassination. Four of the attempted murders were successful. All the victims were white and all save one were deeply involved in Creek politics in opposition to McGillivray. Their "execution" seriously reduced the strength of the anti-McGillivray factions. There is no evidence to suggest that McGillivray ever ordered the political assassination of another Creek. Such an act would have been intolerable. But Hoboithle Mico and Eneah Mico sorely tempted him. In 1785 and 1786 they signed two additional treaties with Georgia which confirmed the 1783 cession and added another large parcel of land to it. Muttering his frustration that "our Customs (unlike those of Civilized people) Wont permit us to treat [them] as traitors by giving them the usual punishment," McGillivray had to be satisfied to order the destruction of all of Hoboithle Mico's property, including his house, personal possessions, crops, horses, and cattle.[23]

McGillivray's Wind clan "constables" were an unprecedented institution in Creek life. Clan kinsmen owed an obligation to one another to right wrongs done by people of other clans, and in this capacity the clan system served Creek society as its legal and judicial machinery. But this function was traditionally reactive. McGillivray's "constables" were an innovation in clan law which twisted the system so that the Great Beloved Man could enforce his will on his political opponents and intimidate the factions into silence if not compliance with his policies. The "constables'" loyalty was to McGillivray, and to the extent that his word was law they evolved into something like a state police. Such use of force to achieve political ends was unheard of. More than a departure from tradition, it was a violation of the respect and tolerance that underlay the ways Creek people functioned together as a society.[24]

Still, the progression of events during the middle 1780s helped McGillivray unify the Nation. Acting on the succession of fraudulent treaties which granted large tracts of land, Georgia laid out two new counties and began to encourage their settlement. Rebuffing the council's protests that the cessions were unauthorized and therefore illegal, Georgians poured into the country claimed by the Creeks. In April 1786, McGillivray convened a special meeting of the National Council and with virtually no debate the headmen agreed to send the Nation's warriors to drive the settlers away. Acting in conjunction with the Cherokees, with whom McGillivray sought an alliance, Creek warriors marched north against the Cumberland Valley settlements in Tennessee as well as east to the disputed territory on the Creek-Georgia frontier. McGillivray's orders to the warriors were "to traverse all that part of the Country in dispute and wherever they found any American settlers to drive them off and to destroy all the buildings on it, but in the progress to conduct themselves with moderation and to shed no blood on no pretence but where self defence made it absolutely necessary. Neither were they to cross over or within the acknowledged Limits of the States." Armed with Spanish weapons, the Creeks swept the country clean. Settlers returned during the ensuing winter, however, and Creek warriors pushed them out again in the spring of 1787.[25]

This military activity kept the war councils active in the duties they knew best and helped to convince the public that a national emergency really did exist. Ironically, the trouble with Georgia also brought Eneah Mico into the McGillivray fold. Poorly armed because they could not get McGillivray's "tickets" for powder, a party of Cusseta hunters was badly mauled by some Georgians out looking for Creeks on whom to vent their anger. The Cussetas, Georgia's most consistent friends in the Nation, were justifiably outraged by the act, and Eneah Mico joined the McGillivray faction, received his "tickets" for guns and powder, and entered the fray with a tardy but genuine enthusiasm.[26]

Creek successes during 1786 and 1787 astonished their Spanish friends. McGillivray had relied heavily on the commandants of Pensacola and St. Augustine and together they had supplied thousands of pounds of powder and ball. By late 1787 Georgia's expansion had been halted and McGillivray's prestige had grown enormously, not just in the Nation but in the United States as well. Georgia and Tennessee made handsome offers to buy his friendship, the American Congress was forming a commission to negotiate with him, and the Great Beloved Man was gaining stature in native councils from the Choctaws to the Mohawks. Spain, on the other hand, viewed the Confederacy simply as a pawn in her imperial game. Creek warriors, inexpensively and surreptitiously armed, were Florida's expendable first line of defense, and McGillivray was their puppet overlord, cheaply purchased with a commissary's salary and a pat on the head. But McGillivray had fooled them, and late in 1787 the Spanish began to see him in a new light. No longer their creature, he now stood like an unpredictable monster beyond their control. The flow of guns and powder stopped, spies entered the Nation to undermine McGillivray's influence, and the Spanish governor at New Orleans demanded that the Creeks make an immediate peace with the United States.[27]

McGillivray eventually was forced to comply. Indeed, talks had already started with an American representative, but McGillivray broke them off when he discovered the United States insisted on Creek recognition of the three Georgia treaties. Negotiations reopened toward the end of 1788, but they were suspended to await the organization of a new American government under the recently drafted Constitution. Therefore, the Great Beloved Man found himself in the extremely disagreeable position of being at odds with his erstwhile Spanish allies, unable to procure an acceptable peace with the United States, engaged in a war with Georgia, and rapidly running out of munitions. The next few years revealed McGillivray's genius at the art of political maneuver as he extricated his nation from this critical situation with a brilliant diplomatic victory.[28]

Much of the Creek military success against Georgia in the mid-1780s depended on the inability of that state to get help, either from her neighbors or from the national government. McGillivray relied on the weakness and poverty of the United States under the Articles of Confederation and was able, so long as that condition prevailed, effectively to block Georgia's expansion. The establishment of the constitutional government vastly increased Georgia's potential, however, as she could now call on a unified national force for protection. Anxious to prevent this from happening, and seeing that the future great power on the North American continent was clearly the United States and not Spain, McGillivray concluded in 1789 to attempt to outflank Georgia, deny her federal military and political support, and gain United States protection for the Creeks. This meant a treaty with the United States which would provide at least the same benefits as the 1784 treaty with Spain—recognition of Creek independence, protection of Creek territory, and the establishment of a guaranteed trade under McGillivray's control.

Negotiations for such a treaty began in August 1789 in the Creek Nation. The United States commissioners, with a haughty and narrow-minded air, demanded a treaty recognizing Georgia's claims to the disputed land, with no suitable compensation for such a radical reversal of Creek policy. McGillivray and the Creek delegation summarily broke off the talks and withdrew.[29] Heartily disgusted with the whole affair, McGillivray closed his interview with one of the Americans with the oath "by G—— I would not have such a Treaty cram'd down my throat."[30]

During the ensuing winter President Washington sent a special envoy to McGillivray with an invitation that the Great Beloved Man, along with the headmen of the Creek Nation, come to New York to negotiate.[31] McGillivray accepted and he and some two dozen Creek leaders spent the summer of 1790 with Washington and Secretary of War Henry Knox, working out the agreement which, when signed on August 7, 1790, became the Treaty of New York.

This treaty was a clear victory for McGillivray. Not only were its terms quite generous to the Creeks, it also did not conflict in any way with McGillivray's previous arrangements with Spain. The document was a second insurance policy guaranteeing the Creek Nation double protection from Georgia. The Creeks acknowledged "themselves and all parts of the Creek Nation within the limits of the United States . . . to be under the protection of the United States." A twin to the Treaty of Pensacola, this now meant that a large national power was under obligation to defend the rights of territory and humanity of all Creeks, regardless of which side of the international border they resided on. The Treaty of New York also stipulated that the "Creek Nation will not hold any treaty with an individual State." At first glance, this provision seemed a restriction on Creek sovereignty, but in fact it was an enormously valuable protection against Georgia. The three treaties of the 1780s, extorted from a handful of headmen, had been for nearly a decade the source of trouble between the Nation and Georgia. Under this article, the danger of a repetition was forever precluded. Georgia was disarmed—she could no longer claim a legal right to treat with the Creeks for anything.

The Treaty of New York offered other advantages. The United States guaranteed to the Creek Nation "all their lands within the limits of the United States," an almost redundant defense against the official acts of Georgia. To deal with the actions of individual Americans, the treaty provided that any non-Indian who "shall attempt to settle on any of the Creek lands . . . shall forfeit the protection of the United States, and the Creeks may punish him or not, as they please." Thus, the Creeks themselves could deal with white squatters, a constant threat to the tranquillity of the Nation. In the past, state agencies had rarely bothered squatters on unceded Indian lands. Indeed, they encouraged such practice as a way to force land cession from the natives. The treaty not only authorized the Creeks to do whatever they pleased with squatters, it also assured the Creeks of federal support if any neighboring state should object. In addition, the treaty forbade Americans to hunt in the Nation or to enter it for any other purpose without a passport issued under federal auspices. Additional provisions outlined procedures for handling crimes committed by whites against Creeks and vice versa, within or outside of the Nation.

The Treaty of New York was an end run around Georgia which reversed the position of the Creek Nation and that state in their relations with the United States. As long as the Creeks continued a defensive policy against Georgia's invasions, the United States was bound by the treaty to support the Nation in their attempts to preserve Creek territory from Georgia's encroachments, frauds, and schemes. No longer could the Georgians legally pursue an aggressive Indian policy in the hope of deliberately precipitating a frontier crisis from which the United States would then, with all its financial and military power, rescue them at the expense of the Creeks.

McGillivray paid a price for these benefits, a price that many Creeks came to believe was too high for the guarantees won. He gave up about two-thirds of the land claimed by Georgia under the spurious treaties of the 1780s. The tract in question was the three-million-acre strip between the Ogeechee and Oconee rivers. McGillivray saved a large parcel south of this grant which included the game-rich Okefenokee Swamp. For this cession the Nation received, in addition to an unspecified amount of goods, a perpetual annuity of fifteen hundred dollars.[32]

In addition, there were two secret articles, one of which commissioned McGillivray a brigadier general in the United States Army, the first commission of that high rank authorized by the Constitutional Congress. His salary was twelve hundred dollars. The other secret article authorized the Creeks to import annually sixty thousand dollars' worth of trade goods, duty free, through an American port and under McGillivray's control. It is important that these secret articles not be misinterpreted. Both were quite consistent with McGillivray's established policy, and temptations to see them as evidence of his self-interest should be overcome. In the age before the founding of the United States Indian

Office and the creation of the agency system, military rank was the best parallel to McGillivray's Spanish commission as commissary. A military commission gave him ready access to the United States government, at the highest levels, and thus important input into its decision-making process. It also gave him influence over the flow of presents. The trade concessions were equally important. Not only did they ensure McGillivray's continued influence over the political climate in his nation, they also offered expanded access to goods at possibly lower prices and assured the Creeks a market that was uninfluenced by the vagaries of British-Spanish relations. Impending war between those two powers over the Nootka Sound crisis threatened the continued flow of British goods into Spanish territory via Panton, Leslie and Company. The articles were secret because McGillivray had pushed the negotiations far beyond what the Spanish had recommended. The Treaty of New York was McGillivray's contingency plan to abandon Spain when such a change in policy would serve the best interests of the Creeks. It was the ultimate play in the game of balance-of-power politics, and there was no benefit for the Creeks in revealing these provisions to the Spanish.[33]

But Alexander McGillivray was no miracle man. There were many weak links in the chain of national unification he was trying to forge. Almost all of McGillivray's connections were in the Upper Towns. His family and friends were there, his service in the British Indian department had been there, and the core of his political support was there. He traveled into the Lower Towns periodically to attend the National Council, but he rarely went farther down the Chattahoochee than Coweta. He knew little of the distant towns and at one point had to admit to not knowing who their headmen were. In addition, McGillivray had several chronic illnesses that incapacitated him for weeks at a time. Had he been stronger and more vigorous he might have tended his fences more assiduously, but he could not. He restricted his traveling almost exclusively to Coweta and his plantation on the Little River, with short jaunts from the latter to nearby Pensacola to visit William Panton, his trading partner, and the Spanish governor, and he paid for those trips with weeks of recuperation.[34]

McGillivray's distance from and ignorance of conditions in the

Lower Towns created a power vacuum that William Augustus Bowles, a former British army officer from Maryland, hoped to fill. Arriving on the Florida coast in 1788, Bowles schemed to gain the confidence of the Lower Creeks through generous presents of gunpowder. Once their trust was gained, he intended to establish a trade from the Bahamas in competition with Panton, Leslie. After laying an economic foundation, he planned to declare himself the "Director-General of the Muscogee Nation." To Bowles's good fortune, he first arrived among the Lower Towns during the Spanish powder boycott and his gifts of ammunition were well received. Yet Bowles failed to capitalize on his initial success, and although he attracted many followers he never succeeded in supplanting McGillivray. Even Spanish and American agents who might have championed the interloper soon realized he lacked the qualities of leadership inherent in the Great Beloved Man and instead they conspired to destroy him.[35]

If Bowles has any importance at all in Creek history, it is because he was a lightning rod who attracted many Lower Creeks dissatisfied with McGillivray's leadership. A man of many promises, Bowles's most popular pledge was his guarantee of inexpensive trade goods. Panton, Leslie's prices were high, partly because the company paid an import duty to the Spanish government, but also because it was willing to exploit its commercial monopoly. By 1792 there was an economic crisis in the Lower Towns and McGillivray's connection with the Pensacola firm had become a liability. Following the Treaty of New York a profitable trade had developed between the Upper Creeks and the Americans at Rock Landing, a trading post on the Creek-Georgia frontier. That location was inconvenient for many Lower Towns, however, and Panton, Leslie's monopoly in their area remained intact. Seizing upon their dissatisfaction, Bowles promised the Lower Creeks that he would supply them with several shiploads of inexpensive merchandise. When his ships failed to arrive, Bowles led a party of disgruntled warriors on a raid of Panton, Leslie and Company's Appalachee store. Creek participation in the attack reflected a long-term bitterness over the company's high prices and the tribe's shortage of trade goods more than any particular confidence in Bowles's leadership.[36]

Bowles also attempted to capitalize on Lower Creek anger over the cession of the Oconee lands in the Treaty of New York. McGillivray had argued, correctly, that the ceded tract had been invaded by Georgians so many times and fought over by Creeks and Americans so continuously that the game was gone. The country had long since ceased being home for most Creeks, and with its value as hunting ground destroyed, it was not worth the benefits received for ceding it. Despite those arguments, many Lower Creeks felt betrayed. They had resisted Georgia's pretensions to the country since 1783. It was land they had long hunted on, and they deeply resented McGillivray, an Upper Creek with no strong personal interest in the area, giving it up. If for no other reason, American occupation of the Oconee lands brought settlers that much closer to the Lower Towns. In this case, McGillivray showed an insensitivity to Lower Creek anxieties that was made to order for exploitation by Bowles.[37]

Meanwhile, Hoboithle Mico, his clan kinsmen, and their friends continued intransigent. This opposition remained the real threat to McGillivray's political reformation of the Creek Nation. Bowles was a troublesome pest, but an outsider whose grandiose schemes were so ludicrous his only defense was his ignorance. But Hoboithle Mico and the others who supported him were on the inside. They understood as well as, perhaps better than, McGillivray how to make the traditional system work. If nothing else, they were always present to disagree. There is no way to estimate the extent of their association with Bowles. But they shared in the hostility to the Great Beloved Man that kept the factionalism of Creek politics flourishing. And Hoboithle Mico was not several hundred miles away on the Gulf Coast; he was barely thirty miles distant on the Coosa.[38]

McGillivray's influence was probably greatest in the two or three years preceding the Treaty of New York, and climaxed with the negotiation of that document. Creek warriors had the clear upper hand against the Georgians and the Cumberland Valley settlers; Heniha Mico had abandoned his old friends and brought Cusseta, one of the four "mother towns" of the Nation, into the McGillivray camp; and the Great Beloved Man's diplomatic juggling appeared successful. Time, the critical dimension, seemed to be on McGillivray's side. Like most reformers, he underestimated the size of his job, but during the late 1780s his efforts to protect his people and their homeland promised some success.

But the pace exhausted him. "I am absolutely worn down with the life I have lived for ten years," McGillivray complained late in 1791.[39] In sixteen months, at age thirty-four, he was dead. He had stalled for time, fought for concessions, and struggled to bridge the gaps that yawned between the many factions, interests, and sections within the Confederacy. Like other Native American leaders in more recent times, he believed the best defense the Creeks could muster began with domestic preparation. Spanish financial and military aid was not enough. Only a united, single-minded Creek Nation could protect its lands and block the onrushing settlers. But it took time, and Alexander McGillivray, Isti atcagagi thlucco, ran out of time.

NOTES

1. The most important recent attempts at scholarly biography are John Caughey, *McGillivray of the Creeks* (Norman: University of Oklahoma Press, 1938); Arthur P. Whittaker, "Alexander McGillivray, 1783–1789," *North Carolina Historical Review* 5 (April 1928): 181–203, idem, and "Alexander McGillivray, 1789–1793," *North Carolina Historical Review* 5 (July 1928): 289–309. Also see Randolph Downes, "Creek-American Relations, 1782–1790," *Georgia Historical Quarterly* 21 (June 1937): 142–84; idem, "Creek American Relations, 1790–1795," *Journal of Southern History* 8 (August 1942): 350–73; and Helen Tanner, "Pipesmoke and Muskets: Florida Indian Intrigues of the Revolutionary Era," in *Eighteenth-Century Florida and Its Borderlands*, ed. Samuel Proctor (Gainesville: University of Florida Press, 1975), pp. 13–39.

2. Albert James Pickett, *History of Alabama*, 2 vols. (Charleston: 1851), 2: 144; B. F. Riley, *Makers and Romance of Alabama History* (n.p., n.d.), p. 461; Willis Brewer, *Alabama: Her History . . . from 1540 to 1872* (Montgomery: Walker & James, 1872), 24; Absalom H. Chappell, *Miscellanies of Georgia* (Columbus: J. F. Meegan, 1874), p. 28.

3. James H. O'Donnell, "Alexander McGillivray: Training for Leadership, 1777–1783," *Georgia Historical Quarterly* 49 (June 1965): 172–86.

4. Henry Rowe Schoolcraft, *Historical and Statistical Information respecting the History, Conditions, and Prospects of the Indian Tribes of the United States*, 6 vols. (Philadelphia: Lippincott, Grambo, & Co., 1851–57), 5:

263; John R. Swanton, *Social Organization and Social Usages of the Indians of the Creek Confederacy*, 42nd Annual Report of the Bureau of American Ethnology (Washington, D.C.: Government Printing Office, 1924–25), pp. 169–70. Also see David H. Corkran, *The Creek Frontier* (Norman: University of Oklahoma Press, 1967), chap. 1.

5. For insights into the role of mixed-bloods as "intermediaries or cultural brokers," see William C. Sturtevant, "Commentary" in Proctor, *Eighteenth-Century Florida*, pp. 43–46.

6. The best source on factionalism prevalent in the Creek Confederacy is Corkran, *The Creek Frontier*, passim. Also see Angie Debo, *The Road to Disappearance* (Norman: University of Oklahoma Press, 1941).

7. John R. Swanton, *Early History of the Creek Indians and Their Neighbors*, 73rd Annual Bulletin of the Bureau of American Ethnology (Washington, D.C.: Government Printing Office, 1922), pp. 434–37.

8. For the Creeks' role in the American Revolution, see Corkran, *The Creek Frontier*, and O'Donnell, "McGillivray: Training for Leadership." Also see James O'Donnell, *Southern Indians in the American Revolution* (Knoxville: University of Tennessee Press, 1973); John R. Alden, *John Stuart and the Southern Colonial Frontier* (Ann Arbor: University of Michigan Press, 1944); and Verner Crane, "The Origins of the Name of the Creek Indians," *Journal of American History* (December 1918): 339–42.

9. Caughey, *McGillivray*, pp. 21–22.

10. McGillivray to Estevan Miro, March 28, 1784, in Caughey, *McGillivray*, p. 73.

11. Memorial to the Spanish Government from Alexander McGillivray, July 10, 1785, in D.C. Corbitt, ed., "Papers Relating to the Georgia-Florida Frontier, 1784–1800," *Georgia Historical Quarterly* 21 (March 1937): 74.

12. Treaty of Augusta, November 1, 1783, in Linda Grant DePauw, ed., *Senate Executive Journal and Related Documents* (Baltimore: Johns Hopkins University Press, 1974), 165–67.

13. McGillivray to Miro, March 28, 1784, in Caughey, *McGillivray*, p. 74.

14. McGillivray to Arturo O'Neill, January 1, 1784, in ibid., pp. 64–66.

15. The Treaty of Pensacola, June 1, 1784, in *American State Papers: Foreign Relations*, vol. 1 (Washington, D.C.: Gales & Seaton, 1832), pp. 278–79; "Tariff for the Trade of the Creek Nation," June 1, 1784, in John Caughey, "Alexander McGillivray and the Creek Crisis, 1783–1784," in *New Spain and the Anglo-American West*, ed. Charles W. Hackett et al., 2 vols. (Los Angeles: Privately printed, 1932), 1:285–86; Miro to McGillivray, June 7, 1784, in Caughey, *McGillivray*, p. 77. Also see Jack Holmes, "Spanish Treaties with West Florida Indians, 1784–1802," *Florida Historical Quarterly* 48 (October 1969): 140–45.

16. McGillivray to Martin Navarro, November 7, 1785, in Cobitt, "Georgia-Florida Frontier," p. 75.

17. O'Neill to Bernardo Galvez, May 30, 1786, in D.C. Corbitt and Roberta Cobitt, eds., "Papers from the Spanish Archives Relating to Tennessee and the Old Southwest, 1783–1800," *East Tennessee Historical Society Publications* 10 (1938): 140.

18. Theron A. Nunez, Jr., "Creek Nativism and the Creek War of 1813–1814," *Ethnohistory* 5 (Winter 1958): 31–33.

19. McGillivray to Thomas Pinckney, February 26, 1789, *American State Papers: Indian Affairs*, vol. 1 (Washington, D.C.: Gales & Seaton, 1832), pp. 19–30.

20. Corkran, *The Creek Frontier*, chaps. 17–18; Schoolcraft, *Indian Tribes*, 5:281.

21. John Pope, *A Tour through the Southern and Western Territories of the United States of America* (Richmond: John Dixon, 1792), p. 65; Schoolcraft, *Indian Tribes*, 5:281; Swanton, *Social Organization*, pp. 324–27.

22. Daniel Murphy to O'Neill, July 11, 1786, in Caughey, *McGillivray*, p. 119; Miro to O'Neill, June 20, 1786, ibid., pp. 117–18; McGillivray to William Panton, August 3, 1786, ibid., p. 123; Miro to McGillivray, June 7, 1784, ibid., p. 77.

23. McGillivray to Viznete Zespedes, November 15, 1786, ibid., p. 139; Schoolcraft, *Indian Tribes*, 5:281; DePauw, *Senate Journal*, 2:167–69, 179–83. Also see Henry Knox to George Washington, July 6, 1789, *American State Papers: Indian Affairs*, 1:15–16.

24. An analysis of the role of the clan as the juridicial institution of southeastern native societies is in John Phillip Reid, *A Law of Blood: The Primitive Law of the Cherokee Nation* (New York: New York Press, 1970). For an insightful criticism of Reid, see Rennard Strickland, *Fire and the Spirits: Cherokee Law from Clan to Court* (Norman: University of Oklahoma Press, 1975), chaps. 2 and 3.

25. U. B. Phillips, *Georgia and States Rights* (Kent, Ohio: Kent State University Press, 1968), pp. 40–41; Milton Heath, *Constructive Liberalism: The Role of the State in Economic Development in Georgia to 1860* (Cambridge, Mass.: Harvard University Press, 1954), pp. 75, 93–96; McGillivray to Miro, May 1, 1786, in Caughey, *McGillivray*, pp. 106–10; McGillivray to Miro, November 20, 1787, ibid., pp. 163–64.

26. McGillivray to O'Neill, April 18, 1787, in Caughey, *McGillivray*, pp. 149–51; O'Neill to Miro, September 17, 1787, in D. C. Corbitt, "Papers from the Spanish Archives," *East Tennessee Historical Society Publications* 12 (1940): 101.

27. R. Caswell to McGillivray, February 24, 1787, in Walter Clark, ed., *The State Records of North Carolina*, vol. 20 (Goldsboro: P. M. Hale, 1902), pp. 619–20; McGillivray to O'Neill, March 28, 1788, in Caughey, *McGillivray*, pp. 172–74; McGillivray to O'Neill, June 20, 1787, ibid.; O'Neill to Miro, October 28, 1788, ibid., pp. 204–5; McGillivray to John Leslie, November 20, 1788, ibid., pp. 206–8; O'Neill to Miro, March 26, 1788, in D. C. Cobitt, "Papers from the Spanish Archives," *East Tennessee Historical Society Publications* 14 (1942): 97.

28. McGillivray to James White, April 8, 1787, *American State Papers:*

Indian Affairs, 1:18–19; White to Knox, May 24, 1787, ibid., pp. 20–21; McGillivray to O'Neill, April 18, 1787, in Caughey, *McGillivray,* pp. 149–51.

29. Lucia Burk Kinniard, "The Rock Landing Conference of 1789," *North Carolina Historical Review* 9 (October 1932): 349–65.

30. McGillivray to Panton, October 8, 1789, in Caughey, *McGillivray,* pp. 251–54. For the commissioners' impressions, see correspondence by David Humphreys in Frank L. Humphreys, *Life and Times of David Humphreys,* 2 vols. (New York: G. P. Putnam's, 1917), 2:4–13; and report of Benjamin Lincoln, Cyrus Griffin, and David Humphreys to Knox, November 17, 1789, *American State Papers: Indians Affairs,* 1:68–77.

31. William W. Willett, *A Narrative of the Military Action of Colonel Marinus Willett, Taken Chiefly from His Own Manuscript* (New York: G. C. H. Carvill, 1831), chap. 9.

32. The Treaty of New York, August 7, 1790, in Charles J. Kappler, ed., *Indian Affairs: Laws and Treaties,* 5 vols. (Washington, D.C.: Government Printing Office, 1904), 2:25–28.

33. McGillivray's description of the treaty can be found in McGillivray to Carlos Howard, August 11, 1790, in Caughey, *McGillivray,* pp. 273–76, and in McGillivray to Miro, June 8, 1791, ibid., pp. 291–93. Also see ibid., pp. 40–46; Whitaker, "McGillivray, 1789–1793," pp. 296–301; Downes, "Creek-American Relations," pp. 181–84; and J. Leitch Wright, "Creek-American Treaty of 1790: Alexander McGillivray and the Diplomacy of the Old Southwest," *Georgia Historical Quarterly* 21 (December 1967): 379–400.

34. McGillivray to Zespedes, August 3, 1786, in Caughey, *McGillivray,* p. 125; Schoolcraft, *Indian Tribes,* 5:252, 260.

35. McGillivray to Miro, August 12, 1788, in Caughey, *McGillivray,* pp. 194–95; McGillivray to Howard, February 10, 1789, ibid., p. 219. Also see J. Leitch Wright, Jr., *William Augustus Bowles: Director General of the Creek Nation* (Athens: University of Georgia Press, 1967).

36. McGillivray to Panton, October 28, 1791, in Caughey, *McGillivray,* pp. 298–300; Pope, *Tour through the South and West,* p. 70; Lawrence Kinniard, "The Significance of William Augustus Bowles' Seizure of Panton's Apalachee Store in 1792," *Florida Historical Quarterly* 9 (January 1931): 156–92.

37. McGillivray to Panton, October 28, 1791, in Caughey, *McGillivray,* p. 298; Kinniard, "The Significance of Bowles' Seizure," p. 163.

38. McGillivray to Panton, January 12, 1789, in Caughey, *McGillivray,* pp. 214–15.

39. McGillivray to Panton, October 28, 1791, ibid., p. 300.

Red Bird

Martin Zanger

"Whitemen came flocking to Fever River, like the *Wolves in the plains to the dead Buffaloe.*"—Kenoka Decora, 1828[1]

"[Red Bird] appeared to be conscious that, according to Indian law, and measuring the deed he had committed by the injustice, and wrongs, and cruelties of the white man, he had done no wrong."—Thomas L. McKenney[2]

EVEN IN the limited frontier sense, the affair known as the Winnebago War of 1827 hardly qualified for designation as a war. Whether measured in terms of "body count" or property damage, the confrontation falls short. The label "Red Bird Uprising," while perhaps more accurate, also bears shortcomings; it carries the distorting connotation of an unprovoked savage outburst rather than one of an important series of responses which the Winnebagos made to American intrusions into their domain.

The Red Bird affair has made a colorful, tragic story in whatever form it has been told—in on-the-scene descriptive passages and romanticized painting in the works of Thomas L. McKenney; in the twentieth-century pageant-drama by University of Wisconsin playwright William Ellery Leonard; and in August Derleth's historical novel, *Bright Journey.* The story takes on an epic dimension with the heroic exploits and seemingly fortuitous presence in Winnebago country of both Lewis Cass, governor and ex-officio superintendent of Indian affairs for Michigan Territory, and McKenney, the federal superintendent. Moreover, on the military side, General Henry Atkinson, who led the army's rapid show of force which overawed the hostile Winnebagos, would four years later command troops in pursuit of Black Hawk's band.

For the Winnebagos, adjusting to changes brought about by a decline in the fur trade and the concomitant heavy influx of miners into the lead district of southwestern Wisconsin, the uprising and its aftermath portended, to most tribal factions, the futility of overt resistance. For interested whites, the uprising conveniently coincided with an upsurge in demands that the government treat for title to the lead region. All aspects of governmental concern—illicit liquor trade, other crimes involving Indians, mining leases—were secondary to an overriding policy that assumed the inevitability of Winnebago removal from this valuable land. Therefore, in 1827, frontier spokesmen and those who formulated policy exaggerated the nature of Winnebago–Anglo-American confrontations as a useful device in appeasing the juggernaut of frontier pressure to annex the lead country.

As staunch supporters of Tecumseh and the Prophet, the Winnebagos fought with the British during the War of 1812. The prominent mixed-blood chief Kenoka Decora (Old Decora) and a Winnebago contingent took part in British campaigns along the Sandusky River and in the Battle of the Thames.[3] Following the war, many Winnebagos remained under the influence of British traders and were not enthusiastic to make friends with the Americans. While at least one band under Choukeka (Spoon or Ladle Decora) signed the June 3, 1816, treaty of amity at St. Louis, other bands refused to participate.

By the early 1820s tensions increased between white Americans and Winnebagos as miners invaded the lead district of southwest Wisconsin. Meanwhile, traders and American military units stepped up their activities between the Mississippi and Lake Michigan. American officials frequently expressed irritation that disaffected Winnebago bands continued to make seasonal visits to Fort Malden or Drummond Island, where they commiserated with, and sought presents and encouragement from, sympathetic British commanders. Government efforts to interdict Indians traveling to these posts by means of directives and speeches were largely ineffective.[4]

In July 1820, observers reported that the Winnebagos were in a "state of considerable agitation" because white Americans had

accused several young Winnebago warriors of murdering two soldiers at Fort Armstrong on Rock Island, in Illinois. Indian and white behavior in this kind of episode warrants closer analysis, for it reveals important cultural divergences in approaches to such matters as retributive justice and punishment or atonement for murder. While the Winnebagos outwardly complied with the justice system of the dominant culture, a number of instances underscore the fact that at least some of them still closely followed traditional tribal practices in these matters. In submitting to Anglo-American legal concepts, the Winnebagos seldom embraced them, and often structured their compliance with an eye to as much conformity with traditionalism as possible.[5]

To American authorities, murders and scalpings appeared wantonly savage acts. Their response was prompt and unequivocal; they summoned leaders of suspected Winnebago bands and gave them an ultimatum to surrender the culprits for trial in state or territorial courts. When such demands were not complied with, various threats, military expeditions, seizure of hostages, and rewards to cooperative Indian leaders—most often in some combination—generally achieved their purpose. Frontier commanders, however, impatient with slow-moving courts, often preferred summary execution by firing squad. In yielding to War Department orders to turn the Winnebagos accused of murder over to civil authorities, Lieutenant Colonel Henry Leavenworth grumbled, "It would have been better to have executed *them & then have tried them*—If they are *tried* they must be *executed* or we shall feel the weight of the Winnebago Tomahawk." Similar attitudes lay behind American policy in the Red Bird affair.[6]

In contrast, Secretary of War John C. Calhoun saw the killings as committed by a few individuals acting "without the knowledge or authority of the Chiefs." The latter, he correctly predicted, would "disavow it, or any hostility on the part of their nation towards the United States." The secretary ordered local officials to inform Winnebago leaders that such atrocities could not be regarded with impunity. Unless they promptly surrendered "the wicked authors," their "whole nation" would suffer the "just vengeance and retribution of the Government." In short, Calhoun asserted that it was somehow within the power of the chiefs to avert "disastrous consequences and annihilation." He expected the culprits to be handed over to federal authorities.[7]

To ensure compliance with this policy, the army held four Winnebago leaders as hostages. They were released when, true to their word, the chiefs brought three men to Prairie du Chien, Wisconsin, "preceded by a white flag, and attended by a large concourse of the tribe." The next day justices of the peace interrogated the three Indians accused of the crime, while their chiefs looked on.[8] When finally brought to trial, two men were found guilty and sentenced to hang in July 1821. One eventually was executed. The other died in prison.[9]

Winnebago villages along the Rock River and its tributaries remained in a disturbed mood throughout the 1820s. Miners commonly set up mining operations on land recognized as belonging to the Winnebagos by the United States. Meanwhile, the War Department became concerned about Winnebagos digging lead in the Fever (Galena) River district and selling it to American traders. The prospect of Indians engaging in a potentially profitable trade that might replace the declining commerce in furs or supplement subsistence hunting and horticulture frightened American officials. They sought to suppress such traffic because it might "create in the minds of the Indians a reluctance in yielding possession of the mine lands." Therefore Secretary of War John C. Calhoun sent instructions that agents were to use their influence to dissuade the Indians from their mining plans.[10]

The discovery of five charred bodies of a French-Canadian family named Methode, in their maple sugar camp across the Mississippi from Prairie du Chien in the spring of 1826, again drew nearby Winnebago bands into the American judicial system. Two of six Winnebagos suspected of murdering the family were apprehended, but within two weeks they escaped. Some American authorities, fearful that the Winnebagos had been treated with too much leniency, thought the tribe viewed the result of a preliminary investigation as a "triumph over the whites." Judge James D. Doty suggested that taking the suspects by military force and holding them would cause the Winnebagos to yield the real murderers. Rather than harbor resentment, he contended, the tribe would be "well satisfied with the justice which has been done them."[11]

American authorities gave band leaders twenty days to come forth with the individuals implicated in the crime. On the last day, July 4, 1826, some eighty Winnebagos came to Fort Crawford to turn over six of their men to Lieutenant Colonel Willoughby Morgan. All of the surrendered men firmly denied their guilt. Morgan had anticipated that even after the interrogation of witnesses he would be unable to place blame on any individuals. He told the Winnebago leaders he intended to hold the men until they named those actually responsible. In mid-July spokesmen for the tribe acknowledged their belief that two or three Winnebagos were guilty, but they were unable to ascertain which ones. They said they held three of the incarcerated young men in high esteem, believed them innocent, and only surrendered them because they had been designated by whites as suspects.[12]

While the suspects were interrogated, at least one prominent Winnebago, The Boxer (He Who Puts All Out of Doors) offered to martyr himself to preserve his people. While admitting his bad reputation among white Americans, he asserted he had never killed so much as a chicken belonging to them. He formally addressed the officials, stating, "If you wish it, let my life be taken for that of those bad men who have committed this murder." Although federal officials refused his offer, they eventually indicted two Winnebagos, Waukookah and Mahnaatapakah, for the Methode murders.[13]

In October 1826, the army decided to abandon Fort Crawford and the two Winnebago prisoners were taken upriver along with troops bound for Fort Snelling, in Minnesota. The move did not bode well for the United States. Some Winnebagos may have envisioned the abandonment of the military post at Prairie du Chien as an indication of weakness by the United States. Others resented the transportation of their fellow tribesmen to Fort Snelling, the site of a recent massacre of Sioux prisoners by Ojibwas. The Winnebagos were particularly concerned because American military officials at Fort Snelling had surrendered the Sioux to the Ojibwas to placate the latter, since a combined Sioux-Winnebago war party had recently attacked an Ojibwa village. The vengeful Ojibwas had promptly killed and mutilated their recently acquired captives, and the Winnebagos feared that Waukookah and Mahnaatapakah might suffer a similar fate.[14]

Sioux leaders in Minnesota played on the Winnebago fears.

Angered over the death of their kinsmen, militants among the Sioux talked of assaulting Fort Snelling. Messengers were sent to the Winnebago villages near Prairie La Crosse falsely informing them that the two Winnebago prisoners had already been killed, and urging them to attack Prairie du Chien. Evidence suggests that Sioux "ambassadors" also chided Red Bird, a leader among the Winnebagos near La Crosse, telling him his reluctance to retaliate against the whites had made him the laughing stock of tribes throughout Wisconsin. Wabasha and other influential Sioux chiefs eventually quashed the militants among their tribe, but Sioux seeds of dissension bore bitter fruit among the Winnebagos.[15]

By the summer of 1827 the Winnebagos were ripe for violence. Seething because of the illegal invasion of their homelands, they deeply resented the miners who extracted lead ore from Indian lands in southern Wisconsin. Other tribesmen were angered over the abuse of Winnebago women by white frontiersmen, especially miners from the Galena region in Illinois. Relatives and friends of the two Winnebagos still incarcerated at Fort Snelling continued to fear for their safety and could not understand American motives for their prolonged imprisonment. Finally, several Winnebago leaders who lived near the Sioux suffered both "great indignities" and "personal violence" from white officials in the region. Although the nature of this abuse remains unclear, the Indians believed they had been sorely mistreated.[16]

Seeking vengeance, "leading chiefs" among the tribe selected Waunigsootshkau, or Red Bird, to "take meat" among the whites. Red Bird was well known to white residents in the Prairie du Chien region, who trusted the warrior and considered him to be their friend. At first Red Bird attempted to placate the other leaders, seeking vengeance symbolically by destroying white property, but taking no scalps. Disappointed, the other Winnebagos called the warrior a coward and taunted him, telling him "if he had the spirit to avenge the wrongs of his people, he could, by going to the Prairie, get as much meat as he could bring home." Thus to "redeem his character as a brave," Red Bird decided that blood must be spilled.[17]

Accompanied by Wekau (The Sun) and Chickhonsic (The Little Buffalo), Red Bird arrived at Prairie du Chien on June 26,

1827. They stopped first at the residence of trader James Lockwood, where Duncan Graham, a former British soldier, talked
them out of any violence. Proceeding to McNair's Coulee, a few
miles from the village, they entered the cabin of Registre Gagnier.
Gagnier received the Winnebagos in a friendly manner and provided them with food and milk. The Gagnier cabin was also
occupied by Gagnier's wife and two children, and by Solomon
Lipcap, a friend of the family. While the Winnebagos were eating,
Gagnier sensed something strange about their behavior and
attempted to take his rifle from its place on the wall, but Red Bird
shot him before he could reach his weapon. Chickhonsic then
shot Lipcap, while Wekau attempted to fire on Mrs. Gagnier.
Although she was washing clothes, the frontier matron reacted
instantly to the attack on her husband, and before Wekau could
level his weapon Mrs. Gagnier pushed him through the doorway
out into the yard, where she wrestled the rifle away from him.
Although she was unable to fire a shot, she snatched up her
three-year-old son and ran to the village to fetch a posse. Enraged
that he had been bested by a woman, Wekau then stabbed and
scalped the only remaining inhabitant of the cabin, the Gagniers'
eleven-month-old infant.[18]

Following the attack on the Gagnier cabin, Red Bird and his
two companions returned to their villages, where other Winnebagos had acquired a large quantity of liquor. After displaying
the scalps to prove that he had struck at the Americans, Red Bird
and his companions evidently joined with many other Winnebago
villagers and began drinking the whiskey. The revelry continued
for two or three days until most of the liquor was consumed and
scouts reported that a small flotilla of American keelboats were en
route down the Mississippi returning from Fort Snelling.
Asserting, "Now we have begun the war we must carry it on—if
we stop, the Americans will hang us and it is better to die bravely
with our arms in our hands," Red Bird encouraged his tribesmen
to attack the keelboats.[19]

One June 30, while the keelboats passed through a narrow
channel in the Mississippi near the mouth of the Bad Axe River,
the Winnebagos fired from ambush. Stationing themselves on the
river bank, on an island, and also in canoes, the Indians fired
some five hundred shots into the *O. H. Perry*. Desperate hand-to-

hand combat, especially the heroics of an old sailor named "Saucy Jack" Mandeville, who supposedly took four Indian scalps, allowed the vessel to escape. Two men aboard were killed and four wounded, while the crew claimed to have killed over a dozen of their attackers. A second boat passed through with no casualties.[20]

If Red Bird believed that the attacks along the Mississippi would inspire a general uprising among the Winnebagos and the Sioux bands in Minnesota, he was mistaken. War messages were sent to other Winnebago bands scattered across Wisconsin, but Winnebago villages along the Rock River and near Lake Koshkonong were reluctant to join Red Bird and his followers. Sioux warriors in Minnesota who had been so anxious to promote the Winnebago attacks also seemed surprisingly cool to Red Bird's overtures. By mid-July the hostile warriors at Prairie La Crosse realized that they were isolated from the majority of their kinsmen and from other tribes. Although they made a few desultory attacks on livestock in the Prairie du Chien region, for all practical purposes the "Red Bird Uprising" was over.[21]

Unsure of just how many Winnebagos had participated in the recent attacks, government officials moved quickly to keep other Indians from joining them. Governor Lewis Cass of Michigan Territory was already in Wisconsin, planning to meet with delegates from several tribes, when he learned of the attacks at Prairie du Chien. From Green Bay he journeyed down the Fox and Wisconsin rivers to Prairie du Chien, where he made provisional arrangements for its defense until military forces arrived. He also sent messages to Winnebago villages along the Wisconsin and Rock rivers, hoping to "detach from the hostile party the residue of the tribe." Meanwhile he ordered Indian agent John Marsh to invite all the Winnebagos to a treaty council at Green Bay. Provisions and presents were offered, as well as ample opportunity for peaceful Winnebagos to describe and seek remedy for injuries they had received from white Americans. The governor gave Marsh a number of other tasks: to advise the Sioux of American policy and urge them to dissociate themselves from the hostile Winnebagos, to invite the Sioux to Green Bay, to use Menominee warriors currently in Prairie du Chien to defend the village and to call in others nearby for the same purpose, and to ask all of them to the treaty. Cass then met with Sauk and Fox leaders near Rock Island before traveling on to St. Louis to seek additional military assistance.[22]

While Cass and Marsh were spending all their efforts attempting to keep the hostiles isolated, Governor Ninian Edwards of Illinois asserted that the uprising had already spread to Potawatomi villagers scattered across the northern sections of his state. Reporting that "daring robberies" were being committed by Indians north of Peoria, Edwards and other Illinois politicians pressured federal officials to use Winnebago "aggressions" to induce the Potawatomis to vacate their lands in Illinois.[23]

Ironically, while Edwards and other politicians were falsely accusing the Potawatomis of depredations, several Potawatomi leaders were already serving as spies for the government against the Winnebagos. Shabbona, an Ottawa married to a Potawatomi woman; Billy Caldwell; and two other Potawatomis prominent at Chicago journeyed to Wisconsin, where Shabbona entered a Winnebago village near Lake Koshkonong. The Winnebago leader, "a one-eyed man," suspected Shabbona of being a spy, but the Ottawa learned that Winnebago war messages were circulating in Wisconsin. Winnebagos near La Crosse had begun the hostilities and now other bands were assembling to find a way to "act in concert." Shabbona reported that the Winnebagos were having difficulty in restraining their young men long enough to deliberate over ways to avoid warfare with the Anglo-Americans.[24]

Responding to Cass's pleas for military assistance, General Henry Atkinson and 580 men left Jefferson Barracks near St. Louis on July 15 and steamed upriver to Rock Island, where Atkinson also used his influence to keep the Sauks and Foxes out of the conflict. On July 23, Atkinson met with Sauk and Fox leaders Keokuk and Wabalah, assuring them that the government intended to move against the Winnebagos. Although Atkinson asked the Sauks and Foxes to stay home and withdraw any of their people who might be among the hostiles, he expected them to turn out willingly if the government should require their services. To sweeten relations, he presented Keokuk with a saddle and bridle and made smaller gifts to other leaders. Meanwhile, other Sauks and a small party of Winnebagos led by

Wabokieshek, the "Winnebago Prophet," met with Indian agent Thomas Forsyth in northern Illinois. Wabokieshek, who was of mixed Winnebago-Sauk lineage, led a small village settled at Prophetstown on the Rock River. The Prophet assured Forsyth that he wanted peace and had no intention of joining Red Bird and his followers.[25]

Although government officials had successfully isolated the hostiles, panic spread throughout white settlements in Wisconsin and northern Illinois. Fleeing their diggings, miners flocked to the Apple River in northern Illinois, where their encampment was reported to extend four miles and contain three thousand people. Residents of Chicago, hearing of hostility among nearby Potawatomi bands, sent American Fur Company trader Gurdon S. Hubbard (the "Paul Revere of the Prairies") on a horseback mission to Danville, where he raised a hundred volunteers to come to the defense of the unprotected village. At Galena, Prairie du Chien, and Green Bay local militia units armed themselves, and residents of these frontier communities remained in a state of "high excitement."[26]

Determined to crush the uprising, American officials mustered all available military forces and sent them toward the Winnebago country. After meeting with the Sauks and Foxes at Rock Island, Atkinson proceeded on through Galena to Prairie du Chien, where he halted, awaiting further instructions from Cass and Thomas McKenney, who planned to meet with friendly Winnebagos and other tribes in eastern Wisconsin. While encamped at Prairie du Chien, Atkinson sent several companies of infantry to scour the surrounding countryside, but the troops encountered no Indians, hostile or friendly. Meanwhile, Colonel Josiah Snelling descended the Mississippi from Fort Snelling. Having seized Winnebagos as hostages, his force arrived at Prairie du Chien in mid-July. Atkinson's and Snelling's combined commands raised the number of troops at Prairie du Chien to nearly seven hundred men.[27]

Regular troops at Prairie du Chien were augmented by several companies of armed militia composed of miners from the Galena region and by almost six hundred mounted volunteers sent north to Wisconsin by Governor Edwards of Illinois. In addition, as McKenney and Cass prepared to meet with the tribes at Butte des

Morts, on the Fox River in eastern Wisconsin, they assembled another force of 60 regulars and 140 armed Menominees, the latter eager to take up the hatchet against the Winnebagos.[28]

The conference between McKenney, Cass, and the friendly Indians took place at Butte des Morts during the first two weeks of August. With American military forces now poised to strike at the Winnebago heartland, Cass and McKenney lectured the Winnebagos on the seriousness of their offenses against the settlers. Those Winnebagos who wished to remain friends with the United States were told to dissociate themselves from the hostiles. As a good-will gesture, the peaceful tribesmen were asked to send representative chiefs to Green Bay, where they would be "looked after" until the crisis ended. Cass also demanded that the Winnebagos surrender those responsible for the recent attacks or the Americans would open a road all the way to the Mississippi with guns, not axes. Indeed, if the hostiles were not surrendered, the Americans would hit the Winnebagos so hard that their children's children would tell of it. "We must," Cass stated, "have blood for blood."[29]

The 450 Winnebagos attending the conference were led by Four Legs, a chief from Winnebago Rapids. Four Legs attempted to placate the commissioners and shift the blame for the recent hostilities away from his tribe. He reminded Cass that the Indians' resentment had been aggravated by miners trespassing on Winnebago lands, but claimed that the Sioux had instigated the recent murders. Asking for pity, he complained that even his own young men were uncontrollable and that it was impossible for him to surrender those responsible for the attacks near Prairie du Chien. Yet he would attempt to arrange the surrender, although it would anger the Prairie La Crosse band. Finally, he excused himself from going to Green Bay, stating that his cornfields required attention.[30]

In reply, American officials made it clear to the assembled Winnebagos that "nothing short of a surrender of the persons who committed the murder at Prairie du Chien and of three or four of the principal men who led the attack upon the boat, should be viewed as an atonement for the offence." McKenney also warned Four Legs that if the Winnebagos refused the government's demands, the "War Chief" Atkinson would proceed up the Wisconsin River to the portage with the Fox, and then strike at the Winnebago heartland. McKenney's warning caused a "good deal of anxiety" among the assembled Winnebagoes, but he was still unsure if Red Bird and his comrades would be surrendered.[31]

Both McKenney and General Atkinson used all their efforts to place the blame for the attacks on the entire Winnebago tribe, not just the Prairie La Crosse band. They believed that if the Winnebagos were allowed to divert all responsibility to the Prairie La Crosse band, the desired surrender would not take place. Peaceful leaders such as Four Legs and Old Decora would claim they had no control over the hostiles, and the murderers would never be brought to justice. The only way to force a surrender was to emphasize group guilt. If the tribe was sincerely inclined toward peace, they would exert pressure on the hostiles to turn themselves in. To emphasize American determination, in late August McKenney proceeded to the portage between the Fox and Wisconsin rivers. Meanwhile, Atkinson ascended the Wisconsin, ominously leading a large force of regulars deep into Winnebago territory.[32]

The American show of force had the desired effect. Fearing for their women and children, Winnebago leaders counseled together throughout Wisconsin. Meanwhile, Red Bird, aware that the consequences of his actions now threatened his people, volunteered to surrender. Although his attack on the Gagnier cabin was justified under Winnebago law, the Americans demanded retribution. Saddened, the Winnebago leader bade his friends and relatives good-by. He would give up his life to spare his people.

On September 3, 1827, Red Bird and Wekau, accompanied by almost one hundred of their kinsmen, entered McKenney's camp at the portage between the Wisconsin and Fox rivers. Singing his death song, Red Bird held a white flag while two other members of the entourage carried American flags, signaling their friendliness. The Winnebago leader had prepared himself meticulously for the occasion. He was dressed in white buckskin, elaborately fringed, and wore a two-inch-wide collar of blue and white wampum encircled with wildcat claws. Half his face was painted red, the other half green and white. He carried a calumet, and while other leaders arranged for his surrender he mixed kinnikinic and tobacco from an otter-skin pouch, then sat quietly, smoking. Visibly impressed, McKenney later commented, "Of all the Indians I ever saw [Red Bird was] the most perfect in form, in face, and gesture."[33]

Speaking for the assembled Winnebagos, Nawkaw Caramani asked McKenney not to put Red Bird and Wekau in irons. He assured the official that the two warriors had voluntarily surrendered and would not attempt to escape. Although the prisoners were willing to accept their fate, Nawkaw Caramani offered to give the Americans some twenty horses "in commutation for the lives" of the two hostages. McKenney declined the offer but praised the tribe for surrendering the prisoners. Moreover, he promised the Indians that Red Bird and Wekau would not be shackled, but would be "treated kindly, and tried by the same laws by which their Great Father's children were tried."[34]

After McKenney finished speaking, Red Bird concluded the drama by slowly rising and approaching the assembled officials. His head held high, he announced: " 'I am ready.' Then advancing a step or two, he paused, saying, 'I do not wish to be put in irons. Let me be free. I have given away my life—it is gone— (stooping and taking some dust between his finger and thumb, and blowing it away)—and like that'— . . . adding, 'I would not take it back. It is gone.' Having thus spoken, he threw his hands behind him, to indicate that he was leaving all things behind him."[35]

Following his surrender, Red Bird and Wekau were taken to Prairie du Chien and imprisoned at the recently regarrisoned Fort Crawford. They were joined in the fort's guardhouse by four other Winnebagos, whom the government accused of leading the attack on the keelboats, and by the two warriors indicted for murdering the Methode family. Cowed, most of the remaining Winnebago leaders signed a document agreeing to allow white miners to continue on tribal lands south of the Wisconsin until the next season, when a commission could "adjust" land titles.[36]

The Winnebagos assumed that the prisoners would be summarily tried and punished, ending the tribe's obligation to the Americans, but they were wrong. Instead of a prompt trial, government officials kept the Winnebago captives imprisoned in the guardhouse at Fort Crawford until arrangements could be made for their prosecution. But the preparations for the trial seemed to drag on indefinitely. Inclement weather hampered government messengers sent to procure witnesses, and many of the witnesses remained reluctant to travel through the Winnebago country to Prairie du Chien. The territorial judge's schedule did not lend itself to a prompt resolution of the Winnebago case, and the government encountered difficulty in securing both prosecutors and attorneys for the defense. Federal officials also were unable to employ an interpreter fluent enough to serve in the court-room.[37]

The extended delay caused confusion among both the Winnebago prisoners and their kinsmen throughout Wisconsin. In early January 1828, Winnebago leaders met with government officials and asked why the prisoners were being kept alive so long. According to the tribesmen:

> The murderers confessed to the nation that they did kill the whites—some of us saw the scalps. . . . *They would not tell the nation a lie*—and we gave them up to you, not to be *tried,* but to be killed. We did so to keep our Nation from a war, our women and children from slaughter, and to save our Country to live and hunt in. . . . If it is your desire to *take your revenge,* they ought to be killed—if not—it would be very good to our hearts if they were liberated. We wish our Great Father to do what shall please him. But now, these Indians' lodges are desolate—they are not in the hunting camps, or war parties—yet we can not mourn them—they are not dead—We come to see our Fathers to offer the hand of friendship, and smoke the pipe of peace around the council fire—we see the high walls that hide the Winne-bago prisoners and *our hearts are very sore:*—We wish to know that the murderers are killed—our white brethren satisfied, and all is forgotten.[38]

Thus if those in custody could be dealt with quickly, all would soon be forgotten; there would be no further "acts of individual revenge." Extended imprisonment, however, meant that the men remained in limbo in the minds of relatives and friends, who entertained false hopes that the Americans intended to spare them.[39]

Uncertain over their kinsmen's fate, many Winnebagos again grew bitter over what seemed to them to be a "cruel and unusual

punishment." Reports reached government officials that Red
Bird's wife had emerged as a leader of anti-American sentiment,
and that the Prairie La Crosse band again were displaying
Gagnier's scalp, this time on a pole erected over the graves of the
men killed in the attack on the keelboat. Other frontiersmen
complained that the Winnebagos seemed "too quiet," as if biding
their time before another attack.[40] Meanwhile, in the spring of
1828 a few Winnebago warriors attempted to extort money and
goods from travelers along the Rock River. Others destroyed a
ferry boat on the same river and drove the ferryman away from
the crossing.[41]

White miners gave the Winnebagos good cause for continued
resentment. With Red Bird imprisoned and the threat of warfare
diminishing, the miners swarmed over Winnebago hunting lands
south of the Wisconsin. Game had been scarce before the
uprising, but with the influx of miners many of the Winnebagos
were hard pressed to feed their families. Most of the tribesmen
withdrew north of the river, but their relocation placed an added
burden on the food supplies in that region. The few Winnebagos
remaining in southern Wisconsin watched in dismay as nearby
whites "turned their cattle and horses loose in the Indian fields,
trampling down and destroying their corn." Some miners even
entered the Winnebago villages "to dig the mineral from under
their feet." Sympathetic Indian agents reported that the Indians
had "much cause to complain of the treatment they have received
from the whites," and that the Winnebagos were conducting
themselves with a "degree of forbearance highly creditable." Still,
white officials feared that events in southern Wisconsin might be
building toward more bloodshed.[42]

If conditions among the Winnebagos in Wisconsin were deteri-
orating, they were worse for Red Bird and the other prisoners at
Fort Crawford. Expecting to be promptly put to death, the
Winnebago captives were bewildered at their prolonged
imprisonment. Before surrendering, they had ritually bid
farewell to their friends and families, singing their death songs
and giving away their possessions. They had expected to sacrifice
themselves as warriors, but now found themselves caged like
animals. The prolonged incarceration was physically and
psychologically devastating for the Indians. Red Bird especially

fared poorly. Developing dysentery, he seemed to lack the will to live, and in January 1828, Winnebago leaders who visited him reported that he seemed weak and had lost considerable weight. His condition continued to deteriorate and one month later, on February 16, 1828, Red Bird died in the white man's prison.[43]

Ironically, Red Bird's death seemed to cause more alarm among the white community than among the Indians. The Winnebagos had resigned themselves to the captives' death when they had surrendered their kinsmen to the Americans. Red Bird's passing therefore was anticlimactic. Indeed, most Winnebagos believed death to be a lesser punishment than prolonged imprisonment. In contrast, American officials were angered that dysentery had robbed them of the opportunity to make an example of the Winnebago leader. Both McKenney and Indian agent Street argued that Red Bird deserved "a violent death" to illustrate "the stern unyielding justice of our laws." "This was a sight," according to Street, "which I devoutly hoped might be exhibited to the Indians, and I counted largely on the beneficial results . . . of the awful scene."[44]

The long delayed trials of the other Winnebagos took place at Prairie du Chien in late August and early September 1828. Judge James Doty who presided over the proceedings expressed serious misgivings about the trials. He questioned whether a competent jury could be impaneled, whether Indians could be admitted as witnesses, whether their confessions, made before or after arrest, sufficed to convict them, and whether, if such actions were indeed part of a "Winnebago war," their "crimes" were punishable in a civil court. Because local authorities failed to notify Winnebago leaders that the trials were starting, most of the Indians that the prosecution planned to use as witnesses were absent. Other tribesmen refused to testify against their kinsmen. When the trial ended, local officials were incensed at the outcome.[45]

The jury found Chickhonsic and Wekau guilty as accomplices of Red Bird in the murder of Registre Gagnier. Chickhonsic was found guilty of killing Solomon Lipcap, and Wekau was convicted of assault and battery with intent to kill upon the Gagnier infant, who miraculously survived the attack. But the Winnebagos accused of attacking the keelboat were never indicted. The government could not present any competent witnesses who would testify against them. Similarly, Waukookah and Mahnaata-pakah, the two warriors accused of killing the Methode family and held in jail since the summer of 1826, also were released because the prosecution's witnesses were unavailable. Therefore, of the eight Winnebagos arrested by the government, only two were convicted.[46]

Chickhonsic and Wekau were sentenced to hang on December 26, 1828, but even these executions never materialized. By late autumn 1828, the government was making preparations to negotiate with the Winnebagos for the remaining mineral lands in Wisconsin. Anxious to facilitate the proceedings, President John Quincy Adams pardoned both Chickhonsic and Wekau while meeting with Winnebago delegates in Washington. Adams's endeavors, coupled with the white invasion of southern Wisconsin, seemed to produce the desired effect. In August 1829, the Winnebagos signed a treaty at Prairie du Chien relinquishing further claims to lands in Illinois and Wisconsin south of the Fox and Wisconsin rivers.[47]

The Winnebago-white confrontation in Wisconsin during the mid-1820s is indicative of Indian-white relations in the Old Northwest during the two decades following the War of 1812. As settlers surged into the area, miners and other frontiersmen completely ignored Indian title to their lands. There was lead in southern Wisconsin. It could be mined at a profit. Other whites had not staked claims to the region, so there was no reason for the miners not to move in. If the Indians protested the encroachment, they could be intimidated into submission. Then the desired lands could be purchased by the federal government. Any violent resistance on the part of the Indians only made them more vulnerable to the government's demands.

The Winnebago reaction to this aggression was a long delayed but spontaneous outburst of violence against those people the tribe held responsible for their problems. Yet the Winnebagos, unlike the whites, subscribed to a concept of group, rather than individual, guilt. The Indians believed that white *people* were the source of their difficulties, so when they lashed out, their attacks fell upon convenient members of that group—the Methodes, the Gagniers, Lipcap, and the keelboat crew—even though these *individuals* were not directly responsible for the intrusion on

Winnebago lands. Of course the frontiersmen saw the attacks as acts of murder carried out against innocent *individuals* and demanded that the tribe surrender those *individuals* responsible for the killings. Still believing in their concept of group guilt, the Winnebagos turned over several warriors to the government. It was important to the Winnebagos not that all of these warriors be participants in the attacks, but that their sacrifice to white justice would absolve the tribe of any further responsibilities in the matter. Ironically, in threatening the entire Winnebago tribe to make them give up the individuals, Cass and McKenney, at least temporarily, also were subscribing to the Winnebago system of group guilt.

To label the events occurring in Wisconsin during 1827 as the "Red Bird Uprising" is a complete misnomer. Red Bird participated in one of the attacks, but so did several other Winnebagos. The attacks were not planned by Red Bird, but rather resulted from a long series of incidents taking place between Indians and whites in the upper Mississippi Valley. Because Red Bird was well known to the white frontiersmen, they focused their resentment on him, mistakenly attributing to him a leadership role he did not deserve. Unfamiliar with traditional Winnebago leadership, federal officials such as Cass and McKenney took their cue from local sentiment and also blamed Red Bird as the instigator of the "uprising." McKenney's participation in the events and his subsequent vivid descriptions of Red Bird in his *Memoirs* has probably been the most important factor contributing to the Red Bird mystique. Thus in retrospect, whites first maximized, then glamorized Red Bird's role in the futile Winnebago attacks of 1827.

Such aggrandizement is not surprising. Although Red Bird's limited leadership fell well within the bounds of Winnebago tradition, whites wanted something more. There was little glory to be gained in subduing a local Winnebago leader from western Wisconsin, but if he were painted in heroic terms, then his conquerors could rise by his fall. Red Bird is not the only Indian whose claim to leadership may have been enhanced by his white opponents. Recent scholarship suggests that Black Hawk, Tecumseh, and Chief Joseph may also have emerged from history considerably larger than life. It is ironic therefore that one of the most widespread concepts of Indian leadership is indebted as much to white fantasies as to red realities.[48]

NOTES

1. Joseph M. Street to the Secretary of War, January 8, 1828, Letters Received, Office of Indian Affairs, Record Group 75, National Archives, microfilm M234, roll 696. Hereafter all records from this group will be cited by their microfilm number only.

2. Thomas L. McKenney, *Memoirs, Official and Personal* (1846; rpt. Lincoln: University of Nebraska Press, 1973), p. 110.

3. Born around 1747, this Winnebago leader also appears in treaty-period sources as Old Gray-headed Decorah, Schachipkaka (War Eagle), Heetshawausharpskawkaw (White War Eagle), and Dekauray, Sr. He died in 1836. See Nancy Lurie, "A Check List of Treaty Signers by Clan Affiliation," in George E. Fay, ed., *Journal of the Wisconsin Indians Research Institute* 2 (June 1966): 63; and Charles P. Hexom, *Indian History of Winnishiek County* (Decorah, Iowa: A. K. Bailey & Son, 1913), n.p.

4. Cass to John C. Calhoun, August 3, 1819, Records of the Michigan Superintendency, National Archives, microfilm M1, roll 7. Also see Cass to Calhoun, October 8, 1819, ibid.; Cass to George Boyd, April 7, 1822, ibid.; Joseph Smith to Jacob Brown, January 5, 1820, ibid. Hereafter all records from this group will be cited by their microfilm number only.

5. Jedidiah Morse, *A Report to the Secretary of War of the United States on Indian Affairs* . . . (New Haven: Howe and Spalding, 1822), pp. 14–15. See also Martin Zanger, "Conflicting Concepts of Justice: A Winnebago Murder Trial on the Illinois Frontier," *Journal of the Illinois State Historical Society*, forthcoming.

6. Francis Paul Prucha, *American Indian Policy in the Formative Years: The Indian Trade and Intercourse Acts, 1790–1834* (Cambridge, Mass.: Harvard University Press, 1962), pp. 192–94; Leavenworth to Daniel Parker, June 10, 1820, quoted in Francis Paul Prucha, *The Sword of the Republic: The United States Army on the Frontier, 1783–1846* (New York: Macmillan, 1969), p. 208. Also see Calhoun to Leavenworth, July 28, 1820, *The Papers of John C. Calhoun*, ed. W. Edwin Hamphill, Robert L. Meriwether, and Clyde N. Wilson, vol. 5, *1820–1821* (Columbia: University of South Carolina Press, 1971), pp. 298–99.

7. Calhoun to Richard Graham, May 11, 1820, Records of the Secretary of War Relating to Indian Affairs, Letters Sent, Record Group 75, National Archives, microfilm M15, role 4. Also see Calhoun to Cass. May

11, 1820, ibid. Hereafter all records from this group will be cited by their microfilm number only.

8. Review of Thomas McKenney, *Tour of the Lakes,* in *North American Review* 25 (October 1827): 345–46; Examinations of Winnebago Indians, June 9, 1820, William Clark Papers, Kansas Historical Society, Topeka, vols. 2–3, pp. 199–212; *Illinois Intelligencer* (Vandalia), June 19, 1821.

9. *Illinois Intelligencer,* May 15, May 26, June 19, and September 4, 1821. Also see Calhoun to Clark, June 11, 1821, M15, roll 5; Calhoun to Jepithah Harding, June 11, 1821, ibid.; and Samuel Hamilton to Daniel Brent, June 9, 1821, ibid.

10. George Bromford to John C. Calhoun, August 5, 1823, *Calhoun Papers,* 8:208–9; Calhoun to Clark, August 6, 1823, M15, roll 5.

11. John Kinzie, Jr., to Cass, May 10, 1826, M1, roll 18; James Doty to Willoughby Morgan, May 11, 1826, M234, roll 315.

12. Report of Lt. Col. W. Morgan, July 9, 1826, M234, roll 931; Kinzie to Cass, July 15, 1826, M1, roll 19. Details of the interrogation of the Winnebago prisoners and the ensuing indictments are in the Boilvin Report, July 6–7, 1826, M234, roll 931; and in "The United States vs. Wau-koo-kah, Indict. for Murder," May 14, 1827, ibid.

13. Boilvin Report, July 6–7, 1826, M234, roll 931. Indictments for both the accused can be found in ibid. Also see George Catlin, *Letters and Notes on the Manners, Customs, and Condition of the North American Indians,* 2 vols. (1841; rpt. New York: Dover Publications, 1973), 2:146, pl. 255.

14. John Marsh to Clark, May 30, 1827, M234, roll 748; Joseph Rolette to McKenney, ibid., roll 419; Rolette to Cass, November 16, 1827, M1, roll 21; Lawrence Taliaferro, Journal, June 13–17, 1827, MS, vol. 4, pp. 15–16, Minnesota Historical Society, St. Paul. Also see speeches by Flat Mouth and Strong Earth (Ojibwas), May 30, 1827, M234, roll 748; and Clark to Barbour, June 14, 1827, ibid.

15. Rolette to Cass, November 16, 1827, M1, roll 21; Rolette to McKenney, November 18, 1827, M234, roll 419; William J. Snelling, "Early Days at Prairie du Chien, and the Winnebago Outbreak of 1827," *Collections of the State Historical Society of Wisconsin* 5 (1907): 143–44. Also see McKenney to the Secretary of War, September 17, 1827, *House Document 277,* 20th Cong., 1st sess., p. 9.

16. McKenney, *Memoirs,* p. 130; Street to the Secretary of War, November 15, 1827, M234, roll 696; Marsh to Cass, November 19, 1827, extract, ibid., roll 419.

17. McKenney, *Memoirs,* p. 130.

18. Ibid., pp. 127–29.

19. John Marsh to Clark, July 20, 1827, M234, roll 748; Street to the Secretary of War, January 8, 1828, ibid., roll 696; Snelling, "Early Days at Prairie du Chien," pp. 145–47. Also see Edward D. Neill, "Occurrences in and around Fort Snelling, from 1819 to 1840," *Minnesota Historical Society Collections* 2 (1889): 34; and "Indian Speech at Drum-

mond Island," *Michigan Pioneer and Historical Society Collections* 23 (1895): 146.

20. Thomas Forsyth to Clark, July 5, 1827, M234, roll 748; James H. Lockwood, "Early Times and Events in Wisconsin," *Collections of the State Historical Society of Wisconsin* 2 (1856): 162–63.

21. John Kinzie to Cass, August 3, 1827, M1, roll 21; John Marsh to Clark, July 20, 1827, M234, roll 748; Marsh to Cass, July 31, 1827, M1, roll 21.

22. Cass to Marsh, July 5, 1827, M234, roll 419; Cass to Forsyth, July 6, 1827, ibid.

23. Clark to Peter Menard, Jr., August 9, 1827, M234, roll 749; Ninian Edwards to the Secretary of War, September 4, 1827, ibid., roll 419; Ninian Edwards to the Secretary of War, August 20, 1827, in Ninian W. Edwards, *History of Illinois from 1788 to 1833; and Life and Times of Ninian Edwards* (Springfield: Illinois State Journal, 1870), pp. 350–51. Also see E. B. Washburne, ed., *The Edwards Papers* (Chicago: Chicago Historical Society, 1884), pp. 298–300; James A. Clifton, *The Prairie People: Continuity and Change in Potawatomi Indian Culture, 1665–1965* (Lawrence: Regents Press of Kansas, 1977), p. 228; and R. David Edmunds, *The Potawatomis: Keepers of the Fire* (Norman: University of Oklahoma Press, 1978), pp. 230–33.

24. Forsyth to Cass, September 10, 1827, M1, roll 21; Kinzie to Cass, August 3, 1827, ibid. Also see Clifton, *The Prairie People*, pp. 222, 228; Perry Armstrong, *The Sauks and the Black Hawk War* (Springfield: Illinois State Journal, 1887), pp. 580–81; and William Hickling and Gurdon S. Hubbard, "Sketches of Billy Caldwell and Shabonee," *Addresses Delivered at the Annual Meeting of the Chicago Historical Society* (Chicago: The Society, 1877), pp. 40–46.

25. Atkinson to Clark, July 24, 1827, M234, roll 748; Forsyth to Cass, September 10, 1827, M1, roll 21.

26. Milo M. Quaife, *Chicago and the Old Northwest, 1673–1835* (Chicago: University of Chicago Press, 1913), pp. 313–17; Grant Goodrich, "Gurdon S. Hubbard: A Settler of Chicago in 1818," in *Early Chicago and Illinois*, ed. Edward G. Mason (Chicago: Fergus Printing Co., 1890), pp. 19–20; McKenney to Barbour, July 19, 1827, M234, roll 419.

27. Marsh to Cass, July 31, 1827, M1, roll 21; "Indian Honor: An Incident of the Winnebago War," *Collections of the State Historical Society of Wisconsin* 5 (1907): 154–55; Roger L. Nichols, *General Henry Atkinson: A Western Military Career* (Norman: University of Oklahoma Press, 1965), pp. 119–28.

28. Ninian Edwards to Secretary of War, August 20, 1827, in Edwards, *History of Illinois*, pp. 350–51; Washburne, *The Edwards Papers*, pp. 298–300; McKenney to Barbour, July 19, 1827, M234, roll 419; Patricia K. Ourada, *The Menominee Indians: A History* (Norman: University of Oklahoma Press, 1979), pp. 83–84.

29. Cass to Marsh, July 5, 1827, M234, roll 419.

30. Treaty Journal, Butte des Morts, August 11, 1827, Winnebago File, Great Lakes Indian Archives, Indiana University, Bloomington, Indiana.

31. Cass to Barbour, August 17, 1827, M234, roll 419; McKenney to Cass, August 19, 1827, ibid.; "Letter from the Secretary of War Transmitting a Report of Gov. Cass and Col. McKenney, on the Subject of the Complaints on the Winnebago Indians," February 5, 1828, *House Document 117*, 20th Cong. 1st sess., pp. 1–7.

32. McKenney to Cass, September 2, 1827, M1, roll 21; Atkinson to Cass, July 31, 1827, ibid.; Atkinson to Cass, July 25, 1827, M234, roll 419. Also see Nichols, *General Henry Atkinson,* pp. 129–30.

33. McKenney, *Memoirs,* pp. 106–10; Joseph Street to Ninian Edwards, December 28, 1827, in Washburne, *The Edwards Papers,* p. 325. Also see Thomas McKenney and James Hall, *The Indian Tribes of North America, with Biographical Sketches and Anecdotes of the Principal Chiefs,* ed. Frederick Webb Hodge, 3 vols. (Edinburgh: John Grant, 1933), 2:426–27.

34. McKenney, *Memoirs,* p. 110.

35. Ibid., pp. 111–12.

36. "Peace Proclamation," September 22, 1827, *Report of the Secretary of War,* 1827, House Executive Document 2, 20th Cong., 1st sess., pp. 152–54; Atkinson to Edmund P. Gains, September 20, 1827, ibid.; Atkinson to Cass, September 10, 1827, M1, roll 21; Brevoort to Cass, September 5, 1827, ibid.

37. Cass to Barbour, January 7, 1828, M234, roll 420.

38. Street to the Secretary of War, January 8, 1828, ibid., roll 696.

39. Street to the Secretary of War, November 15, 1827, ibid.

40. Street to Edwards, December 28, 1827, in Washburne, *The Edwards Papers,* p. 325; Street to the Secretary of War, January 8, 1828, M234, roll 696; Street to Clark, December 10, 1827, ibid., roll 748.

41. Street to Clark, January 26, 1828, M234, roll 748; John McLean to Barbour, April 29, 1828, ibid.; Clark to McKenney, June 20, 1828, ibid.; McKenney to Clark, May 2, 1828, M21, roll 4.

42. Street to Peter Porter, September 9, 1828, M234, roll 696; Clark to the Secretary of War, July 10, 1828, ibid.; Forsyth to Clark, June 25, 1828, ibid.; George Silliman and G. Hunt to Cass, August 26, 1828, M1, roll 23.

43. Street to Clark, January 26, 1828, M234, roll 748; "Indian Speech at Drummond Island," p. 146.

44. Street to the Secretary of War, February 17, 1828, M234, roll 696; McKenney to Clark, April 10, 1828, M21, roll 4.

45. Doty to Barbour, January 31, 1828, M234, roll 696; Street to Clark, August 25, 1828, ibid.

46. "Transcript of Record of Proceedings," September 8, 1828, M234, roll 931; "Bills of Indictment," August 25–September 1, 1828, ibid.; transcript of trial, September 8, 1828, ibid.; Street to Porter, September 9, 1828, ibid., roll 696.

47. Treaty Journal, Prairie du Chien, July 19, 1829, Winnebago File, Great Lakes Indian Archives. Also see Katherine C. Turner, *Red Men Calling on the Great White Father* (Norman: University of Oklahoma Press, 1951), p. 86; "Articles of a treaty . . .," August 1, 1829, in Kappler, *Indian Affairs: Laws and Treaties*, 2:300–303.

48. William T. Hagan, *The Sac and Fox Indians* (Norman: University of Oklahoma Press, 1958), p. 203; Richard Metcalf, "Who Should Rule at Home?: Native American Politics and Indian-White Relations," *Journal of American History* 61 (December 1974): 651–65. Also see "The Shawnee Prophet," a manuscript in the possession of R. David Edmunds, Fort Worth, Texas; and Mark Brown, "The Joseph Myth," *Montana: The Magazine of Western History* 22 (January 1972): 2–17.

John Ross

Gary E. Moulton

CHIEF JOHN ROSS of the Cherokees served his people for more than fifty years in a variety of leadership positions. After establishing a constitutional government in 1827, the Cherokees repeatedly elected Ross to their highest tribal office until his death in 1866. Ross was not tapped for leadership at the moment of some great crisis in Cherokee affairs. Rather, when momentous events occurred, he could lead his people because he had grown to the task through years of increasing responsibility and dedication. He became principal chief of the Cherokees by his own inclinations and because he met the needs of the Cherokees as they were pushed into more frequent encounters with their Anglo neighbors. The Cherokees needed someone committed to their cause who understood the white man's game of negotiations and treaty making. In Ross they found an able and devoted spokesman who would serve them well.

At the beginning of the nineteenth century the Cherokees were rapidly moving through a transitional phase that would see them adopt many customs from the white world. Because Cherokee women married white traders, mixed-blood children displayed a variety of Anglo names such as McDonald, Lowrey, Gunter, Taylor, Adair, and Vann. On October 3, 1790, Ross was born into a family that reflected this changing nature of Cherokee society. Three generations of Scotch-Irish traders had diminished the Indian lineage in his ancestry so that Ross could claim to be only one-eighth Cherokee by blood.[1]

During Ross's childhood, his family traveled throughout the Cherokee country, where the boy was exposed to both Cherokee and white cultures. The third child in a family of nine children, he spent much of his early childhood playing time-honored

Cherokee games with his brothers and sisters. Accounts of Ross's boyhood indicate that he dressed similarly to other Cherokee boys of his age and that he looked forward to participating in tribal ceremonies and festivals. It seems doubtful, however, that he ever had more than a cursory knowledge of the Cherokee language, for even as an adult he never learned to use its written characters.[2]

As Ross approached adolescence, his life began to change. During the late 1790s Daniel Ross, Ross's father, settled near the northern end of Lookout Mountain, in southeastern Tennessee. The elder Ross accumulated books, maps, and newspapers for his home and brought the first tutors into the Cherokee Nation. He also sent his sons to an academy at Kingston, Tennessee, where John boarded with and worked for a merchant. The continued exposure to white culture must have had a profound effect on the young mixed-blood, for after his attendance at the academy he pulled away more from his Indian identity and steadily moved toward the world of the white planter-merchant. About 1814 he established Ross's Landing, a trading post and ferry on the Tennessee River that eventually became Chattanooga, Tennessee. Here, in partnership with a son of the federal agent to the Cherokees, Ross acquired lucrative government contracts to supply both Indians and soldiers. He even attempted to become a factor to the Western Cherokees in Arkansas, but the appointment of a rival and the outbreak of the Creek War thwarted those efforts.[3]

While Ross was acquiring such valuable business experience the Cherokee people were adopting many elements of American culture. Each year white Indian agents among the tribe reported a growing use of agricultural implements, increases in Christian conversions, and greater numbers of Cherokee youth at the frontier mission schools. Moreover, the Cherokees were developing a political system similar to that of the United States. A tribal council was functioning a decade before Ross's birth, and by 1808 it had developed into a regular governing apparatus. In that year the council enacted the first written law for the Cherokees. One year later the Cherokees formed a standing committee of thirteen members, which in time took over the major political functions of the tribe.[4]

Interested in politics, Ross increasingly participated in the gov-

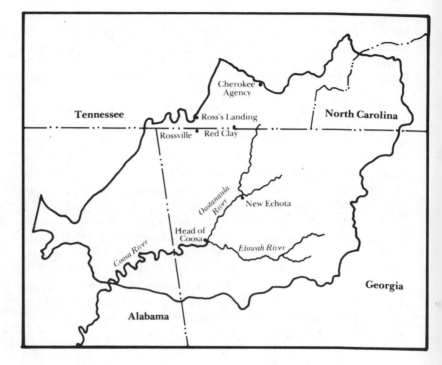

ernment of the tribe. He first served as a clerk to Chiefs Path Killer and Charles Hicks, but by 1811 he was a member of the standing committee and in 1816 he joined the Cherokee delegation which journeyed to Washington to present certain grievances to the United States. Although he protested that public life detracted from his business interests, in mid-1818 he accepted the presidency of the National Committee, as the standing committee was now called. During the next year he joined another Cherokee delegation being sent to Washington, where he helped to negotiate the Cherokee Treaty of 1819.[5]

During the next half decade Ross continued to work at business ventures, but he also remained active in tribal politics. He served as captain of the Cherokee Light Horse, a tribal military unit whose job was to remove white intruders from Cherokee lands. In his position as president of the National Committee, he used his influence to urge his tribesmen to resist any state or federal encroachment on their sovereignty or lands. He also resisted bribery, a common weakness among many Indian leaders during this period. In 1823, after the Creek chief William McIntosh offered him two thousand dollars for his support of a treaty with federal commissioners, Ross stood before a council of his people and declared, "This letter which I hold in my hand will speak for itself, but fortunately the author of it has mistaken my character and sense of honor." The incident raised Ross's prestige and strengthened his role as a principal spokesman for his people.[6]

During 1824 and again in 1825 Ross's talents as tribal spokesman were tested by the federal government. Five years earlier, in 1819, he had served as the principal correspondent in the conferences surrounding the Cherokee Treaty, but in 1824 and 1825 he again traveled to Washington, where he directed the tribe's negotiations with John C. Calhoun, secretary of war, and Thomas L. McKenney, head of the Office of Indian Affairs. The Cherokees had several objectives in these missions: to clarify provisions of several treaties then in effect, to readjust annuity payments divided between the Eastern and Western Cherokees, and to ask for the dismissal of an agent whom they generally disliked. The Cherokees had little success in the negotiations, but Ross gained valuable experience at the bargaining table and favorably impressed many public officials.[7]

The next three years Ross strengthened his position in the Cherokee political arena. He continued to preside over the National Committee, which called forth his talents at its yearly sessions. At two sessions in 1825 the committee forcefully stated that no acts of a public character could be passed by the committee without the consent of the Cherokee people in council. This guaranteed an end to the practice of selling Cherokee lands by a few chiefs who were bribed into compliance. More than thirty other pieces of legislation that year also bore Ross's florid signature and the imprint of his influence. One act provided for the establishment of a national capital at New Echota within the chartered limits of northwestern Georgia. Ross commissioned three persons to lay out the town and to superintend public construction. He also promoted the nascent Cherokee newspaper, the *Cherokee Phoenix,* hoping it would help the spread of literacy and give a wider understanding of tribal affairs. He even volunteered his personal funds to keep the enterprise functioning.[8]

Ross reestablished his family and home near the new capital. From Rossville he moved south to build a house and ferry at the confluence of the Oostanaula and Etowah Rivers, the Head of Coosa, as he named it. He built a comfortable two-story house, seventy by twenty feet, which included a basement and an ash shake roof. Kitchens, workhouses, smokehouses, slaves' quarters, stables, and corn cribs were erected, and Ross's field hands worked the nearly two hundred acres that he controlled. Located within thirty miles of New Echota and easily accessible to the leading men of the Cherokee Nation, Ross tied his fortunes even more closely to the fate of his Indian people.[9]

Ross's widening role in Cherokee affairs was evident during the summer of 1827. Elected as a delegate to the Cherokees' constitutional convention from the Chickamaugah District, he ultimately was chosen as president of that body. Although the written proceedings of the convention are not extant, nor is the author of the finished document known, Ross surely had a dominant voice in all the activities. The convention established the first constitutional government of an American Indian tribe and one strikingly similar to that established under the United States Constitution. Three branches of government were created, with a bicameral legislature, a principal and an assistant chief, and a system of courts. The legislators served two-year terms and were elected by qualified voters, while the chiefs served four years and were chosen by the General Council, the combined legislative bodies.[10]

In 1828, through a formal election in the recently established General Council, Ross was elected principal chief by the overwhelming vote of thirty-four to six. This election marked a turning point in Ross's career, for after accepting the new position he would devote the rest of his life to serving his people. Over the next four decades he maintained his office as principal chief, even when defied by a vocal opposition and discredited by federal officials. Dedicated to the defense of his people, he faced three great struggles in which the authenticity of his leadership was questioned.[11]

From 1830 until the Cherokee removal of 1838 Ross visited Washington almost every year, defending his people against the federal bureaucracy. The Office of Indian Affairs was part of the Department of War during this period, a bureaucratic arrangement that reflected the government's attitude toward the Indian tribes. Since Indian leaders such as Ross were important figures on the frontier, he was granted several audiences with the new president, Andrew Jackson. Jackson had assumed the presidency a few months after Ross was elected principal chief of the Cherokees, but Ross had served under Old Hickory during the Creek War and was already acquainted with him. Although apprehensive of Jackson's policies, Ross was by no means awed by the man.

Ross's primary task in Washington during these years was to forestall the forced removal of his tribe west of the Mississippi River. He lost ground at nearly every turn. Jackson was able to push his Indian Removal Bill through Congress in 1830, officially committing the government to a policy of emigration. The president also withdrew the payment of tribal annuities except as allotments to individuals. This money, owed the Cherokees for former land cessions, served as the sole tribal revenue. Divided into individual payments, the funds amounted to no more than fifty cents per person. Nor was the "frontier president" likely to interfere in the exercise of state sovereignty over Indian property. After gold was discovered on Cherokee lands in Georgia, Jackson did nothing to protect the tribesmen from Georgia's designs in the region. He simply removed federal troops and the state moved in, claiming control over the area and eventually allotting Cherokee lands to white Georgians. Ross and his followers lost their homes, fields, and ferries to lucky ticket holders in Georgia's grand lottery. Returning from Washington in the spring of 1835, Ross found the beautiful Head of Coosa occupied by strangers. He was forced to flee Georgia and take up residence at Red Clay, Tennessee.[12]

Appeals to Congress brought little success. Each session saw Ross and several colleagues preparing a memorial that outlined the abuses the Cherokees had suffered. Included were duplicates of official correspondence, Cherokee resolutions, executive orders, state laws, and pleas for restitution, all copied by hand for the printer. Ross found this a wearisome task, for he personally copied almost all these documents, making drafts which numbered in the dozens. For all his work, he received little reward in terms of reversing federal Indian policy. Northeastern legislators offered sympathy but little hope that they could turn the tide of executive authority and state pressure which urged Indian removal.[13]

Ross also turned to the federal judiciary to find relief for the beleaguered Cherokees. In 1830 he began a lively correspondence with William Wirt, former attorney general of the United States. On one level Ross was interested in getting cases before the state courts to stop the takeover of Cherokee property. He also hoped to establish that the Cherokees were independent of Georgia's jurisdiction. Wirt advised Ross on the employment of the Cherokees' cadre of state lawyers. Wirt's goal was to carry cases to higher tribunals and to force Georgia to acquiesce to Cherokee demands. The issue was sovereignty, and it had to be determined at the highest level, the United States Supreme Court. Ross carried out the specific measures outlined by Wirt and opened the way to the historic case *Cherokee Nation v. Georgia* in 1831. To Ross's disappointment, in this case the justices ruled that the Cherokees were not a "foreign State" but a "domestic dependent nation" and that the court had no original jurisdiction over the case. Another case the next year, although more promising at the outset, proved equally as futile. In *Worcester* v. *Georgia* the court ruled that federal jurisdiction over the Cherokees was exclusive and Georgia had no power to pass laws affecting the Cherokees. Yet Jackson circumvented Chief Justice John Marshall's landmark ruling and the state of Georgia simply ignored the verdict.[14]

With the arrival of the Reverend John F. Schermerhorn, a United States commissioner, in the Cherokee country during the summer of 1835, federal pressure for a removal increased and assaults on Ross's leadership grew more serious. The commissioner was not the first federal emissary sent to treat for migration. Ross had parried the thrusts of repeated representatives who brought promises from Washington of better days for the Cherokees if they would move across the Mississippi. The Cherokees had unequivocally rejected all such offers. Yet where others had failed, Schermerhorn would succeed, for he was prepared to discredit Ross and the Cherokee leadership. He was also willing to disregard orders to abandon his efforts, and to discover Cherokee treaty advocates, no matter how few or how unauthorized their actions. The commissioner found that Ross and several other Cherokee leaders had taken reservations outside the Nation under the Treaty of 1819, some with plans of accepting United States citizenship. Ross's position was very clear in this matter. He had never left the Cherokee Nation, he had never renounced his tribal affiliation, and he could show that the land he obtained was actually part of an ancestral inheritance. Undaunted, Schermerhorn asserted, "These reservees . . . have no more right or authority to dispose of the present Cherokee country, than those members of the Cherokee nation who have actually . . . removed." Since the Cherokees had recently failed to hold tribal elections, he also insisted that "there is not now a single individual belonging to the Red Clay council with John Ross at their head, legally and constitutionally in office." Schermerhorn did admit that this was due to the proroguing of the Cherokee government by surrounding states, but that was of little importance to him. In fact, fear of intimidation and arrest by Georgia had prompted the Cherokees to postpone the elections.

Ironically, the suggestion for such a policy came from Major and John Ridge, leaders of the faction that opposed Ross and advocated removal to the West.[15]

In October 1835, Ross and the proremoval faction agreed to send a joint delegation to Washington to seek a final accord with the federal government. By this time Ross realized that some sort of removal would take place, but he still hoped to negotiate for a western emigration that would be satisfactory to the Cherokees. Ross was no unbending autocrat; he had learned the politics of compromise through years of bargaining. Yet while Ross and other leaders were in the capital, Schermerhorn, in late December 1835, assembled several removal advocates at New Echota, where members of this minority faction put their signatures to a treaty that would force the entire tribe across the "Trail of Tears." In Washington, Ross and his followers were then deserted by the protreaty delegates, who quickly added their names to the removal pact. Despite Ross's protests, the treaty was ratified by the Senate, although by the narrowest of margins. Of course, Jackson eagerly signed it. The Cherokees now had two years to move to new lands in the West.[16]

After the Treaty of New Echota, Ross began a vigorous campaign to have the treaty reversed. He worked incessantly in Washington over the next two years to convince Congress and Martin Van Buren's new administration that the compact was unjust and invalid. In a relentless barrage of letters, pamphlets, memorials, and speeches, Ross pleaded the Cherokees' cause. He displayed numerous resolutions signed by hundreds of his tribesmen deploring the actions of an unauthorized body who would sign away tribal lands. Discouraged, Ross finally ceased his efforts in Washington in mid-1838, when he learned of military pressure against the Cherokees in Georgia. He had achieved some success. He had been able to secure an additional appropriation of over one million dollars for Cherokee removal, and was satisfied that no other changes could be made.[17]

When Ross arrived in the Cherokee country, he found a disheartening situation. Most of his people were confined to crowded camps that had been hurriedly established as staging areas for the subsequent removal. Major General Winfield Scott had been largely ineffectual in getting the Indians underway.

Cherokees resisted his prodding at every stage, thereby adding to their own suffering. In a meeting of the tribe, Ross was asked to take charge of the removal, thus sparing the tribe the humility of being driven west at the point of a bayonet. The chief established a removal committee and organized the tribe into thirteen removal detachments of about one thousand persons each. The logistics of the task were staggering, for this was completely managed by Cherokees, many of whom had little experience in such endeavors. Each detachment had a contingent of conductors, commissary agents, physicians, interpreters, and wagon masters. Agents located along the overland route supplied extra rations, clothing, and advice as needed. Ross supervised every detail: calling in reluctant emigrants, assigning detachment officers, hiring white physicians, transacting complex financial arrangements, and checking the progress of the parties along the route. Ross and his family joined the last small party of invalids and elderly persons who traveled by water in December 1838. When the boat slipped away from Ross's Landing, a long and bitter struggle with state and federal officials had come to an end.[18]

Instead of ending all problems in Cherokee relations with the federal government and opening a golden era for the tribe, removal simply brought a new set of difficulties. Moreover, Ross and his followers would not accept the legality of the tainted Treaty of New Echota. A half-dozen years would pass before the issues over removal were finally resolved.

One immediate problem was the establishment of a new political system. Cherokee emigrants who had settled in the West decades earlier had devised their own governing apparatus and were unwilling to merge with their more numerous brothers from the East. Attempts at compromise on both sides failed, but Ross was able to get enough Western Cherokees to join him that he could declare his following the legitimate power. Ross's followers organized, drew up a new constitution, and elected Ross chief. Other officials in the new government included a considerable number of the Old Settlers, as the Western Cherokees were called.

In June 1839, these tribal political quarrels assumed a more tragic nature with the brutal assassinations of the treaty party leaders: Elias Boudinot, Major Ridge, and John Ridge. Most Cherokees understood the murders, deplorable as they were, for the deaths were part of the ancient "blood law" which forbade the transfer of tribal lands. Although treaty supporters accused Ross of ordering the killings, no evidence ever tied him to the murders. Nonetheless, the two-way split widened when the treaty faction joined the dissident Old Settlers.[19]

Hampering any reconciliation was the interference of Brigadier General Matthew Arbuckle, the area military commander. Although Ross now led the numerical majority of the tribe and many Old Settlers seemed to accept his leadership, Arbuckle was convinced that civil war would soon erupt among the Cherokees. Ross assured the commander that he only intended to wage a "war of reason" against his opponents, but Arbuckle still believed an armed conflict was imminent. Moreover, Arbuckle insisted that Ross turn over those responsible for the Ridge-Boudinot murders. Such an action would have been against the will of Ross's following, and although he considered the killings repugnant, he never moved vigorously to catch the culprits. In retrospect, Ross certainly can be censured for his lack of action in these proceedings.[20]

Undaunted, General Arbuckle continued to support the dissident Old Settlers and the treaty faction. When the dissenters appealed to him to aid them in their bid for control of the tribe, he was only too ready to agree that Ross's government was unauthorized, and he treated the Old Settler chiefs as the legitimate leaders of the Cherokee Nation. After Ross left for Washington in November 1839, Arbuckle and the anti-Ross parties attempted to wreck the new government he had erected. Although Ross's recently established administration was already functioning, Arbuckle demanded another general assembly of the Cherokees. Apparently, he wanted a government formed according to his specifications, which included giving greater power to the Western Cherokees. The Cherokees reconvened in January 1840, but many of the Old Settler leaders balked at attending, obviously realizing the weakness of their position. The extralegal assembly repealed several pieces of legislation earlier passed by Ross and his followers, but Arbuckle felt the assembly had not gone far enough. When Indian agent Montfort Stokes reported back to Washington that the assembly had performed "as favorable as could be expected," Arbuckle complained that the old agent had been "overreached by Ross's friends."[21]

Neither Arbuckle nor Ross's Cherokee opponents were yet satisfied, so they called for further gatherings. Yet Ross's adherents were as uncompromising as ever, and Arbuckle finally realized the futility of his actions. Tragically, the repeated interference of Arbuckle only prolonged Cherokee reorganization in the West. In 1846, when reunification came, it followed Ross's guidelines for the most part and could have been achieved much earlier without the general's steady stream of interruptions. Arbuckle's reluctance to accept the obvious can be explained only by his personal dislike of Ross.[22]

Although a semblance of unity had been achieved, a number of problems continued to vex Ross over the next few years. Treaty party followers thought they had been cheated out of their full share of the removal funds. They also remained vindictive toward Ross and his majority over the murder of the Ridges and Boudinot. In fact, Stand Watie, a relative of the martyrs, kept a private force ready to do battle with his supposed oppressors. A few Old Settlers remained unaligned and demanded their former posts and privileges in the Cherokee government. In the early 1840s threats, killings, and party vendettas plagued the tribe. During these tense times Ross's opponents repeatedly called for his resignation and the division of the tribe into two entities. Again federal authorities vacillated, giving Ross's enemies the idea that Washington would yield to their demands. One perceptive set of United States commissioners noted that as long as the "discontented . . . find a ready audience at Washington," discord among the Cherokees would continue.[23]

In 1841, after President John Tyler gave firm assurances of a new era in Cherokee-federal relations, Ross at first became more optimistic. He was particularly pleased when Tyler promised to negotiate a new treaty. But again, dalliance was the order of the day. Ross traveled to Washington in 1842, 1844, 1845, and 1846, trying with difficulty to accomplish what Tyler had so glibly promised. He finally became exasperated at having to return to each Cherokee legislative session only to tell the tribal representatives that no solution had been reached.[24]

In the winter of 1845–46, all three factions were in Washington with their demands. The Old Settler and treaty party delegates worked together to dislodge Ross and to split the tribe. Ross and his followers worked for a new treaty and insisted on Cherokee cohesion. They pointed to Tyler's promises and stressed that they were the only legitimate Cherokee delegates in Washington. The administration of James K. Polk was not impressed. Polk actually planned to accept the dissidents' plan, but Cherokee Indian agents intervened with new proposals. The three factions were forced to compromise, since none could get a separate treaty, and the settlement they reached became the Treaty of 1846. Ross was kept as chief, and the unity of the Cherokees was maintained. The treaty settled the outstanding difficulties of the tribe and ushered in a peaceful era that prevailed throughout the 1850s.[25]

A decade later external pressures again forced Ross to make difficult and far-reaching decisions. Southern advocates in the surrounding states demanded to know the Cherokee position in case a war erupted between the states. When forced to answer, Ross took a neutral stand on these sectional antagonisms, yet he spoke with ambivalence so as not to appear pro-Union. After the Fort Sumter incident, pressure on the chief mounted. Union sympathizers departed Indian Territory, while Indian agents openly voiced their allegiance to the South. More important, adjacent tribes took a decidedly Southern stance as the Cherokees were slowly isolated from federal aid. Meanwhile, the Cherokee affinity for southern mores made them natural allies with the seceding states.[26]

Albert Pike of Little Rock, Arkansas, was commissioned by the Confederacy to enlist the tribes of Indian Territory in their cause. Pike revealed that he was ready to use tactics reminiscent of Schermerhorn's in his bid to gain Confederate converts. He offered to treat with minority factions who were ready to bear arms for the South. Such a faction existed among the Cherokees. Led by Stand Watie, this proslavery band of Cherokees had already organized themselves into a military regiment. Pike first approached Ross and made him an attractive offer of an alliance. At first Ross refused, biding his time while events unfolded in the West. Meanwhile, the adroit Pike gave Ross much to ponder, for he signed other treaties with area tribes before returning to Tahlequah, capital of the Cherokee Nation. In August 1861, Ross called a national conference of his people and probably surprised a great many when he advocated an alliance with the Confederacy.[27]

The reasons for Ross's change of sentiments are numerous. He may have feared an open rebellion by the Watie contingent. He knew of Confederate military successes and realized how near he was to Southern borders. Pike's other treaties also put him at cross purposes with nearby tribes. Still, the most plausible reason was his desire to keep the Cherokees out of the internecine conflict. The Confederate treaty, signed in October 1861, preserved tribal independence and guaranteed that Cherokee forces would not be used outside their borders. Nevertheless, Ross's heart was never really with the Southern cause. Although he was a slave owner himself, most of his support came from full-blood Cherokees, who largely were not slave holders. Years of Washington negotiations probably had given him a greater identity with the Union position. His undivided loyalty, however, was to the Cherokees, and he would strike any bargain to preserve the tribe and to continue the Cherokees as one people.[28]

By 1862 the Confederacy was losing control of Indian Territory. A federal invasion that year convinced Ross of the futility of staying with the South. Personally, he no longer felt any attachment with the sectional cause, so he moved his family and what few belongings he could carry to Kansas. From there he traveled to Washington to plead the Cherokees' case before the administration of Abraham Lincoln. The thrust of his argument was that the Cherokees were forced into a desperate situation and sided with the South under duress. Ross kept up a steady flow of correspondence to ensure his recognition as chief, to secure provisions for refugee Union Cherokees in Kansas, and to inform Lincoln that the Cherokees had abrogated the Confederate pact and had freed their slaves. Although he showed reluctance, Lincoln seemed ready to accept this reasoning, and at war's end prospects for renewed relations with the federal government seemed bright.[29]

They dimmed rapidly. With Lincoln's assassination and the

inauguration of Andrew Johnson's administration, a new set of officials assumed power in the Indian department. Dennis N. Cooley, the new commissioner of Indian affairs, called the tribes of Indian Territory together at Fort Smith, Arkansas, in September 1865. It was Cooley's intention to make the Indians pay for their disloyalty by signing new treaties that would deprive them of portions of their lands. He also hoped to force them to accept the right of railways to cross their lands, and the consolidation of all the tribes into one administrative unit. These proposals were totally unacceptable to Ross. He insisted that the Cherokees had been loyal to the Union, and he reviewed his discussions with Lincoln. Besides noting the forced nature of Cherokee defection, Ross also pointed to Cherokee units that had served with the Northern armies. In addition, he resisted the loss of lands, the granting of railroad rights of way, and the consolidation of the tribes. Southern Cherokees, also represented at Fort Smith, were more amenable. They were willing to trade lands and rights in return for recognition of their party as the legitimate authority for the tribe. What emerged was the strange situation of the federal government preparing to negotiate with decidedly disloyal elements while ignoring those who had returned to the fold of the Union cause.[30]

No new treaty was signed at Fort Smith, but another round of negotiations was scheduled at Washington. There, as at Fort Smith, the validity of Ross's leadership was questioned. The Southern Cherokees had formed their own government during the war and had elected Stand Watie as Chief. They now came forward, again claiming to be the true voice of the tribe and offering to yield to Cooley's demands. Meanwhile, the commissioner became annoyed at Ross's failure to submit to his requirements, and he was prepared to treat with the Southerners. Cooley even drew up a lengthy pamphlet in which he challenged Ross's loyalty in order to justify his negotiations with Watie's faction.[31]

Ross, seventy-five years old by this time, was bedridden during much of the debates. Yet, a cadre of younger, loyal Cherokees staunchly defended their chief while he carried on a steady flow of correspondence from his room. Cooley actually signed a preliminary pact with the Southern party, but because President Johnson would not accept it, the commissioner had to return to bargaining, this time with the Ross faction. A treaty was quickly worked out in July 1866 and proclaimed in August, shortly after Ross's death on August 1. Although Ross died before the consummation of the treaty, he lived long enough to see himself vindicated. The Northern delegates had insisted at the outset of final negotiations that the treaty carry a designation of Ross as "Principal Chief of the Cherokees." Thus he died bearing a title authenticated once again by the federal government, and one that had never been questioned by the mass of Cherokees who had elevated him to that position.[32]

In his half century of service to the Cherokees, Ross found the validity of his leadership questioned on many occasions. Federal authorities hoped to obtain bargains more easily by discrediting the Cherokees' most articulate spokesman. Ross did not resist federal imposition simply because he valued his office as chief. Rather, he knew that by dislodging him the federal government would weaken the independent foundations of the tribe. The Cherokees would thus become a pawn to every state or national whim.

Ross's authority was based on the sovereign will of the Cherokees, who had established a constitutional government to oppose the capricious demands of the United States. Their loss of lands and power persuaded them to employ the white man's techniques and to beat him at his own game. Ross's success as a leader cannot be measured simply by the fact that he ultimately lost some great contests—the Cherokees were removed, and they were forced into the Civil War. Ross's leadership should be analyzed within the context of his times and in comparison with that of other tribal leaders. In treaties and in negotiations the Cherokees consistently fared better than their neighbors in the South and in Indian Territory. All such achievements remain a monument to Ross's skill and relentless efforts.

Not only did Ross oppose further erosions of Cherokee autonomy, he also pressured the United States to fulfill its treaty obligations. He was never content to accept narrow interpretations that gave the tribe the minimum of payments as in the Treaty of 1835. In the 1860s he could put the blame for Cherokee disloyalty on the American republic, which had failed to protect the Cherokees and made them fall prey to the Confederate appeal. Ross was first selected as chief because the Cherokees recognized his abilities and his commitment to their ideals. He was retained in that office because of his integrity and his unending fight for the survival and unity of his people.

Notes

1. The best account of the Cherokee social transition is Henry T. Malone, *Cherokees of the Old South: A People in Transition* (Athens: University of Georgia Press, 1956), passim. Thomas L. McKenney, *History of the Indian Tribes of North America, with Biographical Sketches of the Principal Chiefs,* vols. (Philadelphia: Rice, Rutler, 1870), 3:291–93.

2. McKenney, *History of Indian Tribes of North America,* 2:291–95.

3. Ibid.; Penelope Johnson Allen, "Leaves from the Family Tree . . . Meigs," *Chattanooga Sunday Times,* January 28, 1834; Gary E. Moulton, " 'Voyage to the Arkansas': New Letters of Chief John Ross," *Tennessee Historical Quarterly* 35, no. 1 (Spring 1976): 46–50.

4. Rennard Strickland, "From Clan to Court: Development of Cherokee Law," *Tennessee Historical Quarterly* 31, no. 4 (Winter 1972): 318–23; Cherokee Chiefs to Return J. Meigs, September 27, 1809, Record Group 75, National Archives, Washington, D.C., Microfilm 208, roll 4, (hereafter cited by the abbreviations NA, RG, M, roll).

5. Charles Hicks et al. to Meigs, November 18, 1811, NA, RG 75, M208, roll 5; Path Killer to the Cherokee Delegation, January 10, 1816, John Ross Papers, Thomas Gilcrease Institute of American History and Art, Tulsa, Oklahoma; Cherokees to John C. Calhoun, June 30, 1818, NA, RG 75, T494 (microfilm), roll 1, 360–65; Path Killer to Cherokee Delegation, December 14, 1818, NA, RG 75, M208, roll 7.

6. McKenney, *History of Indian Tribes of North America,* 2:299–300; McIntosh to Ross, October 21, 1823, NA, RG 75, M208, roll 9; Ross to the General Council, October 24, 1823, John Howard Payne Papers, Newberry Library, Chicago, Illinois.

There is a vast amount of correspondence between the Cherokee delegates and Washington officials for these two years. The material can be found in NA, RG 75, M15, roll 6; M21, roll 1; M234, roll 71; and RG 107, M221, roll 98.

7. *Laws of the Cherokee Nation Adopted by the Council at Various Periods* (Tahlequah, Cherokee Nation: *Cherokee Advocate* Office, 1852), pp. 45–46, 62–63; Annual Message of Ross and William Hicks, October 13, 1828, *Cherokee Phoenix,* October 22, 1828; Miscellaneous Notes, Payne Papers, Newberry Library.

9. Diary of Samuel A. Worcester, 1824–30, Alice Robertson Collection, University of Tulsa Library, Tulsa, Oklahoma; Appraisal of Ross's Possessions, September 21 and December 16, 1836, NA, RG 75, M574, roll 8, 501–2.

10. *Laws of the Cherokee Nation*, pp. 73–76, 118–30; Miscellaneous Notes, Payne Papers, Newberry Library.

11. *Cherokee Phoenix*, October 22, 1828; Miscellaneous Notes, Payne Papers, Newberry Library. I have taken up the internal struggles in another essay. Here I will deal principally with Ross's disputes with federal officials. See Gary E. Moulton, "Chief John Ross and the Internal Crises of the Cherokee Nation," *Indian Leaders: Oklahoma's First Statesmen*, ed. Glenn Jordan and Tom M. Halm (Oklahoma City: Oklahoma Historical Society, 1979), pp. 114–25.

12. Ronald N. Satz, *American Indian Policy in the Jacksonian Era* (Lincoln: University of Nebraska Press, 1975), pp. 19–31; Hugh Montgomery to Ross, June 26 and July 10, 1830, *Cherokee Phoenix*, July 10 and 24, 1830; Ross et al. to the Senate and House of Representatives, June 21, 1836, *House Document 286*, 24th Cong., 1st sess. (serial 292), pp. 5–6.

13. These memorials, too numerous to list here, are scattered throughout congressional documents in the serial set. A representative would be *House Document 286*, 24th Cong., 1st sess. (serial 292).

14. The Wirt-Ross correspondence can be found in Ross Papers, Gilcrease Institute; and Wirt Papers, Maryland Historical Society, Baltimore. The best source for the cases is Joseph C. Burke, "The Cherokee Cases: A Study in Law, Politics, and Morality," *Stanford Law Review* 21, no. 3 (February 1969): 500–531.

15. James William Van Hoeven, "Salvation and Indian Removal: The Career Biography of John Freeman Schermerhorn, Indian Commissioner" (Ph.D. diss., Vanderbilt University, 1972), passim; John Ross, *Letter from John Ross . . . in Answer to Inquiries from a Friend regarding the Cherokee Affairs with the United States* (n.p., 1836), pp. 9–11; Schermerhorn's document "A," September 15, 1835, *House Document 286*, 24th Cong., 1st sess. (serial 292), pp. 67, 77.

16. Ross to Major and John Ridge, and Major and John Ridge to Ross, October 19, 1835, and agreement of the two parties, October 24, 1835, *House Document 286*, 24th Cong., 1st sess. (serial 292). pp. 81–82; Thurman Wilkins, *Cherokee Tragedy: The Story of the Ridge Family and of the Decimation of a People* (New York: Macmillan, 1970), pp. 275–81.

17. Two examples of petitions Ross sent Congress are: *House Document 99*, 25th Cong., 2d sess. (serial 325) and *House Document 316*, 25th Cong., 2d sess. (serial 329). Report of J. A. Slade and J. T. Bender, April 28, 1894, *House Document 182*, 53d Cong., 3d sess. (serial 3323), pp. 9–10.

18. Grant Foreman, *Indian Removal: The Emigration of the Five Civilized Tribes of Indians* (Norman: University of Oklahoma Press, 1953), pp. 286–88, 290–312; Ross's Certificates of Detachment Expenses [May

1840], *House Report 288,* 27th Cong., 3d sess. (serial 429), pp. 57–70; Lucy Butler to John Howard Payne, January 26, 1839, Payne Papers, Newberry Library.

19. Morris L. Wardell, *A Political History of the Cherokee Nation, 1838–1907* (Norman: University of Oklahoma Press, 1938), pp. 12–19; Grant Foreman, *The Five Civilized Tribes* (Norman: University of Oklahoma Press, 1934), pp. 291–95.

20. Wardell, *Political History of the Cherokee Nation,* pp. 20–35; Foreman, *Five Civilized Tribes,* pp. 296–306; Arbuckle to Ross et al., July 17 1839, Ross et al. to Arbuckle, July 20, 1839, Arbuckle and William Armstrong to Ross, September 28, 1839, Ross to Arbuckle and Armstrong, September 30, 1839, *House Document 129,* 26th Cong., 1st sess. (serial 365), pp. 75–76, 79–81, 107–8.

21. Wardell, *Political History of the Cherokee Nation,* pp. 35–37; Foreman, *Five Civilized Tribes,* pp. 306–08; Stokes to Joel R. Poinsett, January 22, 1840, and Arbuckle to Poinsett, January 28, 1840, *House Document 188,* 26th Cong., 1st sess. (serial 366), pp. 50–51, 56.

22. Wardell, *Political History of the Cherokee Nation,* pp. 37–46; Foreman, *Five Civilized Tribes,* pp. 308–10.

23. Wardell, *Political History of the Cherokee Nation,* pp. 47–48, 52–55; Report of the Commissioners, January 17, 1845, in Report of the Secretary of War, *Senate Document 140,* 28th Cong., 2d sess. (serial 457), p. 11.

24. Wardell, *Political History of the Cherokee Nation,* pp. 55–61; John Tyler to Ross, September 20, 1841, *House Report 1098,* 27th Cong., 2d sess. (serial 411), pp. 70–71.

25. Wardell, *Political History of the Cherokee Nation,* pp. 62–75; Foreman, *Five Civilized Tribes,* pp. 338–51.

26. Gary E. Moulton, "Chief John Ross during the Civil War," *Civil War History* 19, no. 4 (December 1973): 314–16.

27. Ibid., pp. 316–18.

28. Ibid., pp. 318–20.

29. Ibid., pp. 321–28.

30. Paul F. Lambert, "The Cherokee Reconstruction Treaty of 1866," *Journal of the West* 12, no. 3 (July 1973): 471–75; Report of the Fort Smith Council, October 30, 1865, in Report of the Commissioner of Indian Affairs, 1865, *House Document 1,* 39th Cong., 1st sess. (serial 1248), pp. 496–532.

31. Lambert, "Cherokee Reconstruction Treaty of 1866," pp. 475–82.

32. Ibid., pp. 482–89.

Satanta

Donald Worcester

"If I were an Indian, I often think I would greatly prefer to cast my lot among those of my people adhered to the free open plains rather than submit to the confined limits of a reservation, there to be the recipient of the blessed benefits of civilization, with its vices thrown in without stint or measure. The Indian can never be permitted to view the question in this deliberate way."—George Armstrong Custer, *My Life on the Plains,* p. 22.

SATANTA (Set-tainte, or White Bear) was born in 1820, the son of Red Tipi, a prominent Kiowa and keeper of the sacred *Tai-me,* the tribal medicine bundles. Though not a large tribe, numbering less than two thousand, the Kiowas produced many notable warriors. Satanta would be one of the greatest of Kiowa warriors during the height of the horse and buffalo era of the plains tribes, widely known for his efforts to preserve his people's lands.

This was the time when the Kiowas roamed freely over the Great Plains, hunting buffalo and sending raiding parties hundreds of miles south to the Spanish settlements on both sides of the Rio Grande. These raiders might be gone for a year or longer, and then suddenly appear with huge herds of horses and mules and captive children to be raised as Kiowas. Prestige depended on success in raiding and warfare, and success was measured by the size of one's horse herd. The Kiowas owned more horses per family than any other plains tribe, with the possible exception of their allies, the Comanches.

The Kiowas were divided according to rank and prestige. At the top were the great warriors and their families—the *Ondes*—who made up about one-tenth of the tribe. Below them were the *Odegup'a,* men of lesser achievements, and the *Kaan,* or poor people. At the bottom of the social scale were the *Damom,* the lazy and inept. Satanta was an *Onde.*

Coming from the northwest, the Kiowas migrated to the region around the upper reaches of the Yellowstone River. For a time they were closely associated with the Crows, from whom they borrowed the *Kado,* or sun dance. Around 1790 they formed an alliance with the Comanches, who had been raiding Spanish ranches and settlements in New Mexico and below the Rio Grande for nearly a century. In 1805 Meriwether Lewis noted that the Kiowas had great herds of horses, which they traded to the Arikaras and Mandans.

Under pressure from the Teton Sioux, and probably attracted by the availability of horses in Mexico, the Kiowas moved to the southern plains, where they remained closely associated with the Comanches. In 1820 Major Stephen H. Long met Kiowas and was astonished at their vast horse herds. It was here on the southern plains that Satanta grew to manhood.

Seeing in Satanta a promising war leader, a famous old warrior named Black Horse gave him his shield. Although Kiowa shields were made of several layers of thick buffalo bull hide, warriors relied more on the supernatural powers of the shield for protection. Black Horse had tested his shield's powers many times and had always come through battle unscathed. He was killed soon after giving the shield to Satanta.

Satanta carried the famous shield with him in countless battles. It protected him on raids into Texas, and he had it with him in Chihuahua when a Mexican vaquero roped him and would have dragged him to death if two other warriors, Frizzlehead and Lone Wolf, hadn't rescued him. He credited the shield with saving his life, and as he rose to prominence among the ranks of Kiowa warriors, he believed that the shield's medicine contributed to his success. By the late 1840s, while still in his twenties, Satanta already rivaled head chief Dohausan for influence among his tribesmen. Moreover, the flamboyant young warrior also was well known as an orator. In return for his good fortune, he hung the shield in his medicine lodge, a place of highest honor.

As Satanta rose to prominence, his people faced a growing threat to their control of the southern plains. Texas joined the

Union in 1845, and during the next decade growing numbers of Texans rode west beyond the cross-timbers, invading the Kiowa hunting lands and killing buffalo. From villages north of the Canadian River, the Kiowas and their Comanche allies struck back, taking scalps and capturing many horses. The Texans complained to the government, and during the 1850s both Indian agents and army officers warned the Kiowas that troops would be sent to punish them if they didn't cease their attacks. Yet when no troops appeared, Satanta and other Kiowa leaders assumed that the government threats were only a bluff and the raiding continued. In October 1859, Indian trader William Bent warned that the warfare might intensify. "A smothered passion for revenge agitates these Indians," he wrote, "perpetually fomented by the failure of food, the encircling encroachments of the white population, and the exasperating sense of decay and impending extinction with which they are surrounded. . . . A desperate war of starvation and extinction is therefore imminent and inevitable unless prompt measures shall prevent it."[1]

No measures were taken and the warfare that Bent predicted soon flared from the Arkansas to the Rio Grande. At first the government was hard pressed to meet the Indians. Bogged down in the Civil War, Union and Confederate forces had few men to spare for defense of the southwestern frontier. Kiowa war parties led by Satanta struck repeatedly at both Texas and supply columns on the Santa Fe Trail. During July 1864, after dancing the scalp dance near Fort Larned in Kansas, Satanta and another Kiowa warrior approached the fort gate, probably intending to go to the sutler's store. The sentry warned them away in a threatening manner. Angered, Satanta quickly put two arrows in the soldier and raced back to camp. While the Kiowa women tore down the tipis and packed the travois, Satanta and his warriors kept the troops from pursuit by running off the garrison's horse herd. To add insult to injury, a few days later the Kiowa chief sent a message to the post commander. He hoped, he told the furious officer, that the quartermaster would provide better horses in the future—the recently captured ones were inferior.[2]

Kiowa and Comanche raids along the Santa Fe Trail and incidents such as the one at Fort Larned did not go unnoticed. General James Carleton, commanding in New Mexico, was particu-

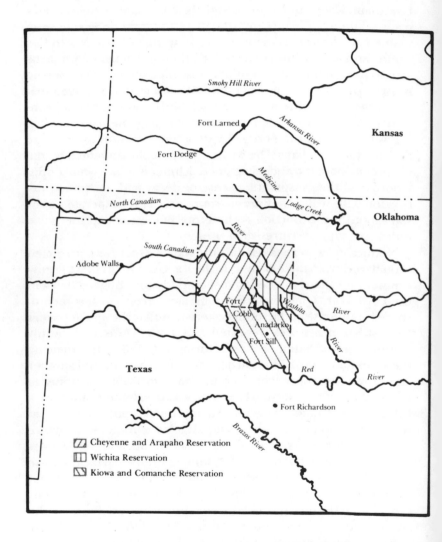

Smoky Hill River

Fort Larned

Arkansas River

Kansas

Fort Dodge

Medicine

North Canadian

Lodge Creek

Oklahoma

River

South Canadian

Adobe Walls

Fort
Cobb

Washita

River

Anadarko

River

Fort Sill

Texas

Red

River

Fort Richardson

Brazos River

☐ Cheyenne and Arapaho Reservation
☐ Wichita Reservation
☒ Kiowa and Comanche Reservation

larly concerned that his supply lines along the Santa Fe trail remain open. Determined to punish the hostiles, in November 1864 he dispatched Kit Carson, with about 350 New Mexico volunteers and several dozen Ute scouts, to attack Kiowa and Comanche camps along the South Canadian River. The battle took place on November 25, but Carson and his troopers were soon put on the defensive. Grossly underestimating their enemy, the New Mexicans faced almost one thousand warriors and were saved from annihilation only by their howitzers. Retreating rapidly, the troops were further confused by a Kiowa bugler, probably Satanta, who kept sounding the advance as the soldiers milled together, unsure of their orders.

In 1865, following Carson's campaign, the Kiowas met with government officials and signed a treaty surrendering their claims to lands in Colorado, Kansas, and New Mexico. Accepting in principle the idea of a reservation, the Kiowa chiefs agreed to remain in the region between the Arkansas and Red rivers, but they had no real comprehension of what a reservation meant. Meanwhile, Dohausan, who had been head chief since 1833, died. In 1866 Lone Wolf replaced him, but in name only, for by that time white pressure had divided the tribe into opposing factions.

A few chiefs, particularly Kicking Bird and Stumbling Bear, had become convinced that the Kiowas must remain at peace with the whites if they were to survive as a tribe. Others, including Satanta, Lone Wolf, and Satank, preferred to fight for their lands. A government physician sent onto the southern plains to vaccinate the Kiowas against smallpox at this time described Satanta as a prominent leader of the hostile faction. After living in Satanta's tipi he reported:

> I was four days in Satanta's (Set-tainte), or White Bear's village, who is, I believe their principle chief. He is a fine-looking Indian, very energetic, and sharp as a brier. He and all his people treated me with much friendship. I ate my meals three times a day with him in his lodge. He puts on a great deal of style, spreads a carpet for his guests to sit on, and has painted fireboards twenty inches wide and three feet long, ornamented with bright brass tacks driven all around the edges, which they use for tables. He has a brass French horn (bugle?) which he blew vigorously when the meals were ready.[3]

The recent treaty had hardly been ratified before Satanta again raided into Texas, capturing a woman and four children. At Fort

Larned the agent refused to ransom the captives (the Box family), and reminded Satanta of his promises to stop raiding. In reply, the Kiowas answered that Texas was not included in the treaty with the United States. Satanta took his captives to Fort Dodge, where the commander ransomed them. The officer was incensed when the Kiowa chief commented that stealing white women was more profitable than stealing horses.[4]

Still hopeful that the Kiowas could be persuaded to give up the warpath, Captain John H. Page visited Satanta in his village in January 1867. Angry, the chief told the officer that all white soldiers must leave the country. The Santa Fe Railroad must not run west of Council Grove, he said, except to bring supplies to the Kiowas.

The next month Satanta paid a visit to Major Henry Douglass at Fort Dodge. "All the country with wood and water and grass," he argued, "belongs to the Indians, and the Government has not paid for it. You have no right to it, and must leave." He also ordered Douglass to stop building houses at Fort Dodge.[5] The whites naturally ignored Satanta's order, but marked him as a dangerous man.

In April, General Winfield Scott Hancock held a council with the Kiowas at Fort Dodge. Kicking Bird and Stumbling Bear represented the peaceful part of the tribe, while Satanta spoke for the rest. "So effective and convincing was the oratorical effort of Satanta," Colonel George Armstrong Custer wrote, "that at the termination of his address the department commander and staff presented him with the uniform coat, sash, and hat of a major general." A few weeks later Satanta, back from a raid in Texas, attacked the post, dressed in his new uniform.[6] He drove off the herders and appropriated the horses of Company B, Seventh Cavalry.[7]

In October 1867, Congress sent a peace commission to make treaties with the southern plains tribes, presumably to remove all causes of warfare. The commissioners were also to assign definite reservations. A huge council was planned for Medicine Lodge Creek in Kansas, and an estimated five thousand Kiowas, Comanches, Kiowa-Apaches, Southern Cheyennes, and Arapahoes assembled there. To guarantee their safety en route, the commissioners persuaded Satanta and other chiefs to meet them at Fort Larned and accompany them to the council.

At Fort Larned, Satanta made a strong impression on all the newspaper correspondents who had assembled to cover the Medicine Lodge Creek council. Especially impressed was Henry M. Stanley, later famous for his successful search for Dr. David Livingston in Africa. Satanta assured the reporters that he was the major spokesman for the Kiowas and informed them that he was eager to leave for the council site because Fort Larned "stink too much white men."[8]

On the trip to Medicine Lodge Creek they came upon a herd of buffalo, and many of the whites rushed out to kill them, leaving the animals to rot on the prairie. This senseless, wasteful slaughter infuriated Satanta, who protested to General Harney. Harney agreed and ordered the hunters to stop.[9] Reporter George C. Brown of the *Cincinnati Commercial,* who disliked Indians and wanted to convince his readers that the commissioners agreed to anything the Indians demanded, wrote concerning Harney's order: "Why was this? Because we were in hostile country and because Satanta and the Indians with us found fault with the killing of their buffalo, since it was their country and their game, and since the animals were . . . left to rot on the prairies to stench up the air that the *Noble Red Man* was to breathe!"[10]

In October 1867, the talks were held among cottonwoods along Medicine Lodge Creek. Most of the warriors sat on their ponies and listened; the chiefs who would speak for the tribes sat on rows of logs facing the commissioners. Prominent among them was Satanta, wearing suspended from his neck a silver medal bearing the profile of President Buchanan.

Senator John B. Henderson opened the meeting by announcing that the government wanted to give the Indians cattle, farm equipment, and farming land. Then he asked what they had to say. This was the customary procedure in negotiating treaties with Indians—talk about what the government would give them and be vague about what it intended to take from them.

Satanta arose and shook hands with each of the commissioners. He had made peace with General Sanborn two years earlier, he said, and he had not broken it. "All the land south of the Arkansas belongs to the Kiowas and Comanches," he told them, "and I don't want to give any of it away."

> I love the land the buffalo and will not part with it. I don't want any of the medicine lodges (churches) within the country. . . . I have

heard that you intend to settle us on a reservation near the mountains. I don't want to settle. I love to roam over the prairies. There I feel free and happy, but when we settle down we grow pale and die. . . . I have told you the truth. I have no little lies hid about me, but I don't know how it is with the commissioners. Are they as clear as I am? A long time ago this land belonged to our fathers; but when I go up to the river I see camps of soldiers. . . . These soldiers cut down my timber, they kill my buffalo; when I see that, my heart feels like bursting; I feel sorry.[11]

Satanta spoke for a long time, forcefully explaining to the shocked commissioners how Kiowas and other Indians felt. "Every line of his strongly marked features," wrote ethnologist James Mooney, "showed the character of the man . . . brave, forceful, untamable."[12] When he sat down the Kiowas shouted their approval; the commissioners were silent. Everyone present was impressed by his eloquence, including reporter H. J. Budd of Cincinnati, who commented, "Satana is a powerful speaker. . . . Even the commissioners could not help expressing their admiration at his magnificent figure. . . . Savage-like as he is, there is a specimen of nobleness in him which two or three of the Commission might do well to imitate."[13]

During the second day Satanta proposed that the Kiowas needed to discuss what they had just been told before making a decision. Ten Bears of the Comanches, who apparently was impatient for the distribution of gifts to begin, remarked that it was unfortunate that Kiowas had to talk so much before they could make up their minds about anything. Satanta pointed out that the Comanches wouldn't make so many mistakes if they talked things over before acting, then angrily stalked away. The commissioners could do little but wait and hope that Satanta would return; without him it was doubtful that the Kiowas, at least, would accept the treaty.

Satanta soon returned; he looked the commissioners over for a time, then told them the Kiowas didn't trust agent Leavenworth and wanted another in his place. Ten Bears said the Comanches trusted Leavenworth and wanted to keep him. Satanta was angry, Ten Bears remarked, because Leavenworth had criticized him for his raids in Texas.

Senator Henderson spoke again. "You say you do not like the medicine houses but you do like the buffalo and wish to do as your fathers did. We say to you that the buffalo will not last forever.

JOSEPH BRANT

From the McKenney-Hall portfolio. Western History Collections, University of Oklahoma Library

RED BIRD

From the McKenney-Hall portfolio. Courtesy of Martin Zanger

John Ross
*Western History Collections,
University of Oklahoma Library*

Satanta

WASHAKIE

Western History Research Center, University of Wyoming

SITTING BULL
National Archives, Indian List #124

QUANAH PARKER

National Archives, Indian List #116

DENNIS BUSHYHEAD
Western History Collections,
University of Oklahoma Li-
brary

CARLOS MONTEZUMA
Chicago Historical Society

PETER MACDONALD
Courtesy of Navajo Nation

They are becoming few and you know it. When that time comes, the Indian must change the road his father trod, or he must suffer and die." He repeated that the government would build a house to hold things they would need, so that when they were naked and hungry they could go there for clothing and food. But the treaty made no such provision, and even though Henderson insisted that the buffalo would soon disappear, the treaty was based on the assumption the tribes would subsist most of the year on buffalo meat. Henderson again went over the terms of the treaty.[14]

"I ask the Commission to tell the Great Father what I have to say," Satanta told him. "When the buffalo leave the country we will let him know. By that time we will be ready to live in houses."[15]

On the third day the treaty was ready for signing. One concession had been made—the Kiowas and Comanches were allowed to hunt on their former lands in southern Kansas and the Texas Panhandle. To the Kiowas this meant that they were expected to live on a reservation but they could leave it whenever they wanted to hunt.

In the end the chiefs of the various tribes made their marks on the treaty, although what they thought it meant is difficult to imagine. Some felt that because they had objected strongly to certain things, those items were no longer part of the treaty or were not binding on them. They did agree to cease molesting the men who were laying railroad tracks across the plains—the railroads would bring their annuity goods much faster than wagons.

The Treaty of Medicine Lodge Creek made it clear that the government's purpose was to confine the tribes to reservations, by force if necessary. The treaty also included provisions for "civilizing" them—the Indians were to be smothered, not simply shoved out of the way of the white man's advance. Although the Kiowas did not comprehend it, after 1868 they were fighting not merely for their lands but for their very survival. Even General William T. Sherman later admitted that the Peace Commission of 1867–68 had prepared the way for the great transcontinental railroads, which, for better or worse, "settled the fate of the buffalo and Indian forever."[16]

After the treaty signing, the promised gifts were distributed—this is perhaps what the majority of Indians were most concerned about. Included were some pistols of unknown manufacture, which the young warriors immediately tested. Every one of the pistols exploded the first time it was fired.

Perhaps the shoddy, exploding pistols were a portent of things to come, for following the treaty the Kiowas rode south into Indian Territory, where they settled near Fort Cobb, on the Washita River. From their new home, Kiowa hunters ranged west into the Texas Panhandle again, seeking buffalo to feed their families. But white buffalo hunters continued to slaughter the herds, and many Kiowas returned to the Washita empty-handed and angry. They demanded that the Indian agents provide them with meat, but the agents had none to give them. When they became threatening, the agents sent for troops. Meanwhile, Kiowa warriors raided nearby Wichita and Caddo villages for both food and horses. The forays were soon extended to Texas and the old pattern of Kiowa raiding seemed to be reemerging.

To the north, Cheyenne and Arapaho warriors also struck at Kansas and eastern Colorado. Determined to suppress the raiding, General Phillip H. Sheridan planned a winter campaign against the hostiles encamped in western Indian Territory. In the winter, the Indian ponies were weak and the tribes customarily "put the war back in the bag" until spring. For a few months the plains nomads were immobile and unprepared to defend themselves. Although Sheridan intended to direct most of his efforts against the Cheyennes and Arapahoes, he also hoped to prove to the Kiowas and Comanches that the United States Army now controlled the plains. Learning that the Kiowas had recently ordered a small troop of cavalry away from their villages, he grimly promised to "take some of the starch out of them before I get through."[17]

While Sheridan was planning his campaign against the Cheyennes and Arapahoes, Colonel W. B. Hazen assumed the position of Indian agent at Fort Cobb. Offering the olive branch to the Kiowas and Comanches, Hazen warned Satanta's people to stop their raiding or troops would be sent against them. He was acting under orders from General William T. Sherman, who wished to neutralize the Kiowas and Comanches and keep them from joining the Cheyennes and Arapahoes. Of course the Kiowas had raided south across the Red River, but Texas was a recent member of the Confederacy and Sherman did not view attacks on Texas as seriously as the Cheyenne-Arapaho incursions into Kansas. If the Kiowas and Comanches would stay north of the Red River, they would be immune from Sherman's retribution. Sherman instructed Hazen: "Every appearance about Fort Cobb should be suggestive of an earnest desire to afford a place of refuge where the peaceable Indians may receive food and be safe against the troops, as well as against hostile Indians who may try to involve them in the common war. If you have not already notified General Sheridan of the fact that some of the Kiowas are peaceful, get word to him in some way, lest he pursue them and stampede your whole family."[18]

Before Hazen could get a message to Sheridan, the latter ordered an attack on the Cheyennes and Arapahoes. On November 27, 1868, acting under Sheridan's orders, a force of the Seventh Cavalry commanded by Lieutenant Colonel George A. Custer struck Black Kettle's Cheyenne village on the Washita River. Learning of the encounter, Hazen knew that most of the Kiowas could not have taken part in the battle, for Satanta and several other war chiefs had slept in his tent the night before the engagement. He promptly wrote Sheridan that all Indian camps south of the battlefield were peaceful. "If this reaches you," he said, "it would be well to communicate at once with Satanta or Black Eagle, chiefs of the Kiowas . . . who will readily inform you of the positions of the Cheyennes, Arapahoes, [and] also of my camp."[19]

Hazen sent two couriers with this message, but Satanta and Lone Wolf intercepted them and personally delivered the message to Sheridan and Custer under a flag of truce. Custer wanted to hang them on the spot, but Sheridan restrained him. They seized the two chiefs despite the flag of truce and held them as prisoners on the march to Fort Cobb. Sheridan, who had planned to attack any Indians they encountered, was incensed at Hazen's note. The Kiowas, shocked at what they considered an unprovoked attack on Black Kettle's people, feared a similar attack and fled. Sheridan and Custer, who followed an old trail the Kiowas had made from the Washita to Fort Cobb, were certain that Kiowas had fought alongside the Cheyennes. Some Kiowas under Big Bow probably were with the Cheyennes, but they had never been to Hazen's agency. The Kiowas' flight from Fort Cobb as the troops approached confirmed Sheridan's belief that they were trying to escape just and proper punishment.

Interpreter Philip McCusker, who was at Fort Cobb at the time, explained that "on the approach of General Sheridan the Kiowas stampeded, not because they had been in the battle of the Washita, but like all wild Indians, they were alarmed at the approach of so large a body of troops knowing they had destroyed a Cheyenne village a short time before."[20]

On reaching Fort Cobb, Sheridan announced that if the Kiowas did not return by sunset the next day, he would hang Satanta and Lone Wolf. The two chiefs sent messages to the various bands, asking them to come for a council. All but a few arrived before the deadline. Custer and other officers were surprised at the devotion shown to Satanta by his followers. They also were surprised at the war chief's open display of affection toward each of his four wives and their children.[21]

Sheridan held Satanta and Lone Wolf until mid-February 1869. Sherman had suggested that he hang them and all others who had raided white settlements. Although he heartily approved of the idea in theory, Sheridan concluded that it would require too large an army to punish all those warriors he considered guilty. He finally gave Satanta and Lone Wolf a warning lecture, then let them go.

The arrest of Satanta and Lone Wolf embittered both chiefs and their followers, but their subsequent release was interpreted as a sign of the army's weakness by the Kiowas. Meanwhile, in 1869, President Ulysses S. Grant introduced his Peace Policy, and the army was restrained from attacking Indians unless requested by the agents or Indian Bureau. The new policy further convinced the Kiowas that the army was afraid of them.

Under the Peace Policy, Quaker Lawrie Tatum replaced Hazen as Kiowa-Comanche agent. Satanta bluntly informed Tatum that he took hold of that part of the white man's road that was represented by the breech-loading gun, but he didn't like the ration of corn, for it hurt his teeth. Indians who listened to white men, he said, got nothing. Those who didn't listen were the only ones who were rewarded. Satanta wanted guns and ammunition, not shovels.

During the same year the Board of Indian Commissioners inspected the western Indian agencies. The Kiowas, especially Satanta, gave them a cool reception. "We have tried the white man's road and find it hard; we find nothing but a little corn . . . no sugar, no coffee," he told them. Satanta reminded them that the plains belonged to the Indians. "But the whites have divided it up to suit themselves. I don't know that my heart feels good about this business."[22] In response, the commissioners recommended that the Kiowas receive increased rations, hoping that the extra food would keep them quiet.

The plan failed. During 1870 Satanta and his warriors again raided into Texas, returning with large numbers of stolen horses. In response, Texans preyed upon the Kiowa horse herds, and the number of stolen animals crossing and recrossing the Red River increased. In August, Tatum and Colonel Benjamin Grierson, commander of the recently established Fort Sill, met in council with the Kiowas, warning them to give up the warpath and to try the white man's road. The officials urged the Kiowas to emulate the Caddos and Wichitas, who were settled peacefully near the fort, halfheartedly trying their hand at farming. In reply Satanta again asserted that only those Indians who were strong and opposed the whites were well treated. The Caddos and Wichitas were scratching in the dirt like women. They received little food and were in a miserable condition. Only warriors like the Kiowas were rewarded.

To emphasize his point, during the following spring Satanta led a mixed Kiowa-Comanche war party south into Texas. Accompanying Satanta were war chiefs Eagle Heart and Big Tree. Also in the party was Maman'te, a powerful Kiowa medicine man who relied on the spirits of his sacred owls for his visions. After crossing the Red River the war party camped for the night and Maman'te received his vision. The owls instructed him that on the next day the warriors would see two parties of Texans. The first would be small; they must let it go through. The second would be larger, and their attack on it would be successful.

Late the next morning the Kiowas saw an army ambulance with a cavalry escort pass quickly along the road to Fort Richardson. They did not know it, but General William T. Sherman, who was on a tour of inspection of the western forts, was in the ambulance.

Sherman was convinced that the Texans' complaints about Indian attacks were greatly exaggerated. Many of the young warriors were eager to convince him of his error, but Maman'te restrained them.

That afternoon a wagon train came slowly along the road. Satanta blew a blast on his bugle and the Kiowas raced, shrieking, to the attack. They killed seven of the teamsters; five escaped. The Kiowas looted the wagons and unhitched the mules. One of the wounded teamsters limped into Fort Richardson and informed Sherman of the raid. Sherman ordered Colonel Ranald S. Mackenzie and troopers of the Fourth Cavalry after the raiders, but a heavy downpour obliterated their tracks. MacKenzie continued on toward Fort Sill, hoping to pick up the trail again.

In the meantime Sherman traveled on to Fort Sill, where he asked Tatum if any Kiowas had been absent from the reservation. When the Kiowas came in to draw their rations a few days later, Tatum asked them if they knew of the attack on the wagon train.

"Yes," Satanta replied, "I led the raid. I have heard that you have stolen a large part of our annuity goods and given them to Texans." He probably referred to payments for damages that were customarily made out of the annuities. "I have repeatedly asked for arms and ammunition," Satanta continued, "which you have not furnished. . . . You do not listen to my talk," Satanta added. "Some years ago they took us by the hair and pulled us here close to Texas, where we have to fight them. When General Custer was here some years ago he arrested me and kept me in confinement several days, but that is played out now. There are never to be any more Kiowas arrested. I want you to remember that. On account of these grievances, I took, a short time ago, about 100 of my warriors, with the chiefs Satank, Eagle Heart, Big Tree, Big Bow, and Fast Bear."

At this point Satank interrupted him, warning him not to name any more of the Kiowas who had gone on the raid. "We found a mule train, which we captured, and killed seven of the men. Three of our men got killed, but we are willing to call it even."[23] By this he meant that there would not be any reprisal raids to avenge the slain warriors, as tribal custom usually demanded. He apparently did not understand that the whites had different rules.

Satank, Eagle Heart, and Big Tree confirmed what Satanta had said. Sherman ordered Satanta, Satank, and Big Tree arrested and taken to Jacksboro, Texas, to stand trial for murder under Texas law. Colonel Mackenzie arrived at Fort Sill a few days after Sherman departed; he had not been able to find the raiders' trail after the storm. Sherman had left orders for him to escort the prisoners to Texas.

Satank was put in one wagon, and Satanta and Big Tree in another. When they had gone a short distance from Fort Sill, Satank called to a Caddo scout who rode alongside the wagon, asking him to tell the Kiowas that Satank was dead. He told the Caddo to tell the Kiowas to give the agent the mules they had taken, and not to do any more raiding around Fort Sill or in Texas. The wagons had traveled about a mile when Satank sang his death chant and slipped his hands out of the manacles. Drawing a knife he had concealed under his robe, he attacked his guard. Moments later he fell dead from the gunfire of the soldiers.

The trial of Satanta and Big Tree took place in the court of Judge Charles Soward. The prosecutor, S. W. T. Lanham, later governor of Texas, knew how to sway the cowboy jury. Although he had nothing kind to say about Big Tree, most of his colorful prose was directed against Satanta, "the arch fiend of treachery and blood—the cunning Cataline—the promoter of strife—the breaker of treaties signed by his own hand—the inciter of his fellows to rapine and murder . . . abject coward . . . canting and double-tongued hypocrite."[24]

It is not surprising that such eloquence prevailed and the two Kiowas were found guilty. Judge Soward offered them a chance to speak before he pronounced sentence. In halting Spanish Satanta said that if he were allowed to return to his people they would never again make war on Texas, but if he were killed the frontier would run with blood. Soward sentenced both to hang.

Agent Tatum wrote Soward that it would have a better effect on the Kiowas if the two chiefs were imprisoned rather than executed, and asked him to use his influence with Governor Edmund J. Davis of Texas. Soward complied, and although Davis was bitterly criticized throughout the state, he commuted the sentences to life imprisonment. The two Kiowas were taken to the state prison at Huntsville.

When informed that the sentence had been commuted, Sherman was angry. "Satanta ought to have been hung," he said, "and that would have ended the trouble, but . . . I know these Kiowas well enough to see that they will be everlastingly pleading for his release. He should never be released, and I hope the War Department will never consent to his return to his tribe."[25]

Despite Sherman's animosity toward Satanta, Custer acknowledged that there was at least some right on the Kiowa chief's side. "His eloquence and able arguments upon the Indian question in various councils to which he was called won for him the deserved title of 'Orator of the Plains,' " he wrote. "Aside . . . from his character for restless barbarity, and activity in conducting merciless forays against our exposed frontiers," he continued, "Satanta is a remarkable man—remarkable for his powers of oratory, his determined warfare against the advances of civilization, and his opposition to the abandonment of his accustomed mode of life, and its exchange for the quiet, unexciting, uneventful life of a reservation Indian."[26]

Captain R. G. Carter, one of the officers in the escort to Jacksboro, described Satanta on his way to prison. "He was over six feet in his moccasins, and . . . he seemed to be even taller than he really was. . . . His immense shoulders, broad back, deep chest, powerful hips and thighs, contrasted singularly with the slight forms of the Ton-ka-was grouped about him. The muscles stood out on his gigantic frame like knots of whip cord. Proud and erect in the saddle, his immobile face and motionless body gave him the appearance of polished mahogany."[27]

If the Texans believed that Satanta's confinement in the prison at Huntsville would break the spirit of the aging war chief, they were sorely mistaken. A newspaper reporter who visited him in prison described the Kiowa leader as follows:

> In the corridor of the penitentiary I saw a tall, finely-formed man, with long, flowing brown hair, a man princely in carriage, on whom even the prison garb seemed elegant, and was told it was Satanta, the chief of the Kiowas who with his brother chief was held on account of murder. . . . Satanta had come into the work room where he was supposed to labor, but where he never performed a stitch of work. He motioned me to be seated with as much grace and dignity as though he was a monarch receiving a foreign ambassador. His face was good, there was a delicate curve of pain on his lips which contrasted oddly with his strong Indian caste of features. Although he is well past sixty

years old, he hardly seemed forty, so strong, erect, elastic and
vigorous was he. . . . When I questioned him, if he ever expected
liberation and what he should do if it came, he responded in Spanish
with the most stoical indifference, "Quien Sabe?"[28]

While Satanta remained in prison, Captain H. E. Alvord, who
knew the Kiowas well, was sent to their agency in 1872 to investigate conditions there. Because of the Kiowas' strong desire for
the liberation of Satanta and Big Tree, he decided to take a
delegation of chiefs and headmen to Washington for a meeting
with the commissioner of Indian affairs. None were willing to
make the trip; all suspected that Texans had already killed the
two chiefs. When Alvord assured them that Satanta and Big Tree
were alive, they insisted on proof. If the Kiowas would
accompany him to Washington, Alvord promised, they could see
Satanta and Big Tree. Lone Wolf, Stumbling Bear, Fast Bear,
Red Otter, Sun Boy, Woman's Heart, Wolf-Lying-Down, and
Tohausan immediately accepted.

Satanta and Big Tree were, with other prisoners, laboring on
the railroad tracks being laid between Dallas and Houston. Governor Davis had them sent by train, under guard, to St. Louis,
where they had an emotional reunion with Alvord's delegation.
Alvord had planned for them to accompany him to Washington,
but Davis, under political pressure, refused to allow it. In Washington the commissioner of Indian affairs promised the Kiowas
that if they refrained from raiding for six months, the two chiefs
would be released from prison. When agent Tatum learned that
Satanta would be freed, he resigned.

Satanta and Big Tree were prisoners of the state of Texas, not
the United States, and it required considerable federal pressure
on Governor Davis before he finally had them delivered to the authorities at Fort Sill in August 1873. For Davis the freeing of
Satanta and Big Tree was political suicide, but he went to Fort Sill
and insisted on receiving the Kiowas' assurances that they would
not raid in Texas again before agreeing to order the prisoners released from the guardhouse. He also demanded that they surrender their guns and horses and promise to settle down to farming.
The Kiowas objected strenuously; they had agreed to abstain
from raiding, and had kept their promise. Now they wanted
Satanta and Big Tree returned.

124   *American Indian Leaders*

Although many Kiowas pleaded with the officials for Satanta's release, perhaps the most poignant entreaty came from Red Tipi, Satanta's aged father. "I am a poor old man," he said. "I want you to pity me and give up my son. The Indians love their children as much as the white people do theirs. You have your wife and children. Take pity on me and gladden my heart by the immediate release of my son. Never again will we raid upon Texas."[29]

Satanta also spoke. "I want all the chiefs present here to make a new road, and particularly the Quahada Comanches," he said. "I want them to quit raiding into Texas, to listen to whatever Commissioner Smith brings them from Washington, and to do whatever he says. We have been treated kindly in Texas. I heard that the Kiowas were told that we were dead, but the Texans treated us well. My heart feels big today and I will take my Texas father to my breast and hold him there. . . . Whatever the white man thinks best I want my people to do. Strip off these prison clothes, turn me over to my people and they will keep their promise."[30]

When Davis continued to insist on his conditions, the Kiowas felt betrayed. "Washington" had promised them that if they ceased raiding, the chiefs would be freed unconditionally. The governor's demands were impossible, for they needed guns to protect themselves and to hunt. Lone Wolf and others began talking of war.

Overnight, Commissioner Smith and superintendent of the plains tribes Enoch Hoag persuaded Davis to soften his demands, thereby saving his life and their own. At the council the next morning the warriors had concealed weapons under their robes or blankets. If the two chiefs were not set free, the Indians were determined to kill all of the white men and rescue the prisoners. Po-ah-rite (Big Buttocks), son of the friendly Comanche chief Horseback, saw two of his white friends. "This is a good day to die," he told the astonished men, who very likely disagreed. "I will stay with you and we will die together." Before trouble could start, Governor Davis announced that the Kiowas had complied with their promises, and he ordered the two chiefs released. They were freed on parole, he reminded them. If they violated it in any way they would be arrested and taken back to prison. These conditions clearly broke the government's earlier promise to the Kiowas.[31]

At the sun dance in the summer of 1874 Satanta made it clear that he had abandoned the warpath; he gave his famous medicine lance to Ato-tain (White Cowbird), brother of Chief Sun Boy, and his ancient shield to his son. Without shield and lance he could never lead his people on raids or in battle, for they were his medicine that ensured success. He had, in effect, resigned as chief in favor of Ato-tain.

Unfortunately, the peace that Satanta now championed never was attained. By the mid-1870s white hide hunters had taken such a toll upon the buffalo herds that Kiowa and Comanche hunters could not feed their families. In desperation, some of the Kiowas were forced to eat their ponies to avoid starvation. Although the Texas legislature discussed protecting the remaining herds, many frontiersmen opposed such a measure. If the hide hunters finally killed off the buffalo, then the plains tribes would be at the white man's mercy. As General Sheridan pointed out to the Texas legislature, "Let them kill, skin and sell until the buffalo is exterminated, as it is the only way to bring lasting peace and allow civilization to advance."[32]

In June 1874 the Comanches discovered a large group of white hunters at Adobe Walls, in the Texas Panhandle. In desperation, Comanche, Kiowa, and Cheyenne warriors attacked them. With their powerful long-range buffalo guns the hunters killed or wounded many warriors before they could come into range of their own carbines, and the attack was abandoned. Some whites believed that Satanta took part in the attack, but without the supernatural protection of his lance and shield, he would not have risked his life. "Satanta, since his release from the Texas State Prison," Custer wrote, "has led a comparatively quiet and uneventful life."[33]

Humiliated by the recent defeat, Lone Wolf led a Kiowa war party south for a revenge raid against Texas. In retaliation, Sherman suggested to President Grant that all peaceful Indians should be ordered to report to their agencies and enroll by name. Frequent roll calls by army officers should be held; those who refused to enroll or were absent from the reservations should be regarded as hostile. The worst offenders should be tried and punished; those against whom there was insufficient evidence for conviction should be sent to some distant fort and held as prison-

ers of war. The president approved these measures—for the
Kiowas and Comanches, the Peace Policy was terminated. On July
20, 1874, the agent and post commander at Fort Sill received instructions to transfer management of the Indians from the Indian Bureau to the War Department—from the agent to the post
commander.

Meanwhile, hostile Kiowas and Comanches continued to
thwart the government's efforts. On August 21, Colonel John
Davidson received a message from the Wichita agency at Anadarko that sixty lodges of renegade Noconee Comanches under
Red Food were camped nearby and trouble was expected. Lone
Wolf and his band of irreconcilable Kiowas were also there. With
four troops of the Tenth Cavalry, Davidson left Fort Sill and hur-
ried to Anadarko.

On his arrival the next day Davidson summoned Red Food and
ordered him to surrender with his people. He sent forty troopers
with Red Food to his camp to collect the weapons and receive the
prisoners. Trouble arose when the troopers demanded that the
Comanches hand over bows and arrows as well as guns; those who
had surrendered earlier had been allowed to keep their native
weapons.

While a messenger was on his way to get Davidson's instructions
concerning the bows and arrows, Lone Wolf and his Kiowas took
shelter in the brush around the Comanche camp. They loudly
taunted Red Food for being afraid of the soldiers—if there was
any fighting, they said, they would help the Comanches. Stung by
these jeers, Red Food gave a whoop, waved his blanket to frighten
the cavalry horses, and headed for the brush with bullets whistl-
ing around him. The "Battle of Anadarko" lasted a full ten minutes; the atmosphere was riddled by dozens of bullets, but no one
was wounded on either side.

Satanta had been hunting buffalo when these events occurred,
and had gone to the Wichita agency for a friendly visit. He
panicked when the cavalry appeared and the shooting began.
Afraid to return to Fort Sill, he camped in the Red Hills and
avoided the columns of troops now crisscrossing western Oklahoma. On September 29, Big Tree slipped into the Cheyenne
agency at Darlington to inform Colonel Thomas Neill that Satanta wanted to surrender.

Colonel Neill wired this information to General John Pope, commander of the Department of Missouri. Pope instructed him to do everything possible to apprehend Satanta. Neill sent a Kiowa-Apache man and a Kiowa woman to Satanta's camp to urge him to come to the agency. On October 3, Satanta, accompanied by Woman's Heart and Poor Buffalo, with thirty lodges of their people, rode up to the agency and surrendered. Woman's Heart and Poor Buffalo, two former raiders, had turned back when Lone Wolf, Maman'te, and the Kiowa-Comanche hostiles had headed out into the Panhandle of Texas.

Satanta and Big Tree both admitted to Neill that they had made an unauthorized but friendly visit to the Wichita agency. When the troops arrived and fighting broke out, they became frightened and fled. They had not taken any part in the fighting. Even so, Neill had no choice but to send them as prisoners to Fort Sill.

Reservation teacher Thomas C. Battey supported Satanta's claim of innocence. "Sometimes the Indians reported on the war-path have been sick in their own lodges, on their reservations, or running buffalo hundreds of miles from the scene of the reported depredation," he wrote. "This has lately been the case with Satanta and Big Tree, whose doings in Texas since their release have furnished hundreds of paragraphs for the newspapers while to my certain knowledge the latter was at home, sick in his lodge, and the former enjoying—after two years' confinement in prison—the pleasures of the buffalo chase, in territory assigned for the purpose."[34]

On October 4, Sheridan wired the War Department recommending that Satanta be returned to prison in Texas. Secretary of War William W. Belknap concurred and forwarded the recommendation to President Grant. Commissioner of Indian Affairs Edward P. Smith, supported by superintendent of plains tribes Enoch Hoag, urged clemency, for Satanta had been guilty of nothing more than momentary fright. That did not, they maintained, justify returning him to prison.

Enoch Hoag had earlier protested that Satanta and Big Tree had been released on parole "conditioned upon the future behavior of the tribe, and liable to rearrest on the evidence of further raiding by Kiowas into Texas (notwithstanding they were in equity entitled to unconditional release in accordance with promises of the government), remained peaceable and loyal. . . . No evidence has reached this office of any hostility on their part, and they have recently, without compulsion, voluntarily surrendered to the military, and are confined at Fort Sill. I recommend official clemency in their case."[35]

Despite Smith's and Hoag's pleas, President Grant ordered Sheridan's recommendations carried out. Satanta was hastily removed to Texas before anyone else could come to his defense. Not even a token attempt was made to determine whether or not he had in any way violated his parole.

General Sherman also recommended that all Indians who had committed murders or stolen livestock in the previous two years be tried by a military commission. Grant authorized separating the ringleaders and confining them in some distant military post. About twenty-five Kiowas and Comanches were, as a result, shipped off to Fort Marion in St. Augustine, Florida. They were not tried—peaceful chief Kicking Bird was instructed to name the ones who deserved punishment.

Kicking Bird named Lone Wolf, Maman'te, and other raiders who were too well known to be excluded, then selected unimportant warriors to make up the rest, sparing as many of the prominent Kiowas as possible. Maman'te sullenly warned Kicking Bird that he would die for what he had done. When the prisoners were on their way to the railroad, Maman'te communed with his owls, then assured the other prisoners that Kicking Bird would indeed die, but that for causing the death, he, Maman'te, must also perish.

Two days later Kicking Bird died of a mysterious ailment despite efforts of the agency physician to save him. Later in the year Maman'te died with a similar illness. Although he appeared to be in good health, the Kiowa medicine man informed his comrades that the end was near. He pulled a blanket over his head; when his friends removed it, he was dead.

Four years passed, and Satanta remained imprisoned at Huntsville. He had often said that when he was free to roam he was happy, "but when I settle down I grow pale and die." On August 15, 1878, prison superintendent Thomas Goree wrote Kiowa agent P. B. Hunt: "Satanta is here in declining health and very feeble. If he remains here he can not live long. Will heartily second any effort for his release."[36]

On September 10, Satanta asked a deputy marshal if he would ever be released. The marshal's answer was no. The next day Satanta threw himself headfirst from an upper floor of the prison hospital and died a few hours later. He was buried in Texas, but in 1963, James Auchiah, Satanta's grandson, received permission to remove his remains to Fort Sill. There Satanta was reinterred with military honors in the post cemetery. At last the chief had returned to his homeland.

Like Sioux chiefs Red Cloud and Crazy Horse, Satanta fought desperately to preserve his people's lands and way of life. Like them, too, he was defeated by overwhelming forces, beaten into submission if not submissiveness. Not the least of the whites' instruments for crushing the plains tribes was the rapid extermination of the buffalo herds, for it spelled their certain doom with or without help from the cavalry.

To white men, Satanta, because he fought for his land and his people, was an arch-fiend, as such men have ever been represented by those whose encroachments they resisted. To his own people Satanta was a tragic hero who forcefully expressed their sentiments and courageously battled to uphold them. Above all, Satanta was a man who cherished his freedom intensely—without it he could not go on living.

NOTES

1. James Mooney, *Calendar History of the Kiowa Indians*. Seventeenth Annual Report of the Bureau of American Ethnology (Washington, D.C.: Government Printing Office, 1898), pp. 182, 183.

2. Wilbur Sturtevant Nye, *Carbine and Lance: The Story of Old Fort Sill* (Norman: University of Oklahoma Press, 1942), p. 357.

3. Mooney, *Calendar History*, p. 177; Carl Coke Rister, "Satanta, Orator of the Plains," *Southwest Review* 17 (Autumn 1931): 78.

4. Mooney, *Calendar History*, p. 181.

5. Wilbur Sturtevant Nye, *Plains Indians Raiders: The Final Phase of Warfare from the Arkansas to the Red River* (Norman: University of Oklahoma Press, 1968), p. 65.

6. George Armstrong Custer, *My Life on the Plains; or, Personal Experiences with Indians* (1874; rpt. Norman: University of Oklahoma Press, 1962), p. 59.

7. Nye, *Plains Indian Raiders,* p. 59.

8. Douglas C. Jones, *The Treaty of Medicine Lodge* (Norman: University of Oklahoma Press, 1966), p. 52.

9. Mooney, *Calendar History,* p. 207.

10. Jones, *Treaty of Medicine Lodge,* p. 68.

11. Mooney, *Calendar History,* pp. 207, 208.

12. Ibid., p. 206.

13. Ibid., p. 114.

14. Ibid., p. 127.

15. Ibid.

16. Ibid., pp. vii, viii.

17. Nye, *Carbine and Lance,* p. 56.

18. Ibid., p. 72.

19. Custer, *My Life on the Plains,* p. 386; Nye, *Carbine and Lance,* p. 73.

20. Custer, *My Life on the Plains,* p. 407.

21. Ibid., p. 310.

22. Mildred P. Mayhall, *The Kiowas,* rev. ed. (Norman: University of Oklahoma Press, 1962), pp. 258, 259.

23. Lawrie Tatum, *Our Red Brothers and the Peace Policy of President Ulysses S. Grant* (1899; rpt. Lincoln: University of Nebraska Press, 1970), pp. 116–17; Nye, *Carbine and Lance,* pp. 130, 135.

24. Rister, "Satanta," p. 92.

25. Nye, *Carbine and Lance,* p. 147.

26. Custer, *My Life on the Plains,* p. 22.

27. Rister, "Satanta," p. 91.

28. Mooney, *Calendar History,* p. 209.

29. Nye, *Carbine and Lance,* pp. 169, 170.

30. Ibid.

31. Mooney, *Calendar History,* p. 197.

32. William H. Leckie, *The Military Conquest of the Southern Plains* (Norman: University of Oklahoma Press, 1963), p. 187.

33. Custer, *My Life on the Plains,* p. 378.

34. Thomas Battey, *The Life and Adventures of a Quaker among the Indians* (1875; rpt. Norman: University of Oklahoma Press, 1968), p. 240.

35. Report of the Commissioner of Indian Affairs for 1874, *House Executive Document 1,* 43d Cong., 2d sess. (serial 1639), p. 523.

36. Leckie, *Military Conquest,* p. 219 n.

Washakie

Peter M. Wright

CAPTAINS MERIWETHER LEWIS and William Clark departed from St. Louis in the spring of 1804 to explore the Missouri River and to discover a route to the Pacific Ocean. They were the advance agents of American territorial expansion and the first official party from the United States to enter the country of the Shoshones. Lewis and Clark learned about these Indians while encamped in the Mandan villages on the Missouri River during the winter of 1804–1805, and they hoped the tribesmen would assist them in completing their mission by providing supplies, horses, and information about their country and the route to the mouth of the Columbia River.

After reaching the Three Forks of the Missouri in present-day Montana, a small party led by Lewis set off to locate the tribe. On August 11, 1805, Lewis sighted a mounted warrior approaching at a distance of about two miles. Using his telescope, the captain recognized that the man did not belong to any Indian group the party had already encountered. The warrior carried a bow and quiver of arrows and rode a saddleless horse with a string attached to its lower jaw as a bridle. The distance between Lewis and the Indian closed to a mile when the Indian suddenly halted. Lewis signaled for a parley, but two other members of the expedition advanced toward the warrior. Lewis tried to maintain the attention of the Indian by holding up a mirror, trinkets, and beads. Then, unarmed, Lewis approached nearer to the warrior, but at two hundred yards the Indian turned his horse and moved slowly away. Lewis shouted, "Tabba bone!" ("white man") and rolled up his sleeve to show the color of his skin. However, when the Indian and Lewis were only a hundred paces apart, the warrior put his whip to his mount and disappeared into some willows.[1]

For the first time, a Shoshone tribesman had seen a representative of the government of the United States. From then on the Shoshones would face the dilemma that all Native Americans confronted when they encountered the white Americans, whose appetite for the territory of others seemed never satisfied: to resist, make war, and block the advance of the white men, or to fraternize, seek an accommodation, and share the land. This became an increasingly important decision as the authority of the United States grew relative to the power of the Indians. As white Americans ignored the preemptive rights of red Americans, killed or drove off the game, and fenced the land, Indian leaders had to decide whether to fight to maintain their traditional way of life or to cooperate and through negotiation retain as much of the land as possible to guarantee the continuation of at least part of the tradition of their fathers while surrounded by an alien people and culture.

The Shoshones chose friendship with white Americans, and that policy became a tradition into the twentieth century. Chief Cameahwait, the brother of the "Bird Woman" (Sacajawea), provided horses and guides to facilitate the successful completion of the penetration of the Rocky Mountains by Lewis and Clark. Later, Chief Washakie continued that friendship and avoided much of the bloodshed that plagued other tribes in the West. Washakie secured a large territory for his people in their homeland, while other tribes, such as the Sioux and Cheyennes, forfeited their range as punishment for depredations against white American emigrants and settlers.

The reluctant tribesmen Lewis encountered spoke the Shoshonean tongue, a branch of the Uto-Aztecan language family. Shoshonean-speaking people occupied the Great Basin and an area reaching from Canada to present-day California. Besides the Shoshones themselves, these Indians included the Bannocks, the Paiutes, and the Utes, all of whom spoke distinct dialects of the same language but could understand one another. They resided in the prehistoric period in the basin, a desert area surrounded by mountains: the Sierra Nevada of California; Oregon's Cascade, Blue, and John Day mountains; the Rocky Mountains; and the Bitter Root and Salmon River ranges of Idaho. The limited rainfall in the basin did not flow to the sea, but often remained to form saline areas, the most prominent of which was the Great Salt Lake. To the south, the Grand Canyon of the Colorado River defined that limit of the basin. On the perimeters of the Great Basin flowed the Snake, Green, and Colorado rivers, although most of the region, varying in altitude from 4,000 to 13,000 feet above sea level, was essentially a desert characterized by sparse plant and animal life and an occasional oasis where people could survive.

Native Americans in the basin lived in small family groups because the limited food sources could not support large, concentrated populations. They were gatherers who relied on what nature provided in the region for shelter, clothing, and food. For nourishment, they harvested the roots of bulrushes, shoots of clover, and the bulbs of the camas lily. The rivers on the edges of the area yielded fish, especially salmon in the Snake River, which could be dried. Grasshoppers, crickets, and locusts all served as food, and the Indians occasionally killed some larger animals, such as deer and antelope, in the areas that are now Idaho and western Wyoming. Jackrabbits provided food and clothing. The Indians took rabbits in drives in the late fall when groups of people came together under the direction of the rabbit-drive boss. Working as a community, they herded the long-legged animals into a net made from milk weed where they could easily be slaughtered. The fur made leggings and robes; the hide formed a usable rope after being dried.

Despite the constant struggle to subsist in a desert area, the natives developed an abundant culture including a simple religion. As time passed, they built habitations from woven grass and made some pottery. Tools were fashioned from flint: knives, scrapers, and arrow points. Clothing remained basic and consisted of a fur apron, or skirt, for women and a breechcloth for men. Skin moccasins were worn. Willow basketry became a major form of artistic expression, and the Indians decorated their work with geometric designs. Shamans and medicine men exercised their talents during times of sickness or crisis and derived their powers from instructions received in a personal vision. And from time to time when larger congregations of people came together for the rabbit drive, other religious ceremonies took place.[2]

Gradually some basin dwellers drifted east into the Rocky

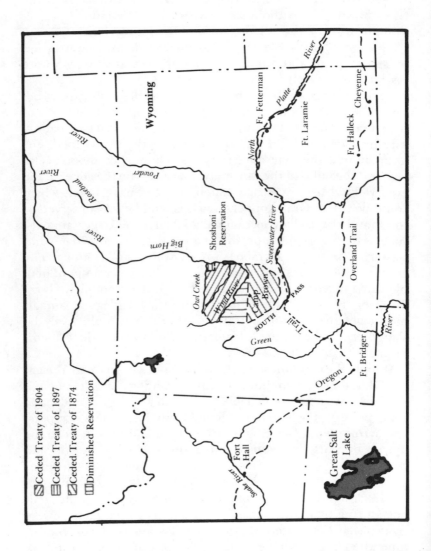

Mountains and onto the plains. Larger groups or bands formed when food supplies increased, and the bison made it possible for an evolution in life-style to take place. Some of the Indians acquired horses and developed a modified plains culture. These people became known as the Shoshones, while their brethren who remained afoot in the basin were called Shoshokos. Around 1700, after the Shoshones obtained many horses, accelerating the change in the pattern of their lives, skin tipis came into use and the tribesmen wore more elaborate skin clothing decorated with colored beads. Eagle feather headdresses adorned chiefs and headmen of bands. Soldier societies were formed, and the Shoshones adopted the sun dance. Their expanded mobility provided them with a more complex economic, social, religious, and political life.

The mounted Shoshones ranged from the Snake River for salmon to the High Plains of present-day Wyoming for bison. While the Shoshones moved east, however, other tribes, also hunting bison, were migrating west onto the Great Plains. To hold their new hunting lands in Wyoming, the Shoshones needed arms to defeat this host of new enemies. Crow and Blackfoot hunters pressed in from the north while Sioux, Cheyennes, and Arapahoes threatened their eastern range. These opponents were better armed than the Shoshones and gradually forced them back into the Rockies. Therefore, when the white Americans appeared, Shoshone leaders envisioned them as a possible source of firearms to be used against their enemies.[3]

Following the reports of Lewis and Clark, American trappers journeyed into the Shoshone homeland and trade between the two peoples rapidly developed. The Shoshones gradually obtained firearms and struck back at their enemies, defending their remaining hunting lands in central and western Wyoming. But the trade with the Americans was a double-edged sword: although the Shoshones now had muskets, they soon became dependent upon white traders for many of the necessities of life. They welcomed American merchants into most of their villages, and when the fur traders met at the great rendezvous on the Green River in eastern Wyoming, Shoshone warriors always were present. At the 1840 rendezvous Father Pierre Jean de Smet recorded that many "Shoshonis, or . . . Snakes" greeted the whites with a parade: "Three hundred of their warriors came up in good order and at full gallop into the midst of our camp. They were hideously painted, armed with war clubs and covered all over with feathers, pearls, wolves tails, teeth and claws of animals. . . . After riding a few times around the camp, uttering at intervals shouts of joy, they dismounted and all came to shake hands with the whites in sign of friendship."[4]

Yet the 1840 rendezvous was one of the last, for by the 1840s many of the streams had been overtrapped and the Rocky Mountain fur trade was declining. Mountain men and traders once common in the Shoshone country now packed their horses and moved west, seeking pelts in Washington and Oregon. Deprived of their primary source of guns and ammunition, the Shoshones also faced other problems. Sioux and Cheyenne war parties swept in from the east, forcing the Shoshones from their hunting lands along the Platte and Sweetwater. Meanwhile, the tribe suffered a crisis in its leadership. Padashawaunda, an old chief who had led the Shoshones for several years, died and was succeeded by Mowoomhah, his brother. Mowoomhah was a popular leader, supported by several minor chiefs, including Inkatushepoh, Fibebountowat, and Washakie, whom trapper and journalist Osborne Russell described as "the pillars of the Nation and at whose names the Blackfeet quaked with fear." But Mowoomhah also died within a few months, leaving the Shoshones confused and divided.[5]

Out of this confusion Washakie emerged as chief. Washakie, first named Pina Quahah (Smell of Sugar) by his parents, was born sometime between 1798 and 1804 in the Bitterroot Valley of Montana. His father, Pasego, belonged to the Flathead tribe, but was of mixed Indian blood—Umatilla, Flathead, and Shoshone. His mother came from the Lemhi band of Shoshones, the group that Lewis and Clark encountered. In the early 1800s, after Blackfoot raiders attacked their Flathead village and killed Pasego, Washakie, two brothers, and two sisters fled with their mother to the Salmon River and took refuge with a group of Lemhis.

Although he grew up among his mother's people, as a young man Washakie joined with a band of Bannocks, spending several years in their company. White trappers regarded the Bannocks as the most hostile of the Shoshonean-speaking peoples, and Washakie undoubtedly fought alongside his adopted brothers against both Indians and whites. Having developed his military abilities, he then returned to the Shoshones and never left. His reputation increased after battles with the Blackfeet and Crows. Because he carried deep scars from a Blackfoot arrow that pierced his left cheek, his enemies called him "Scar Face" or "Two Scar Chief." His tribal name, Washakie, stemmed from his first bison kill. After skinning the head, the young Shoshone removed the hair and tied the skin around a hollow stick. He then blew the skin up like a balloon and put stones in it. After the skin dried, the stones rattled. Washakie carried the noisemaker into battle to frighten his enemies' horses and thus earned his name, which meant "the Rattle."

Washakie was married several times, once to a Crow captive, and was a devoted father to his twelve children, from whom he extracted absolute loyalty. Standing over six feet tall and of a lighter complexion than most Shoshones, he projected a dignified bearing that commanded respect from both Indians and whites. Although known primarily as a warrior, Washakie was also highly regarded by the Shoshones as a singer and accompanied his songs with a gourd rattle. In addition, he was skilled in arrow making and constructed bows from elk horns, which he strengthened with sinews and coats of pitch from pine trees. Late in life he took up painting and decorated elk skins with recollections of his battles, hunts, and bison chases. Washakie possessed all the virtues that attracted other warriors: maturity, good judgment, oratorical ability, generosity, and success in war.

In the early 1840s, Washakie established an encampment on the Green River in southwestern Wyoming. Other Shoshones gradually drifted into his camp, and by 1844 he was the leader of a band that ranged from the North Platte and Wind rivers southwest to the Great Salt Lake. Like other Shoshone leaders, Washakie never enjoyed absolute power over his followers, but chiefs who led their bands into his region submitted to his authority. Since increasing numbers of emigrants were passing through his country en route to Oregon, Washakie demanded that horses not be stolen from the white men. Although this friendship was based upon tradition, it was also dictated by self-interest on the part of the Shoshones. They were surrounded by hostile tribes and needed the resources of the Americans.[6]

In later years Washakie asserted that he had always been friendly to white Americans. In 1897, he informed Nelson Yarnall, a white friend, that he had originally met Americans during the fur trade era and had earned his first money by herding ponies for a trapping party. When the trapping season closed, the Americans promised to return the following year and Washakie agreed to meet them. "My first experience with them was so pleasant I had determined to go," Washakie explained, "[and] . . . they had promised to bring me a gun." After acquiring the firearm, Washakie said, "All the young men of my tribe followed me, because I could shoot further than they." Since Washakie "had learned to eat the white man's bread, and drink their coffee," he promised the trappers "never to go on the war path against white men, and to try to prevent . . . [his] people from doing so."[7]

By the late 1840s, white Americans made Washakie's promises of peace difficult to keep. Gold seekers poured through Shoshone lands en route to California, and although they established no permanent settlements, the large number of white emigrants did increase the possibility of a Shoshone-white confrontation. The Mormons posed a more serious problem. In July 1847, Brigham Young and his followers established a permanent village on the Great Salt Lake, and during the following year over fifteen hundred more Saints flocked to the settlement. Washakie watched in alarm as these sturdy pioneers occupied the southern flank of his hunting grounds. Although the Mormons traded with the Shoshones, they also traded with the Utes, enemies of Washakie's people.

Meanwhile, armed conflicts between white emigrants and Sioux and Cheyenne warriors along the Oregon Trail forced the federal government to take action. Congress decided that the wagon road had to be garrisoned to protect travelers, and the War Department developed plans to obtain old fur posts or to build new forts for that purpose. Fort Kearny (Nebraska), Fort Laramie (Wyoming), and Fort Hall (Idaho) became army outposts. In addition, the government hoped to persuade the Indians to vacate the area between the Platte and the Arkansas to free the transportation routes from the danger of attack. The government's new policy was to concentrate Indians into large but definite regions and to abandon the "one big reservation" policy that had assigned tribesmen to the entire "Great American Desert."

Thomas Fitzpatrick, agent for the Upper Platte and Arkansas Indians within the Central superintendency, called the "chiefs, headmen, and braves" of the Sioux, Cheyennes, and Arapahoes to Fort Laramie in 1851 to formalize the government's new policies in a treaty. Federal officials at first did not invite the Shoshones because they were under the jurisdiction of the Utah Superintendency. Through Brigham Young's influence, however, the Shoshones and Utes announced they would attend.

Enroute to Fort Laramie, Washakie's party was attacked by a war party of Cheyennes near South Pass. Two Shoshones were killed and scalped before the Cheyenne warriors could be driven away. Angered by the attack, Washakie arrived at Fort Laramie expecting trouble. He was not disappointed. Not only were the hostile Cheyennes camped nearby, but as the Shoshone chief approached the fort he was challenged by a Sioux warrior who rode toward him brandishing a rifle and demanding revenge for one of his relatives killed by Washakie. A government interpreter managed to disarm the Sioux, but the atmosphere remained charged with tension. Washakie demanded that the Cheyennes return the two scalps taken near South Pass and give assurances that no scalp dance had been performed before he would allow the conference to begin. Through government pressure, the Cheyennes reluctantly agreed, but the Shoshones were forced to make amends to the Cheyennes for one of their warriors who had died from wounds received in the recent skirmish.

Starting under such unfavorable circumstances, the treaty negotiations did not bode well for Washakie and his people. The Shoshone leader assured the Americans, "I have come a great distance to see you and hear you . . . and I am glad and my people are glad we have come. Our hearts are full; all our hearts are full of your words. We will talk them over again."[8] The government generally ignored the Shoshones' interests. After eighteen days of deliberations, the council ended in a treaty dividing the northern plains into specific regions to be occupied by the Sioux,

Cheyennes, Arapahoes, Crows, Assiniboins, Gros Ventres, Mandans, and Arikaras. Refused full status as participants in the proceedings, the Shoshones learned that their northeastern hunting range, a vast tract between the Powder River and the Wind River Mountains, had been assigned to the Crows.[9]

Disgruntled by the treaty, Washakie turned away from the federal government and sought closer ties with the Mormons. Ironically, in 1850 Congress had authorized the organization of Utah Territory and President John Tyler recently had appointed Brigham Young as superintendent of Indian affairs for the Utah Superintendency, but Washakie still considered the Mormon leader to be apart from the general structure of the United States government. Young, who sought closer ties with both the Utes and the Shoshones, welcomed Washakie's overtures. Envisioning an eventual expansion of Mormon settlement east onto Shoshone lands, Young encouraged his followers to send traders and missionaries among Washakie's people.

The traders were welcome. The missionaries encountered a cooler reception. Mormon James S. Brown met with Washakie and offered to teach him agricultural techniques and Mormon religious doctrines. Washakie received the missionary politely, but when Brown presented him with a copy of *The Book of Mormon*, he replied that the volume was "no good for Indian[s]." Washakie also refused the missionary's request that Shoshone women marry Mormon settlers, for such unions would have given the Mormons too much influence within the tribe. In contrast, the Mormons' offer of agricultural assistance interested the chief. The game herds were declining, and Washakie realized that his people would need a broader economic base.[10]

During the mid-1850s Washakie remained on friendly terms with his Mormon neighbors. Although he did not try his hand at farming, he encouraged other Shoshones to learn the white man's methods; and Bazil, a subchief and adopted son of Sacajawea, cleared a small plot of farmland along the Green River and raised several crops of grain. Meanwhile, Washakie used his new ties with Brigham Young to press for a return of the former Shoshone hunting lands between the Wind and Powder rivers.

Unfortunately for the Mormons, their new-found influence among the Shoshones ended in 1857. The Mormon War began, and President James Buchanan removed Brigham Young as governor of Utah. Problems had always existed between the Saints and territorial officials of the United States, who found their authority in Utah limited by Young's influence. Mormon polygamy offended the sensibilities of Utah's growing Protestant population, and their complaints brought an army under Colonel Albert Sidney Johnston to assert the sovereignty of the United States over Utah Territory. To meet this threat, Young called all his loyal followers back to defend Zion, and the Mormons abandoned their Green River settlements among the Shoshones. Meanwhile, Mormon agents sought the assistance of the Shoshones and Utes in repelling Johnston's forces. Young ordered that the Indians be informed "that they have either got to help us or the United States will kill us both."[11]

Washakie had been willing to accept agricultural advice from the Latter-Day Saints, but he was too shrewd to side with the Mormons against the United States Army. Dr. Jacob Forney, Young's replacement as Indian agent, accompanied Johnston, and while the army spent the winter of 1847–58 encamped at Fort Bridger, Washakie met with the new agent. Washakie convinced Forney that the Shoshones were loyal to the United States. He told the agent of his rejection of Young's proposals and asked him to send government agricultural experts to replace those Mormons who had fled back to Salt Lake City. Washakie also used the conference to plead for a Shoshone reservation, assuring Forney that his people wished to occupy the "Warm Valley," the protected, well-watered region assigned to the Crows by the Treaty of Fort Laramie.

Forney and other officials were so impressed with the Shoshones' importance that the government established a new agency for Washakie and his people. Opened at Fort Bridger in 1861, the agency soon found it difficult to maintain the peace between the Indians and the many settlers moving through their hunting lands. In 1859, Frederick Lander had blazed a new route along the Sweetwater to the Snake River. The trail cut across both the Shoshone and Bannock hunting lands, and many Indians resented the growing traffic, which drove bison and other game out of their country. Although Washakie tried to keep his young warriors at peace, many slipped away from his village on the Green

River to join Bear Hunter, a militant Shoshone leader, or Pash-ego, a hostile Bannock chief. Renegade Utes joined the malcon-tents, and during 1862 they began to raid immigrant parties and isolated settlements near the Utah-Idaho border.

Although hard pressed by the Civil War, the government was determined to suppress the hostiles. In 1862, federal officials es-tablished Fort Halleck, near Elk Mountain, Wyoming, to protect travelers on the Overland Trail. Meanwhile, Colonel Patrick E. Connor and the Third California Volunteers arrived at Salt Lake City to conduct an active campaign against the unfriendly Indi-ans. During 1863, his troops attacked a hostile village on the Bear River in Idaho, killing over two hundred Indians, including Bear Hunter, and taking many captives. By the summer of 1863 most of the hostile Shoshones were suing for peace.[12]

Washakie had counseled his people against taking up the hatchet against the United States and had refused to participate in the fighting. By the summer of 1863, many of the young men who had originally ignored his advice were dead. Others had sur-reptitiously returned to his village on the Green River, hoping to escape retribution from the Americans. Because Washakie had remained friendly to the United States, federal officials worked through him in negotiating the peace settlement. In July 1863, he and the other leaders signed a treaty officially reestablishing peace between the government and the Shoshones. The Indians agreed not to molest whites traveling west along the immigrant routes and to allow the construction and maintenance of both telegraph and railroad lines through their country. In return the government promised to pay the Indians an annuity of twenty thousand dollars for twenty years (later changed to ten years by the Senate) to compensate the tribesmen for the game destroyed by emigrants and for the agricultural or mining settlements al-ready established on Shoshone lands. The treaty commissioners also distributed six thousand dollars' worth of presents—provi-sions and clothing—to the Indians at the close of the treaty con-ference.[13]

Washakie's stature among both the Shoshones and the Ameri-cans was much enhanced by the conclusion of the treaty. Many of those warriors who had disregarded his advice and fought against the Americans were either dead or defeated. Moreover, in the years following the treaty, government officials often followed Washakie's advice in distributing the annuities, giving him considerable economic influence within his tribe. Meanwhile, he again urged federal agents to establish a new reservation for his people in the Wind River region. He argued that the Green River valley was ill suited for agriculture and that if his people could move to the Warm Valley, many would become farmers. Although the Crows and Shoshones had traditionally been enemies (Washakie had killed the Crow chief Big Robber in single combat near Crowheart Butte, Wyoming, in 1858), they had recently made peace and were both willing to assist the government against the Sioux.

By the mid-1860s, the government needed such assistance. During the Civil War, army engineers had opened the Powder River Road north from the Platte River to the gold fields in Montana. Angered over the intrusion, the Sioux struck back, attacking army outposts and, in 1866, annihilating Captain William Fetterman's command in northern Wyoming. Two years later President Andrew Johnson dispatched a peace commission to the plains tribes, planning to restore peace across the plains and to concentrate the Indians into smaller tribal territories. Officials hoped that under the watchful eye of the army the tribesmen could be converted into farmers, Christianized, and educated in the tradition of the white man.

Sioux chiefs and government commissioners met at Fort Laramie in April 1868 and signed a treaty that established a large reservation in the Dakota Territory. The treaty also permitted the Sioux to hunt west of their reservation, into the Powder River region of Wyoming. The Shoshones did not attend the Fort Laramie negotiations, but two months later they met with federal officials at Fort Bridger. Brevet Major General Christopher Augur informed Washakie that the government wanted to locate the Shoshones on a new reservation far removed from the Union Pacific Railroad, which was laying track westward across southern Wyoming from Cheyenne. Once again, Washakie took the opportunity to assert the Shoshone claim to the Wind River region, suggesting that his people would trade their lands on the Green

River for the more fertile Warm Valley. After several days of negotiations, the government and the Indians reached an agreement.

The resulting Treaty of Fort Bridger, signed on July 3, 1868, was Washakie's greatest accomplishment. The government "set apart for the absolute and undisturbed use and occupation of the Shoshonee Indians" a permanent reservation of over three million acres located in the Wind River drainage of west-central Wyoming. The government also agreed to provide about twenty thousand dollars for the construction of agency buildings and a school. To encourage the Shoshones to take up agriculture, federal officials promised that every Shoshoni head of family could claim 320 acres as a farm for his exclusive possession. The government would give aspiring farmers one hundred dollars' worth of seeds and implements to get them started, an additional twenty-five dollars' worth of such commodities for the next three years and twenty dollars "in necessities" for the ten years that followed. In addition, Indian agents pledged to award five hundred dollars in prizes annually for three years to the ten Shoshones who grew the best crops. The government also agreed to provide a school and teacher for the children and to furnish one yearly issue of clothing to all Shoshones for the following thirty years.

In return, the Shoshones gave up their claims to their remaining lands in Wyoming and Utah and promised to settle permanently on the reservation and to remain at peace with their white neighbors. They also agreed that other tribes might be settled on the reservation, but only "with Shoshoni approval and the consent of the United States."[14]

After a decade of effort, Washakie had finally secured a large reservation, located within his homeland, which provided his people with protected, well-watered farmland, free from the immigrants that streamed westward toward the Great Salt Lake. Ironically, however, other Indians—Sioux, Cheyennes, and Arapahoes—kept Washakie and his followers from occupying their new home. Ostensibly at peace with the whites after the Treaty of Fort Laramie, Sioux, Cheyenne, and Arapaho raiders struck at Shoshone camps in north-central Wyoming, creating havoc and taking several scalps. Washakie wanted to move to the new reservation, but he knew his outnumbered warriors would be

hard pressed to defend the Wind River region from their enemies. Aware that the government was anxious to remove his people from the path of the oncoming railroad, Washakie demanded
that federal troops drive the hostiles from the Wind River. Until
he received military assistance, he intended to remain in southwestern Wyoming.

Giving in to Washakie's demands, military officials established
Camp Augur (later Camp Brown) in 1869, on the new Wind
River Reservation. But the hostile raids still continued, spilling
over into the burgeoning new mining settlements near South Pass
City, north of the Sweetwater. These "diggings" soon expanded
north, onto the new reservation lands, increasing the Shoshones'
resentment. To Washakie and his people the new reservation
now seemed a cruel joke. Not only could they not occupy their
home because of inadequate military protection, but they
watched in dismay as the southern portions of the reservation
were invaded by white miners. Disgusted, Washakie withdrew his
village from the Green River valley in 1871, and moved westward
into Utah.

To remedy the situation, the government offered two proposals. In the fall of 1872, Washakie and many of his followers journeyed to Camp Brown, where federal officials suggested that the
Shoshones give up the southern portion of their reservation in
exchange for similar acreage which would be added to the northern limit of their reserve. Since the southern region was poorly
watered and had little game, it would serve as a buffer zone between the miners and the Indians. In addition, the government
promised to station more troops at Camp Brown if the Shoshones
would settle permanently at Wind River.

Washakie was willing to cede the southern reservation lands,
but he refused to accept the additional acreage along the northern border of the reservation. Arguing that the northern lands
belonged to the Crows, Washakie offered to relinquish the southern tract if the government would pay the Shoshones twenty-five
thousand dollars in five equal installments over the next five
years. The money would be used to purchase cattle to form the
nucleus for a tribal herd. The agreement was signed on September 26, 1872.[15]

Washakie also agreed to settle permanently on the Wind River

Reservation, but the Shoshones were still plagued by attacks from hostile Indians. In late June 1874, scouts reported back to Washakie that several villages of Sioux, Cheyennes, and Arapahoes were approaching the reservation from the north, planning to raid the Shoshones. After consulting with military officials, Washakie decided to take the offensive. In early July, a combined force of U.S. cavalry and Shoshone warriors left Camp Brown, intent on intercepting the raiders. Traveling at night, they moved north undetected, and on July 4 they discovered the Arapaho village, which had split off from the Cheyennes and Sioux. Although their attack on the Arapahoes lacked coordination, the combined force of Shoshones and cavalry was successful, killing twenty-five of the enemy and capturing six hundred horses. Alarmed by the attack, the Cheyennes and Sioux withdrew to their own country.[16]

Washakie and his people remained on the Wind River Reservation, but Sioux raiders continued to mount sporadic forays against the Shoshone pony herds. Angered, Washakie in May 1876 sent a large war party of his tribesmen to assist General George Crook, who was assembling troops at Fort Fetterman for a campaign against hostile Sioux in southern Montana. Meanwhile, the Shoshone chief remained near Camp Brown, awaiting war parties of Bannocks and Utes who also planned to join with the army. In mid-June, before Washakie could arrive with the Bannocks and Utes, Crook and his Indian allies engaged large numbers of Sioux under Crazy Horse on the Rosebud River in southern Montana. The Shoshones, armed with "glittering lances and brightly polished weapons of fire," fought well, and Shoshone and Crow warriors turned back several Sioux charges that threatened to overrun the American position. In contrast, the cavalry remained on the defensive, and although the Sioux eventually withdrew, Crook refused to press forward until he received reinforcements.[17]

Throughout June, Washakie waited at Camp Brown, anticipating the arrival of the Utes and Bannocks. In early July, when both tribes still failed to appear, he assembled another war party of his tribesmen and left for the Rosebud, arriving at Crook's camp on July 11. During August he accompanied Crook north up the Rosebud, where they encountered General Alfred Terry and a force of cavalry on August 10. Crook and Terry combined their commands and pursued the hostiles east toward the Powder River, marching slowly through heavy rains and mud. Since Shoshone scouts brought back information that the Sioux were short of food and were eating their dogs and horses, Washakie knew that the enemy would soon split into small bands and scatter over the countryside. Discouraged by the slow pursuit, he informed the officers that he and his warriors were too far from home and were unfamiliar with the terrain. In late August they returned to their reservation.[18]

Later in the fall, Washakie's two sons, Konaya and Saraguant, led about one hundred warriors to assist other government efforts against the hostiles, and in November 1878 Washakie's warriors rode with Colonel Ranald S. Mackenzie against Dull Knife's Cheyennes, who were encamped near the Big Horn Mountains. In the attack on the Cheyennes, the Shoshones were again in the thick of the fighting and suffered several casualties, but captured many horses. By the following spring most of the fighting had ended. Crazy Horse, Gall, and other Sioux chiefs surrendered. Sitting Bull fled to Canada.[19]

With a tentative peace restored to the northern plains, Washakie's service to the United States did not go unrecognized. Earlier, the government had given him a silver medal as a reward for his friendship, and in 1878 the army renamed Camp Brown Fort Washakie in his honor. During the same year President Ulysses S. Grant presented a silver-mounted saddle to the chief through the Indian agent at Wind River. Deeply moved, the aging chief replied: "Do a kindness to a . . . [white man], he feels it in his head and his tongue speaks; do a kindness to an Indian, he feels it in his heart. The heart has no tongue."[20]

Yet the strong ties between the Shoshones and the United States were severely strained by government Indian policy following the Sioux wars. Attempting to shatter the coalition of recently hostile tribes, federal officials during the late 1870s, sought to place the Sioux, Cheyennes, and Arapahoes on widely separated reservations. The Sioux were scattered across reservations in Nebraska and the Dakotas. The Cheyennes were sent to Indian Territory. Unfortunately for the Shoshones, the Arapahoes were brought to the reservation at Wind River. Over Washakie's strong objections, 938 Arapahoes were settled "temporarily" on the southeastern portions of the Shoshone reservation in March 1878. The Arapahoes were destitute, near starvation, and Washakie reluctantly agreed that they could remain, but he repeatedly asserted that the newcomers had no claim to the lands. Moreover, he warned them to stay on the flatlands and not to venture into the western portions of the reserve, where the Shoshones remained camped close to their beloved mountains.[21]

During the summer of 1878, Governor John W. Hoyt of Wyoming Territory visited the reservation, and Washakie expressed his growing frustration to the territorial official. Speaking with politeness and great deliberation, he said:

> I shall . . . speak to you freely of the many wrongs we have suffered at the hands of the white man. . . . But I cannot hope to express to you the half what is in our hearts. They are too full for words. . . . The white man, who possesses this whole vast country from sea to sea, who roams over it at pleasure, and lives where he likes, cannot know the cramp we feel in this little spot, with the enduring remembrance of the fact, which you know as well as we, that every foot of what you proudly call America, not very long ago belonged to the red man. The Great Spirit gave it to us. There was room enough for all his many tribes, and all were happy in their freedom.

But, according to the chief, the white man knew things the Indian did not, "how to make superior tools and terrible weapons," and drove the Indians off their lands. He reminded the governor that the United States had promised to keep whites and other Indians off Shoshone lands if Washakie and his people accepted the reservation. *"But it has not kept its word!"* the chief protested, "and so, . . . we are sometimes nearly starved and go half naked."[22]

Hoyt was so moved by Washakie's eloquence that he pledged to use his influence to rectify the mistake and provide justice for "two to three thousand of the most deserving of the nation's wards." Unfortunately, however, the governor's efforts proved useless and the Arapahoes remained on the Wind River Reservation. Finally, in 1891, the government gave de facto recognition to their right to occupy the lands, and only in 1938, long after Washakie's death, did the government pay the Shoshones for those lands occupied by the Arapahoes."[23]

Washakie's disenchantment with the government resulted from other causes besides the settlement of the Arapahoes on the Shoshone reservation. Reservation life itself was far from fulfilling. Although the government assigned agents to Fort Washakie and constructed schools, flour mills, corrals, and a blacksmith shop, Washakie and many of his followers longed for the old days when buffalo herds filled the plains and warriors were free to hunt them. But by the late 1870s the great herds were dwindling and the Shoshones were forced to rely more heavily on government annuities. To make matters worse, white interlopers continued to trespass on reservation lands, hunting the few buffalo that remained and killing large numbers of deer and antelope. In 1875, Indian agents issued five thousand Texas cattle to Washakie and his people, but over half were stolen, driven away by white rustlers. The Shoshones tried their hand at farming, but most of Washakie's kinsmen soon found the occupation not to their liking. Accordingly, Shoshone dependence on the government increased.

To provide more federal assistance for his people, Washakie agreed in 1896 to the cession of a small tract of land, ten miles square, at the northeastern corner of the reservation. Bordered by Owl Creek and the Bighorn River, the land held a thermal spring famous for its medicinal properties. In return for the ceded land, the Shoshones and the Arapahoes shared a government payment of sixty thousand dollars. Sharp Nose signed the reservation agreement as chief of the Arapahoes; Washakie signed for the Shoshones. It was the last time the aging chief would put his mark on a reservation agreement.

The years had taken their toll of the old Shoshone. Well into his nineties, Washakie was in failing health and senile. Although he was still much admired by his followers, the reins of leadership passed from his hands to younger, more able leaders. Realizing he was nearing the end of his trail, Washakie expressed a renewed interest in religious matters. He used his influence to oppose the Ghost Dance, was skeptical of peyote, but urged his people to continue such traditional celebrations as the sun dance.

Moreover, in 1897, after a personal crisis in which his wild, younger son was killed in a barroom brawl, Washakie accepted Christianity and was baptized as an Episcopalian. Soon thereafter many other Shoshones became Christians.

As he sat beside his campfire, the old chief must have pondered the impact of his leadership upon his tribe. He had led his people into friendship with the white man; surrounded by traditional enemies, his people had no other choice. They needed the guns and assistance of the Americans if they were to hold their lands against the more populous Sioux, Cheyennes, and Arapahoes. Moreover, unlike his enemies, who had been scattered across desolate reservations chosen by the government, Washakie had secured a place for his people in the choicest part of their homeland. Of course, reservation life posed major problems, but given the expansionist policies of nineteenth-century America, what other alternatives were available? A conservative, tribal people, the Wind River Shoshones certainly had no wish to assimilate into the white society of the United States.

Washakie was not a white man's Indian. He had fought with the Anglo-Americans against the Sioux because the latter posed a traditional and immediate threat to the Shoshones and their homeland. Like most other nineteenth-century Indian leaders, he had no concept of pan-Indianism. His loyalty was first to his family, then to his band, and finally to his tribe. A realist, Washakie was willing to utilize any alliance that would serve his people's purpose.

Aged and infirm, Washakie was blind by 1899 and had developed a partial paralysis of his lower limbs. Finally, on February 20, 1900, the old Shoshone fell asleep in his cabin, attended by his wife, two sons, and daughter. He did not awaken. The War Department ordered a full military funeral for the "white man's friend." A creaking gun carriage carried the chief's body to its final resting place, at Fort Washakie, in the shadow of his beloved Wind River Mountains. From there Washakie began his great journey to what he called "Dâm Apuā Ungam"—"Our Father's Home."

NOTES

1. Meriwether Lewis, *The Expedition of Lewis and Clark,* 2 vols. (Ann Arbor, Mich.: University Microfilms, 1966), 1:354–56.

2. Robert F. Spencer, Jesse D. Jennings, et al., *The Native Americans: Prehistory and Ethnology of the North American Indians* (New York: Harper & Row, 1965), pp. 273–81.

3. Virginia C. Trenholm and Maurine Carley, *The Shoshonis: Sentinels of the Rockies* (Norman: University of Oklahoma Press, 1964), pp. 17 ff.

4. Pierre Jean De Smet, *Letters and Sketches, with a Narrative of a Year's Residence among the Indian Tribes of the Rocky Mountains,* ed. Reuben G. Thwaites (Cleveland: Arthur H. Clark Co., 1906), pp. 163–64.

5. Osborn Russell, *Journal of a Trapper,* ed. Aubrey L. Haynes (1955; rpt. Lincoln: University of Nebraska Press, 1965), pp. 114–15.

6. Grace R. Hebard, *Washakie: An Account of Indian Resistance of the Covered Wagon and Union Pacific Railroad Invasions of Their Territory* (Cleveland: Arthur H. Clark Co., 1930), pp. 21–30, 225–40.

7. Nelson Yarnall, "A Good Indian," *Recreation* 8 (July 1897): 20–21.

8. Trenholm and Carley, *The Shoshonis,* pp. 116–26.

9. Charles J. Kappler, comp. and ed., *Indian Treaties, 1778–1883* (New York: Interland Publishing, Inc., 1972), pp. 594–96.

10. James S. Brown, *Life of a Pioneer* (Salt Lake City: George Q. Cannon & Sons Co., 1900), pp. 304 ff.

11. Norman F. Furniss, *The Mormon Conflict* (New Haven, Conn.: Yale University Press, 1966), pp. 162–63.

12. Robert M. Utley, *Frontiersmen in Blue: The United States Army and the Indian, 1848–1865* (New York: Macmillan, 1973), pp. 219–25.

13. Kappler, *Indian Treaties,* pp. 848–50.

14. Ibid., pp. 1020–23.

15. Charles J. Kappler, comp., *Indian Affairs: Laws and Treaties,* 5 vols. (Washington, D.C.: Government Printing Office, 1903), 1:153–55.

16. Nelson Yarnall, "Captain Bates' Fight with the Arapahoes," *Recreation* 6 (February 1897): 90–93.

17. John G. Bourke, *On the Border with Crook* (1891; rpt. Glorieta, N. Mex.: Rio Grande Press, 1971), pp. 303, 337.

18. Robert M. Utley, *Frontier Regulars: The United States Army and the Indian, 1866–1891* (New York: Macmillan, 1973), pp. 236 ff.

19. U.S. Congress, *House Executive Document 1,* 39th Cong., 2d sess. (serial 1284), p. 31.

20. Quoted in Trenholm and Carley, *The Shoshonis,* p. 258.

21. *Report of the Commissioner of Indian Affairs . . . 1878* (Washington, D.C.: Government Printing Office, 1878), p. 148.

22. Quoted in Hebard, *Washakie,* pp. 211–13.

23. Kappler, *Indian Affairs,* 1:624–27.

Sitting Bull

Herbert T. Hoover

"Sitting Bull legends seem . . . to have no relation to facts at all. They are in general mere fabrications many of which were concocted by war correspondents, and were embodied in a book written by the Indian agent during whose term of office Sitting Bull was killed. And the worst of it is, these yarns are not artistic—not half so colorful and interesting as the truth turns out to be."—Stanley Vestal

FAR MORE LEGEND than truth has been written about Sitting Bull because he was active in dramatic episodes of resistance to Anglo-American frontiersmen and federal Indian policies during the last half of the nineteenth century. In that period, no dispute over territory along the Anglo-Indian frontier caused more problems for federal negotiators than their dealings with Teton Sioux chiefs and headmen over the disposition of the sixty-million-acre Black Hills region. No military confrontation generated greater concern among congressmen and War Department leaders than the Great Sioux War. No incidents involving Indians attracted wider attention across the country than the Battle of the Little Bighorn and the Ghost Dance crisis. For his prominent roles in these and other important developments, Sitting Bull has been portrayed by most observers and scholars who have written about him as either a villain or a saint. Only a few have characterized him properly as a person of unusual intelligence and ambition who rose from obscurity to a position of power through dedication to a single purpose: the perpetuation of a segregated existence for traditional Teton people in the vicinity of his birthplace.[1]

He was born during the early 1830s near a site called Many-Caches, where Hunkpapa people stored supplies along the

Grand River in western Dakota, and grew up in an area between the mouth of the Grand and the Yellowstone River basin. As a youngster he was called Slow, because of his deliberate mannerisms, but as he came of age he lived down the stigma of his childhood name by "becoming a man" according to rules of tribal tradition. When he was ten years old he demonstrated his prowess as a hunter by killing a buffalo. At age fourteen he gained recognition as a soldier by counting coup on an enemy and by receiving public acclaim for his courage in a ceremony during which his father assigned him the adult name Sitting Bull. The same year he displayed potential as a medicine man by completing a vision quest and "making spiritual contact." A short time later he achieved social status among Hunkpapas by earning membership in the Strong Heart warrior society—a prestigious soldiers' lodge that policed encampments, governed hunting expeditions, and defended territorial boundaries. And in 1856 he gained political power by taking charge of the society following an engagement during which he killed a Crow chief and sustained a gunshot wound that caused him to limp for the rest of his life.[2]

As head of the Strong Hearts, Sitting Bull held status equal to that of any other person except a chief, and in the ensuing years his prestige and influence continued to grow because of the services he rendered and feats he performed in the interest of tribal survival. The Hunkpapas relied heavily on buffalo for food to sustain them through the harsh winters, robes to cover their tipis, sinew to manufacture clothing, and other materials. To ensure adequate supplies of these necessities, Sitting Bull supervised several hunting expeditions each year, and when buffalo were scarce he battled the military forces of other tribes to enlarge the hunting range of his own people. Over a period of twenty years he carried on territorial wars against the Crows, Arikaras, Mandans, Gros Ventres, Hidatsas, Assiniboins, Blackfeet, Flatheads, Piegans, and Shoshones, and claimed personal victory over more than sixty enemy soldiers.[3]

At about the time he began his career in the warrior society, non-Indians launched a succession of encroachments on the northern Great Plains that lasted until Sioux claims to most of the Black Hills region were extinguished. Clearly these early intrusions threatened the future security of all Tetons. But they occurred along the southern edge of the region, where the Brulés

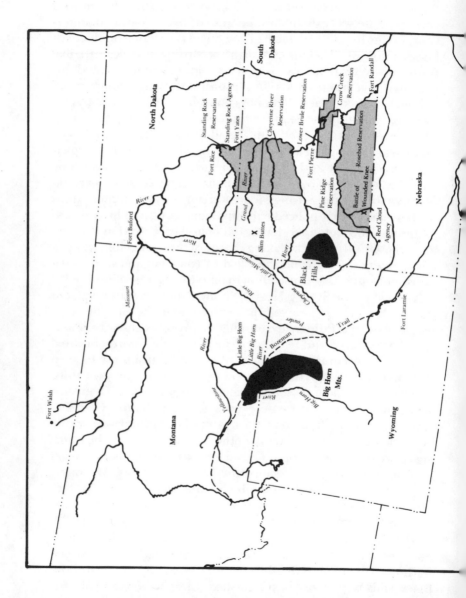

and Oglalas lived, and Sitting Bull refused to lead his Strong Hearts in resistance as long as whites did not violate the sanctuary of the Hunkpapa people. He did not engage in the negotiations that led to the signing of the Treaty of Fort Laramie in 1851, for example, even though the treaty called for restrictions on the movements of all Tetons and guaranteed safe passage for non-Indians traveling across Sioux country on the Oregon Trail. Sitting Bull gave no assistance to Brulés and Oglalas who fought General William Harney at the Battle of Ash Hollow in 1855, where eighty-six Indians were killed, and offered no resistance when Harney established military posts along the Missouri River from Fort Randall to Fort Pierre in 1856. He was not perturbed by encroachments on the eastern edge of the Black Hills region that accompanied the establishment of the Yankton Reservation in 1859 and the founding of Dakota Territory in 1861. With unwavering consistency, he avoided contact with all white people except traders until Generals Henry Hastings Sibley and Alfred Sully led punitive expeditions to the edge of Hunkpapa country in pursuit of eastern Sioux *(Isanti)* refugees during 1863 and 1864. Their presence finally forced him to change his stance, and he led the Strong Hearts into action against them.[4]

These brief encounters with Sibley and Sulley caused Sitting Bull to fear the intrusions of whites as much as invasions by other tribes, and as he learned of other developments in the mid-1860s he gradually came to view the activities of non-Indians as the greater threat. Less than two hundred miles east of Hunkpapa territory a steady stream of pioneers filed in to occupy homesteads between Fort Randall and the headwaters of the Red River. Along the southwestern edge of the Black Hills region U.S. troops guarded work on the Bozeman Trail through the Powder River country until Red Cloud's Oglalas forced an end to the construction with the annihilation of Captain William J. Fetterman's ill-fated column. Up the Missouri came the Northwest Indian Commission headed by Dakota territorial governor Newton Edmunds to negotiate with representatives of "stay-around-the-fort-people" at Forts Sully and Rice. Edmund's several meetings with these pliable Sioux spokesmen produced no permanent treaties, but they gave the governor ample opportunity to announce the intention of the United States government to confine all Teton people to reservations where they could be "civilized" under the supervision of federal agents.[5]

Fears engendered by the governor's aggressive discussion evidently intensified Sittting Bull's growing resentment toward non-Indians, for at the next sign of trespass on Hunkpapa land he initiated a war that quickly earned him national recognition as an Indian military leader. The construction of Fort Buford at the confluence of the Yellowstone and Missouri rivers in 1866 provoked devastating attacks by the Strong Hearts on troops garrisoned at the post as well as against civilians who lived nearby. The raids themselves attracted widespread attention because in the course of one battle the post commander shot and killed his wife, at her own request, to save her from captivity among the Sioux.[6] The Fort Buford raids generated more publicity for Sitting Bull in the following years, too, for they caused him to abandon his policy of defensive resistance in favor of more aggressive tactics. From then on, the Strong Hearts became "the terror of mail carriers, wood-choppers and small parties in the vicinity of the post [Fort Buford], and from 100 to 200 miles from it either way, up and down the river," according to one observer. "From 1866 to 1870 . . . this band . . . several times captured and destroyed the mail," stole "200 head of cattle and killed near a score of white men in the immediate vicinity of the fort."[7]

Hoping to stave off further aggression by the forces of Sitting Bull and other western Sioux war leaders, veteran missionary Pierre Jean De Smet accepted an appointment as "envoy extraordinary of the Government" and traveled up the Missouri River on successive peace missions in the years 1867 and 1868. His specific charge was to persuade recalcitrant leaders along the middle and upper Missouri Valley to join the stay-around-the-fort-people near the agencies, where they and their followers could be schooled in the fundamentals of non-Indian culture. Upon completion of the first expedition, Father De Smet said he was "firmly convinced" by talks with leaders from several tribes at Fort Rice that if they and their followers were treated decently, and were given the tools necessary for survival in a sedentary existence, they all would soon cease their depredations and join the stay-at-home people near the forts.[8] Following a historic conference at the junction of the Yellowstone and Powder rivers the next year, De Smet was equally optimistic about peace as he reported his visit with Sitting Bull and a cortege of Teton dignitaries: "I took possession of a large lodge, pitched in the center of the camp, which had been prepared for me by order of the generalissimo of the warriors, Sitting Bull. . . . When I awoke, I found Sitting Bull beside me, together with Four Horns, head chief of the camp, Black Moon, his great orator, and No Neck."[9] Several men spoke of how they had taken up arms only in response to offenses committed against their constituents by obtrusive whites. Then Sitting Bull explained his posture:

> Black-robe, I hardly sustain myself beneath the weight of white men's blood that I have shed. The whites provoked the war; their injustices, their indignities to our families . . . shook all the veins which bind and support me. I rose, tomahawk in hand, and I have done all the hurt to the whites that I could. To-day thou art amongst us, and in thy presence my arms stretch to the ground as if dead. I will listen . . . and as bad as I have been to whites, just so good am I ready to become toward them.[10]

His previous reluctance to wage war against non-Indians, until they threatened the security of his own tribe, gave credence to the Hunkpapa leader's expression of desire for peace. Yet by the time he talked to De Smet his responsibilities outweighed his own inclinations and even his obligations to his own tribe. Now he was "generalissimo"—principle military leader and strategist—for more than ten thousand Tetons who refused to accept reservation life, and he would not honor any commitment to peace that might at some future time undermine the traditional existence of his constituency.[11]

Because of the advantageous terms of the 1868 Fort Laramie treaty, more than half a decade passed before Sitting Bull was forced to choose between peace and the defense of his followers. Guided partly by fear of the power of the Tetons and partly by change in the policies of officials in Washington, D.C., federal negotiators agreed to withdraw from the Bozeman Trail; to set aside an area bounded on the west by the 104th meridian, on the north by the 46th parallel, on the east by the Missouri River, and on the south by the Dakota-Nebraska border as the Great Sioux Reservation; and to abandon an unceded area between the 104th meridian and the Big Horn Mountains as western Sioux hunting ground. The negotiators agreed, moreover, to prevent further white intrusions into the Black Hills region until such time as three-fourths of the adult males in the signatory tribes agreed to amend the terms of the treaty.[12]

Except for occasional raids in the vicinity of Fort Buford, Sitting Bull continued to keep his distance from non-Indians as long as the boundaries established at Fort Laramie in 1868 remained inviolate. However, signs that treaty terms alone could not hold back the Anglo-American frontier were soon in evidence. As early as 1872 prospectors, who had exhausted placer gold deposits elsewhere in the West, began to explore the Black Hills, and over the next three years they filed into the hills in ever increasing numbers.

Federal officials attempted to deal with their intrusions by several means, but without success. Officers stationed near the scene tried warnings and occasional arrests, but prospectors were not intimidated. Colonels George Custer and Richard Dodge led expeditions into the hills to assess the value of the gold deposits, realizing that negative results would discourage further illegal entry. But both men returned with reports of gold in substantial quantities at several places. When these tactics failed, cabinet-level officials summoned Sioux leaders from several tribes to the national capital in the hope of negotiating the purchase of the Black Hills. But even the most pliable chiefs would not take responsibility for the cession of land within the boundaries of the Great Sioux Reservation without a general plebiscite.[13] When these discussions aborted, Congress dispatched Senator William B. Allison, of Iowa, with a commission to further explore the possibility of a negotiated purchase, but in June 1875 he returned from the frustrating experience to suggest an ultimatum: set a reasonable price for the Black Hills and offer it "as a finality."[14]

General George Crook labored through the summer of 1875 to expel intruders from the gold fields while congressmen considered Allison's plan. Yet by early fall most observers could see that the failure of the government either to enforce the terms of the 1868 treaty or to negotiate the purchase of the Black Hills had set the stage for a major war. During the third week of September, twenty thousand Indians (stay-around-the-fort-people as well as traditionalists) assembled in general council near the Red Cloud

Agency, and out of the council emerged an army of Tetons and Cheyennes under Sitting Bull and Two Moon that soon reached a size of three thousand warriors or more. In the spring of 1876, Sitting Bull assembled this grand army between the Big Horn and Powder rivers in preparation for the defense of the Black Hills region. In response, the United States Army mustered a force of twenty-five hundred men and drew up plans for attacks on the Sioux-Cheyenne encampments: General Crook would move up from the south, General Alfred Terry from the east, and Colonel John Gibbon from his station in Montana.[15]

As these three military units advanced toward the Big Horn Mountains in the middle of June, Sitting Bull, who by then had become more a spiritual leader than a front-line soldier, participated in a sun dance and saw a vision: "soldiers and some Indians on horseback coming down like grasshoppers, with their heads down and their hats falling off. They were falling right into our camp."[16] Victory was inevitable, in other words, if the Sioux and Cheyennes would stand their ground.

On the morning of June 25, Crazy Horse, Gall, and other tactical leaders answered the call and drew their forces into battle lines. Sitting Bull took up a position to observe and plan strategy from a distance. George Custer led his Seventh Cavalry into a trap, and the grand army of Tetons and Cheyennes won the opening engagement of the Great Sioux War with ease.

Soon, however, the war turned into a succession of reverses and frustrations for Sitting Bull and his men. With Colonel Nelson Miles on his trail, he assembled two thousand men in a defensive position near Twin Buttes on the Grand River. But by early fall so many of his men had slipped away in search of food that he could not marshal a force sufficient to relieve the band of American Horse when it came under siege by a small unit from Crook's army at Slim Buttes.[17] By that time, former Indian commissioner George Manypenny was on his way with word that Congress would pay no more benefits under existing treaties until the Tetons signed a new "agreement" to relinquish claim to the Powder River country and to surrender a large area in the Great Sioux Reservation that contained the Black Hills. Fearing reprisals for continued resistance, numerous Teton chiefs and headmen stepped forward to affix their marks to the agreement and, as though oblivious to the provision in the 1868 treaty that forbade a reduction in the size of the Great Sioux Reservation without the consent of three-fourths of the adult males, they advised their followers to submit to federal demands and accept reservation life.[18] People quickly packed their belongings and headed for the agencies; by October of 1876, Sitting Bull was left with only a few chiefs and a following of no more than one thousand of the most determined traditionalists who still believed he could save them from forced acculturation on the reservations.

To protect this group, he embarked on an odyssey that prevented his return to the Grand River area for nearly seven years. It began with a retreat into eastern Montana, where Colonel Nelson Miles appeared with an army of 394 men to demand his surrender. During the first of three meetings between the two men, according to Miles, Sitting Bull displayed confidence: "He was a strong, hardy, sturdy looking man of about five feet eleven inches in height, well-built, with strongly-marked features, high cheek bones, prominent nose, straight, thin lips, and strong under jaw, indicating determination and force. . . . He was very deliberate in his movements and somewhat reserved in his manners [and presented a demeanor] . . . that was civil and to some extent one of calm repose." In a second meeting, the Hunkpapa leader showed defiance when Miles threatened attack if the Indians refused to surrender, ordered his Tetons to fire the grass, and directed them to a more advantageous position forty miles away. At the third meeting, Sitting Bull revealed a strong determination to carry on resistance to the United States government, whatever the odds; even though five chiefs in his party surrendered their arms to Miles and led their constituents off toward the agencies, "Sitting Bull, Gall, Pretty Bear, and several other" leaders "broke away from the main camp . . . with nearly four hundred people . . . and retreated north" to seek refuge in Canada.[19]

As he crossed the Canadian border, Sitting Bull must have thought of the six hundred eastern Sioux refugees from the Minnesota Sioux Uprising of 1862 who lived in Manitoba. They had received permission from Dominion officials to stay in Canada in return for the support their forebears had given the British during the War of 1812. He could not ask the same privilege for any service rendered by his Teton ancestors, but he could at least hope for a sympathetic reception. The most any Canadian official would ever say on behalf of Sitting Bull and his followers, however, was that the "traversing of an imaginary boundary line by nomadic Indians in search of their means of subsistence is not an offense against international law."[20] For the most part, Dominion officers took a posture similar to that of Interior Minister David Thompson, when he spoke of the "anomalous position" of the Tetons in his country.[21] Census takers marked them down as "American Sioux" or "stragglers" without official status. The Royal Mounted Police refused to give them food or other assistance and extended no more hospitality than reluctant tolerance for their presence as long as they caused no trouble.[22] Even *Isanti* leaders were uneasy about their presence; at one assembly these chiefs would "scarcely acknowledge that they knew" who Sitting Bull was for fear any association with him might jeopardize their own security north of the border.[23]

In spite of the cool reception he received, Sitting Bull made clear his determination to stay in Canada when General Terry led a commission to Fort Walsh in September 1877 to offer a general pardon to him and his followers if they would return to the United States. The motivation for Terry's generous overture lay not in benevolence but in recognition that Sitting Bull and his exiled traditionalists remained as great a threat to peace on the western Sioux reservations in the United States as they had been before they moved to Canada. "This body of refugees is not a distinct section of the Sioux nation," the commissioners explained. "It is made up by contributions of nearly every agency . . . of young men, whose families still remain at various Sioux agencies." Were it composed of a "distinct band that had separated itself . . . it would soon be forgotten. . . . But the intimate relationship, the ties of blood between the refugees and the agency Indians, forbid us to hope for such a result." Accordingly, Terry gave unqualified assurance that neither Sitting Bull nor his followers would be in any way harmed or punished if they would surrender, but the appeal was in vain. Fully convinced that he would be killed if he crossed the international boundary, Sitting Bull stated his determination to "stay here," and told the commissioners to "take it easy going back" to the United States.[24]

He remained in Canada until his position became untenable.

Without food to supplement the meat taken from the dwindling buffalo herds, his group, which at one point exceeded one thousand, was on the verge of starvation most of the time. When his followers staged raids into Montana to steal horses or to acquire supplies, U.S. officials applied pressure upon leaders in Ottawa, and officers on the Canadian frontier threatened to drive the Tetons back across the border. Because he could get neither material assistance nor official recognition from the Canadian government, Sitting Bull's authority deteriorated steadily and groups began to break away from his encampments. Gall surrendered a party of three hundred to Major Guido Ilges near Poplar Creek Agency, for example, and Patriarch Crow (Crow King) turned over a substantial group to Major D. A. Brotherford at Fort Buford. By the spring of 1881, Sitting Bull had only a remnant of his original following, and the people who remained with him to forage on the barren Canadian plains between Wood Mountain and Lake Qu'Appelle were in desperate straits.[25]

As the plight of Sitting Bull and his remnant became hopeless in the spring and early summer of 1881, Major Brotherford announced that a reward might be forthcoming to anyone who could persuade the Hunkpapa leader to give himself up, and several men worked to earn the reward. After Sitting Bull arrived at Fort Buford, Gus Hedderich, an employee of a trading company at Wood Mountain, insisted that he had persuaded Sitting Bull to come in. Fred Hans, a self-seeker from the United States, claimed that his influence had made the difference. Edwin Allison, a scout-interpreter at Fort Buford who made three trips to Canada and persuaded many Tetons to go into Poplar Creek Agency, said his efforts had caused the Hunkpapa leader to give himself up. Jean Louis LeGare, the principal trader at Wood Mountain, who between May 1 and July 3 brought 235 Sioux across the border, presented documents before the U.S. Court of Claims to show that he had persuaded Sitting Bull to surrender.

Whoever had the greatest influence, it was LeGare who finally brought Sitting Bull and approximately two hundred followers across the Canadian border to Fort Buford at noon on July 19, 1881. There the distraught leader gave up his horses and weapons and threw himself and his followers on the mercy of Major Brotherford, leaving behind only thirty-five families, who remained in Canada to found small reservations at Wood Mountain and Cypress Hills before the outset of the twentieth century.[26]

At Fort Buford, Sitting Bull and his party boarded the steamboat *General Sherman* for a journey down the Missouri River. At the time they were led to believe they would go directly to Fort Yates near the Standing Rock Agency for a reunion with their relatives and friends. But before they landed at Fort Yates they learned the truth. Despite an emotional appeal from the Hunkpapa leader and the recommendation of Standing Rock agent James McLaughlin that they be permitted to return to their homes, they were scheduled for detention at Fort Randall until officials in Washington were convinced that their return to the Grand River area would create no disturbance.

During his two years of confinement at Fort Randall Sitting Bull enjoyed the deference and respect due a person of high rank. People from around the world wrote him letters of praise and sympathy. Leaders of several Sioux tribes appeared to seek his advice on political matters. Officers at the fort treated him like a chief and sought his companionship. Except for homesickness, he probably suffered no discomfort. On May 10, 1883, he boarded the steamer *W. J. Behen* with his 187 followers and returned to his birthplace.[27]

Detention at the fort had given Sitting Bull time to recover his composure. Indeed, newsman James Creelman had visited him before he left Fort Randall and found him as self-confident as ever: "There was an inexpressible dignity in the strong face of the old chieftain, as he stood there on the prairie, with one moccasined foot thrown lightly forward, while the weight of his sinewy body rested solidly on the other foot. . . . The red and yellow paint smeared on his cheeks, and the gaudy girdle of porcupine quills and beads seemed trivial and out of harmony with the eagle nose, straight, powerful mouth, and the general sense of reserved power, which expressed the born commander of men."[28]

The composure and self-assurance reflected in Sitting Bull's demeanor as he returned to Standing Rock in 1883 posed a problem of no little concern to James McLaughlin. Because of his marriage to a mixed-blood *Isanti*, Marie Buisson, and his previous service among the Sioux at Fort Totten, McLaughlin had been appointed agent at Standing Rock in 1881. William T. Sherman had chosen him for his apparent ability to integrate prisoners from Forts Buford and Randall into reservation society without disturbing the processes of acculturation that were required by federal policy. With help from priests, teachers, Indian police, and most of all Chief Gall and Charging Bear (John Grass), the agent had met little opposition to the conversion of the traditional seminomadic hunters into Anglicized, sedentary ranchers during his first two years at Standing Rock. When Sitting Bull came home, however, the work of acculturation was in serious jeopardy.

McLaughlin held the Hunkpapa medicine man's influence in check for several years by sending him off the reservation at every opportunity. In 1883 Sitting Bull went to Bismarck, North Dakota, at the agent's suggestion, to celebrate the opening of the Northern Pacific Railroad. That same year he also led the last organized buffalo hunt on record by the Teton Sioux. During 1884 he accompanied Colonel Alvaren Allen on tour to St. Paul and other cities, where he was erroneously displayed as the man who killed Custer. The next year he traveled with Buffalo Bill Cody and the Wild West show across the eastern United States and into adjoining regions of Canada. Although Sitting Bull was ridiculed in the eastern states, in Canada he was applauded for his determined resistance to the Indian policies of the federal government.[29]

After his eastern excursion in 1885, Sitting Bull traveled only once more on an itinerary created by the agent—when he went to the Crow Agency in Montana to exchange memories and to make peace with his long-time enemies. The next year he rejected an invitation to accompany the Wild West show to England and made clear his intention to settle down in a log cabin near his birthplace on the Grand River to oppose the processes of forced acculturation.[30]

Signs of dramatic change were everywhere. Children came home from school with their hair cut short, spouting ideas that challenged the wisdom of their elders. Parents shuttled back and forth between their homes and the agency to draw rations rather than hunt and gather food by traditional means. Compliant "BIA chiefs"—Gall, Mad Bear, Charging Bear, Big Head, and others—espoused the goals of the agent for their clans. The Indian police force that was intended to replace the ancient warrior societies

promoted adaptation to the social and religious habits of non-Indians and enforced regulations that forbade traditional practices
and rites handed down among the Sioux from antiquity. Indian
dances were permitted only under close supervision. The peace
pipe religion was under attack by missionaries and agency officials. Values and philosophies that Sitting Bull had cherished and
supported throughout his life were threatened with extinction.[31]

Although these changes generated severe tension between Sitting Bull and McLaughlin, it was the land issue that finally caused
the two men to become bitter enemies. In 1882, while Sitting Bull
remained in custody at Fort Randall, former Dakota governor
Newton Edmunds toured the Grand River district, urging the
Sioux to relinquish more of their territory. Because the United
States had triumphed in the Great Sioux War, he argued, the
Teton tribes should sell eleven million acres of land along a corri-
dor between the Missouri River and the Black Hills for about
eight cents an acre; formally recognize the subdivision of their remaining communal holdings into five reservations (Pine Ridge,
Rosebud, Lower Brulé, Cheyenne River, and Standing Rock);
and accept allotments of half a section for every family head on
each reservation, thereby releasing surplus land for entry by non-
Indians. With guarded threats and cajolery, Edmunds and other
members of his commission gathered signatures from pliable
BIA chiefs at all of the agencies and returned to the national
capital confident that they had amended the Treaty of Fort Laramie of 1868. Reformers prevented the implementation of the
1882 agreement, however, because it called for further reduc-
tions in the size of the Great Sioux Reservation without the consent of three-fourths of the adult males. But Edmunds had introduced a plan for major land reform in Teton country that was
soon fashioned into other agreements.[32]

In 1888 another commission headed for the western Sioux
agencies bearing a proposal that contained terms similar to those
in the agreement of 1882. The Tetons should sell eleven million
acres at fifty cents an acre, define boundaries for five reservations
on the remaining lands, and accept allotments of land in severalty
as prescribed by the General Allotment Act of 1887. At Standing
Rock, McLaughlin worked diligently to gain support among compliant leaders, but on this occasion Sitting Bull was there to thwart

his efforts. Even the most pliable BIA chiefs supported the old Hunkpapa medicine man in the rejection of the offer, then applauded him when he traveled to Washington, D.C., to shake the hand of the president and to extract a promise from the secretary of the interior that if the Tetons surrendered any more land they would receive no less than $1.25 an acre.

After returning to the reservation, Sitting Bull spoke out against the surrender of more land at any price. But in 1889 veteran soldier-negotiator George Crook led another commission west, again seeking control of the Sioux homeland. This commission had orders to negotiate land reform by seeking signatures from three-fourths of the adult males on the reservation so the reformers could not negate the agreement later on. For a short time Sitting Bull was able to resist the commission's effort, but before long Crook and McLaughlin devised a combination of tactics that succeeded. Threats that no more rations would be distributed until the people ratified a land-sale agreement elicited support from such compliant leaders as Gall and Charging Bear. The careful deployment of Indian police prevented Sitting Bull and his principal supporters from participating in public discussions. Gall, Charging Bear, and Bear Face were persuaded to sign the agreement in Sitting Bull's absence, and their signatures precipitated a movement that produced the required number of votes. The Standing Rock people joined Tetons at other agencies in support of amendments to the 1868 Fort Laramie treaty that contained terms similar to those in the 1882 and 1888 agreements.[33]

Sitting Bull's lifelong efforts to maintain a segregated existence for traditional Teton people through military tactics and diplomacy all but failed with the ratification of the '89 agreement. Now he turned exclusively to the Great Spirit, and for the remainder of his life he made almost continuous supplication. This was not a ruse, as some writers have suggested. During the previous twenty years or more Sitting Bull had earned recognition as a leading medicine man in the peace pipe tradition, and it was natural that he conduct ceremonies almost daily in the sweat lodge outside his cabin in the belief "that he was divinely commissioned to maintain the old Dakota nationality intact." This activity "overshadowed everything else to the last," according to Aaron Beede, a seasoned

Episcopal priest who understood the medicine man's motives well.[34]

It was natural, moreover, that Sitting Bull turn to forms of worship other than his own, for the peace pipe religion to which he belonged was thoroughly ecumenical. He relied most heavily upon the pipe as intermediary with the Great Spirit, to be sure, but there is strong evidence that he developed more than a token commitment to Christianity. "I have it on good authority," wrote Father Beede, "that Sitting Bull not infrequently prayed to Jesus."[35] And though he refused to embrace Christianity openly at Standing Rock, because to do so would have been an admission of support for the Indian policy of the federal government, he confessed to a Catholic baptism and took instruction from Congregational missionary Mary Collins.[36]

For a medicine man with ecumenical beliefs, it was even more natural to accept the religion of another tribe, such as the messianic Ghost Dance, which promised deliverance for Indian people. This new faith had been founded earlier near Walker Lake, Nevada, by a Paiute named Wovoka, who experienced a vision. The Great Spirit and the ghosts of deceased Indians assured him that Native American people could enjoy better times if they would reject non-Indian culture, dance the Ghost Dance, and perform other rites. The new dogma came to the Teton country through Kicking Bear and Short Bull in a somewhat enlarged version, which promised that Ghost Dancers could, through rigorous prayer, produce a messiah with the power to cause non-Indians to vanish, buffalo to reappear, and traditional culture to return as it had existed before white people arrived. On the Standing Rock Reservation, Sitting Bull became the leading exponent of the new faith and called believers (dressed in shirts of white muslin painted with figures of the moon, stars, and buffalo) to his cabin to dance and to seek visions.[37]

By the autumn of 1890, John Carignan, a teacher at the day school a mile and a half from the medicine man's home, reported that about two hundred men and their families were dancing daily. While the Ghost Dance was in progress, only three of ninety students enrolled in his school appeared for class. On one occasion, he escorted a curious reporter to the scene to record the size and the drama of the dance:

Indians, men and women, stood side by side, forming a circle from 75 to 100 feet across, depending upon the number of participants. The tom-tom was placed in the center and the "musicians" stood around it, or sat, as they often did, and sang the most weird songs imaginable. By the side step movement the great circle of ghost-dancers slowly revolved, keeping perfect time, and often some would join in singing. Others would cry in high, falsetto tones, making you think it was the wailing of a banished people, or a people in sore distress. . . . They kept everlastingly at it until they dropped from sheer exhaustion, as many did.

As soon as one dropped, he was immediately carried into a tepee where Sitting Bull waited for him to recover sufficiently to tell of his "dream" or of what he saw in his "vision." In nearly all cases the vision would concern dead relatives or ghosts of friends, hence the affair was called the "ghost dance." Sitting Bull would interpret the vision. . . . Thus, day by day, he was working them into a mental state approaching that of irresponsible fanatics.[38]

That they became "irresponsible fanatics" was questionable, but there was no doubt that Sitting Bull encouraged Ghost Dancers to unite in opposition to reservation conditions, which had worsened steadily during the 1880s. Rigorous attacks on cultural traditions plus negotiations for land reform had undermined the morale of the traditionalists. Epidemics of measles, influenza, and whooping cough brought affliction and death to most of the villages. Droughts interspersed with blizzards in the years 1886–88 caused extreme hardship for the entire reservation population.[39]

Agent McLaughlin and the Indian police managed to confine the activities of the Ghost Dancers to the Grand River area during the fall of 1890, but they were unable to curb its growth in that district. One officer later reported that "the number of Indians on this reservation seriously affected by the prevailing craze" reached "about one-fourth of all, counting by families, including some 300 males from 16 years old and upwards."[40] Nor could the agent and his police prevent the Ghost Dance community at Standing Rock from communicating with dancing communities on other reservations. By late October, as a result, both agency personnel and military officers at Fort Yates expressed the belief that Sitting Bull had enough support to start a general uprising among the western Sioux.

In response, the acting commissioner of Indian affairs advised the secretary of the interior that Sitting Bull, as a leading symbol of resistance to federal authority in Sioux country, should again be arrested and confined to a military compound far from his home until he ceased to be a threat to peace. The secretary of the interior immediately sent word that Sitting Bull should be seized, and McLaughlin began to make preparations.[41]

Subsequent events have been interpreted as steps in a murder plot by some writers, and as a sequence of bureaucratic blunders by others. The former view lacks supporting evidence, but the latter view has been well documented. For late in December 1890, Congress demanded an investigation after word reached some of its members that it had been "charged in the public press and elsewhere . . . that certain Indian reservation police officers, acting under the authority of the civil and military powers of the United States, did, in arresting the late Sitting Bull . . . unjustifiably kill" him and "afterwards barbariously [sic] mutilate his remains."[42]

Documents prepared at the scene suggested that had one plan of action existed, and had that plan been executed without interference from Washington, Sitting Bull might have survived to die a natural death. Several plans were developed in an atmosphere of fear and confusion, however, which almost inevitably led to the medicine man's assassination. First William Cody traveled to the reservation to ask his old friend to give himself up, but before Cody could leave the agency for Sitting Bull's cabin, McLaughlin requested and received orders that authorized cooperative action by himself and the commander at Fort Yates.[43] Because McLaughlin had been unsuccessful in his efforts to persuade Sitting Bull to call off the Ghost Dance, he proceeded to make plans to arrest the medicine man on December 6. Two days before he was to leave for the Grand River, however, the agent got word from the Indian commissioner that he should take no action without approval from military officials.[44] Eight more days passed before Colonel William F. Drum, the commander at Fort Yates, received the necessary approval. During that time McLaughlin convinced Drum that the best plan of action was to send the Indian police to make the arrest, and to dispatch Captain Edmund Fechet from Fort Yates with a support unit. Once the two men agreed on this plan, they set the date for December 20, for at that time most of Sitting Bull's followers would be at the agency drawing rations. But while they waited, John Carignan sent an urgent message to McLaughlin warning that Sitting Bull had begun preparations to travel to Cheyenne River and perhaps to Pine Ridge. In order to prevent Sitting Bull from slipping away, McLaughlin quickly changed the time of arrest to December 15, and during the night of December 14 he sent Indian police officer Captain Bullhead with forty-three men to the vicinity of the medicine man's cabin while Captain Fechet drew his support unit into position approximately three miles away.

Both Fechet and Bullhead had their forces in position by daybreak on December 15, and Bullhead went to Sitting Bull's cabin to make the arrest. Prolonged discussion between the two men inside the cabin allowed more than 150 Ghost Dancers to assemble and to devise plans to free their leader. When Bullhead emerged from the cabin with his prisoner and faced the assembly of dancers, he and two other officers closed ranks around Sitting Bull: Bullhead and Sergeant Shavehead on either side and Sergeant Red Tomahawk to the rear. At that moment, the Ghost Dancers opened fire, and shooting continued until both the police and the Ghost Dancers suffered tragic losses. Strike-the-Kettle shot Sergeant Shavehead in the abdomen; Catch-the-Bear hit Captain Bullhead in the right side; Bullhead turned and shot Sitting Bull in the left side as Red Tomahawk shot the medicine man in the head; and the three men fell together. Others were drawn into the fight, and by the time Fechet arrived to relieve the Indian police seven policemen and eight Ghost Dancers had fallen to the ground, either dead or severely wounded.

After Fechet drove off the Ghost Dancers, an intense argument took place among the Indian police over the proper disposition of Sitting Bull's body. Red Tomahawk, who took command after his senior officers had fallen, believed the medicine man's remains should be taken to Fort Yates on a wagon, but his subordinates took exception to the transportation of Sitting Bull's body on the same vehicle with the bodies of their fallen comrades. After considerable discussion, Red Tomahawk arranged a compromise; all of the bodies would be transported on the same wagon, but the bodies of the policemen would ride on top of the remains of Sitting Bull.[45]

In this fashion the body of Sitting Bull reached the agency, but debates continued there over its proper disposition. "The dead policemen were buried with military honors in the agency cemetery," Captain Fechet later recalled, but "the surviving Indian Police and their friends objected so strenuously to the interment of Sitting Bull among their dead that he was buried in the cemetery" at Fort Yates.[46] The body of Sitting Bull was taken "by the police, without removal from the wagon in which it was brought from Grand River" to Fort Yates and was placed there "in charge of the military authorities," recalled McLaughlin, who "was present in the afternoon of December 17, 1890, in the Military Cemetery and saw" the grave.[47] To corroborate McLaughlin's story, the post surgeon at Fort Yates wrote: "I received the body of Sitting Bull . . . and it was in my custody until it was buried on the 17th." "During that time it was not mutilated or disfigured in any manner. I saw the body sewed up in a canvas, put in a coffin and the lid screwed down and afterwards buried in the northwest corner of the post cemetery in a grave about eight feet deep" in full view of "Captain A. R. Chapin . . . Lt. P. G. Wood . . . and myself."[48]

The intense interest in the death of Sitting Bull and the disposition of his remains only underscored his great importance. For his devotion to the perpetuation of a segregated existence for traditional Teton people in the Black Hills region, he rose from common origins to become the most famous Sioux, and one of the most famous Native Americans in the United States, during the nineteenth century. "Since the days of Pontiac, Tecumseh and Red Jacket," Captain Fechet reflected, "no Indian has had the power of drawing to himself so large a following of his race and molding and wielding it against the authority of the United States."[49] More than any other Indian leader, he exemplified the tenacity with which traditional Indians resisted Anglo-American encroachments and federal Indian policies in the nineteenth century. Better than any other incident, except perhaps the subsequent massacre at Wounded Knee, his death and burial commemorated the tragic plight of Native American people who refused to submit to non-Indian civilization throughout American history.

NOTES

1. The Tetons, who lived as one of seven council-fire groups of Sioux in prehistoric times, were subdivided into seven tribes—Brulé, Oglala, Two Kettle, Sans Arc, Blackfoot, Miniconjou, and Hunkpapa—after they moved from the Minnesota woodlands to the Black Hills region during the eighteenth century.

2. Stanley Vestal, *Sitting Bull: Champion of the Sioux* (New York: Houghton Mifflin, 1932), pp. 8–18, 27–30; Shannon Garst, *Sitting Bull: Champion of His People* (New York: J. Messner, 1946), pp. 12–15, 43–51.

3. *Senate Executive Document 52*, 44th Cong., 1st sess. (serial 1664); Vestal, *Sitting Bull*, p. 34; Matthew William Stirling, *Three Pictographic Autobiographies of Sitting Bull* (Washington, D.C.: Smithsonian Institution, 1938), p. 3.

4. 11 *Stat.*, 749; Vestal, *Sitting Bull*, pp. 51–76; Herbert S. Schell, *History of South Dakota*, 3d ed., rev. (Lincoln: University of Nebraska Press, 1975), pp. 66–68, 72–76.

5. Schell, *South Dakota*, pp. 86–88.

6. Willis Fletcher Johnson, *The Red Record of the Sioux: Life of Sitting Bull and the History of the Indian War of 1890–91* (Edgewood, S. Dak.: Edgewood Publishing Co., 1891), pp. 25, 60; Alfred B. Gilbert, *The Way of the Indian* (Portland, Oreg.: F. E. Gotshall, 1908), p. 40; Alexis A. Praus, *A New Pictographic Autobiography of Sitting Bull* (Washington, D.C.: Smithsonian Institution, 1955), pp. 1–2.

7. Johnson, *Red Record of the Sioux*, p. 25.

8. Hiram Martin Chittenden and Alfred Talbot Richardson, eds., *Life, Letters and Travels of Father Pierre-Jean DeSmet, 1801–73,* 4 vols. (New York: Francis P. Harper, 1905), 3:881–86.

9. Ibid., 3:911.

10. Ibid., 3:912.

11. Vestal, *Sitting Bull*, pp. 87–91; Robert G. Athearn, *Forts of the Upper Missouri* (1967; rpt. Lincoln: University of Nebraska Press, 1972, p. 279.

12. 15 *Stat.*, 635.

13. Schell, *South Dakota*, pp. 126–31.

14. Francis Paul Prucha, *American Indian Policy in Crisis: Christian Reformers and the Indian, 1865–1900* (Norman: University of Oklahoma Press, 1976), pp. 170–71.

15. *Senate Executive Document 30*, 44th Cong., 1st sess. (serial 1664); Schell, *South Dakota*, pp. 132–34.

16. Vestal, *Sitting Bull*, p. 153.

17. Schell, *South Dakota*, p. 137.

18. Prucha, *Indian Policy in Crisis*, pp. 170–71.

19. *Personal Recollections and Observations of General Nelson A. Miles* (Chicago: Werner Co., 1896), pp. 226–44.

20. *House Executive Document 1*, 47th Cong., 1st sess. (serial 2009).

21. *Sessional Papers*, 1878, no. 10, p. xvii.

22. Vestal, *Sitting Bull*, pp. 230–35; "Statement of Jean Louis Legare," September 30, 1882, Letters Received, Office of Indian Affairs, Record Group 75, National Archives (hereafter cited as RG 75, NA).

23. *Sessional Papers*, 1879, no. 7, p. 58.

24. *Commission Appointed . . . to Meet the Sioux Indian, Chief Sitting Bull, with a View to Avert Hostile Incursions into the Territory of the United States*

from the Dominion of Canada (Washington, D.C.: Government Printing Office, 1877), pp. 3–12.

25. Judson Elliott Walker, *Campaigns of General Custer in the Northwest, and the Final Surrender of Sitting Bull* (New York: Jenkins and Thomas, 1881), pp. 59–62; Edwin H. Allison, *The Surrender of Sitting Bull: Being a Full and Complete History of the Negotiations . . . Which Resulted in the Surrender of Sitting Bull and His Entire Band of Hostile Sioux in 1881* (Dayton, Ohio: Walker Litho and Printing Co., 1891), pp. 1–15; District Commander Ruger, Helena, M.T. to Adjutant General, Department of Dakota, February 21, 1881, Letters Received, RG 75, NA.

26. *House Report 277*, 51st Cong., 1st sess. (serial 2807); *House Report 841*, 53d Cong., 2d sess. (serial 3271); Vestal, *Sitting Bull*, pp. 236–37; Allison, *Surrender of Sitting Bull*, p. 53; Walker, *Campaigns of General Custer*, pp. 73–74; Fred M. Hans, *The Great Sioux Nation* (Chicago: M. A. Donohue & Co., 1907), p. 561; Usher L. Burdick, *Tales from Buffalo Land: The Story of Fort Buford* (Baltimore: Wirth Brothers, 1940), pp. 24–35; Brigadier General Alfred H. Terry to General Sherman, July 20, 1881, and "Statement of Jean Louis Legare," September 30, 1882, Letters Received, RG 75, NA.

27. Vestal, *Sitting Bull*, p. 243; Frank Bennett Fiske, *Life and Death of Sitting Bull* (Fort Yates, N.Dak.: Pioneer-Arrow Print, 1933), p. 17; Thomas Bailey Marquis, *Sitting Bull and Gall, the Warrior* (Hardin, Mont.: Custer Battle Museum, 1934), p. 7; Garst, *Sitting Bull*, p. 152; Usher Lloyd Burdick, *The Last Days of Sitting Bull, Sioux Medicine Chief* (Baltimore: Wirth Brother, 1941), p. 35; Sitting Bull to the Commissioner of Indian Affairs, August 29, 1881, telegram from James McLaughlin to the Commissioner of Indian Affairs, September 8, 1881, Bishop Martin Marty to Mother M. Paul, January 7, 1882, telegram from Fort Randall Commander Swaine to Assistant Adjutant General, April 28, 1883, Letters Received, RG 75, NA.

28. James Creelman, *On the Great Highway: The Wanderings and Adventures of a Special Correspondent* (Boston: Lothrop Publishing Co., 1901), pp. 294–95.

29. Vestal, *Sitting Bull*, pp. 254–57; Burdick, *Last Days of Sitting Bull*, pp. 25–29; Garst, *Sitting Bull*, pp. 153–57; Jan M. Dykshorn, "Leaders of the Sioux Indian Nation," *Dakota Highlights* 3 (1975): 2–3; Alvaren Allen to the Secretary of the Interior, September 7, 1884, telegram from Agent McLaughlin to the Commissioner of Indian Affairs, September 16, 1884, Letters Received, RG 75, NA.

30. Vestal, *Sitting Bull*, pp. 262–65.

31. Garst, *Sitting Bull*, pp. 160–63; James McLaughlin, *My Friend the Indian; or, Three Heretofore Unpublished Chapters of the Book I Published under the Title of My Friend the Indian* (Baltimore: Proof Press, 1936), p. 18.

32. Prucha, *Indian Policy in Crisis*, p. 173; Schell, *South Dakota*, pp. 322–23.

33. Vestal, *Sitting Bull*, pp. 265–69; Garst, *Sitting Bull*, pp. 164–65;

Schell, *South Dakota*, p. 323.

34. *Sitting Bull-Custer* (Bismarck, N.Dak.: Bismarck Tribune Co., 1913), p. 42.

35. Ibid., p. 44.

36. Ibid., p. 45; Garst, *Sitting Bull*, pp. 161–62.

37. Brig. Gen. Thomas H. Ruger to the Adjutant General, U.S. Army, Washington, D.C., October 19, 1891, in Col. W. F. Drum, *Sioux Indian Troubles, Dept-Dakota, 1890–91* (n.p., n.d.) pp. 1–3; Garst, *Sitting Bull*, pp. 167–72.

38. Fiske, *Life and Death of Sitting Bull*, pp. 35–36.

39. Edmund Gustav Fechet, "The Capture of Sitting Bull," *South Dakota Historical Collections* 4, (1908): 186.

40. Ruger to Adjutant General, October 19, 1891, in Drum, *Sioux Indian Troubles*, p. 4.

41. Ibid.; *Senate Executive Document 4*, 51st Cong., 2d sess. (serial 2818).

42. *House Miscellaneous Document 80*, 51st Cong., 2d sess. (serial 2869).

43. Fiske, *Life and Death of Sitting Bull*, pp. 37–40; Burdick, *Last Days of Sitting Bull*, p. 49.

44. James McLaughlin, Indian Agent, to Herbert Welsh, January 12, 1891, Indian Rights Association Papers, Philadelphia.

45. Ibid.; Fechet, "Capture of Sitting Bull," pp. 186, 190–92; Fiske, *Life and Death of Sitting Bull*, pp. 48–50; Ruger to Adjutant General, October 19, 1891, and Lt. Col. W. F. Drum, 12th Infantry, Commanding Post, Fort Yates, N.Dak., to Assistant Adjutant General, Department of Dakota, St. Paul, Minn., February 27, 1891, in Drum, *Sioux Indian Troubles,* pp. 2–5; *Chicago Herald and Examiner*, August 7, 1931.

46. Fechet, "Capture of Sitting Bull," pp. 192–93.

47. McLaughlin, *My Friend the Indian*, p. 15.

48. Ibid., p. 14.

49. Fechet, "Capture of Sitting Bull," p. 193.

Quanah Parker

William T. Hagan

ON MARCH 31, 1911, about fifteen hundred people gathered at the Post Oak Mission cemetery, near Cache, Oklahoma, to see Quanah Parker lowered into his grave to the accompaniment of "Nearer My God to Thee." Never before had so many people, both white and Indian, assembled for a funeral in southwest Oklahoma. The funeral cortege, principally wagons and buggies of every description with a few automobiles and saddle horses interspersed, had stretched for a mile and a half along the dusty road.[1]

The great turnout of people was confirmation of the celebrity of Quanah, the son of a white captive, Cynthia Anne Parker, and a Comanche war chief, Peta Nocona. As a young man he had followed the buffalo herds, raided the Texas settlements, and harried the Utes and other tribes with whom the Comanches were perpetually at war. Nevertheless, after being forced to settle on a reservation, Quanah had rapidly adjusted to his new situation. He rose to the rank of principal chief of the Comanches, a title he cherished, and exercised a degree of leadership among all Comanches impossible until the tribe located on the reservation.

The tribe into which Quanah had been born about 1852 had had no central political organization. At any given time it would have been divided into a dozen or more autonomous bands. Even these lacked the stability of comparable groupings among more sedentary tribes. Extended family relationships usually provided the nucleus of a Comanche band, but the membership was in constant flux. Individuals and groups freely detached themselves from bands to join others or perhaps launch new ones. Despite this continual change, some bands had a long life, although their size varied. For example, the Penetethkas, the first band to settle

175

on a reservation, lost or attracted members depending on the fortunes of the bands still roaming the plains. If the other bands
were under pressure from the cavalry, some Cochetethkas,
Noconies, or Yamparekas might decide to seek shelter among the
Penetethkas at the agency. But the following spring when the
grass was high enough to support the Indian ponies and the buffalo were reported temptingly near, or a war expedition was being organized against the Utes or white settlements, agency Indians would slip away to the plains bands.

Within each Comanche band there were acknowledged
leaders. Usually one was recognized as the principal band chief,
and white men frequently identified the band by his name. However, he shared decision making with others. Any warrior could
try to initiate a war party, his degree of success being conditioned
by his reputation. Although the Comanches had no such term,
white observers used *war chief* to designate particularly influential
warriors. The Comanches did have a term for what the white man
identified as a *peace chief*. Generally older men, they were
acknowledged leaders with whom the principal chief would consult whenever important decisions faced the band.[2]

It was into such a relatively unstructured society that Quanah
was born in about 1852. He suffered the serious misfortune of
losing both parents by the time he entered his early teens. Cynthia
Anne was recaptured in 1860, and Peta Nocona was killed two or
three years later. Late in life Quanah recalled the first years following his father's death as very unhappy ones. His mixed-blood
status had exposed him to the taunts of his peers and he was dependent on the grudging charity of fellow band members.[3]

However, Comanche society was one in which inherited position was not the most important factor. Success as a hunter and
fighter was, and any young Comanche could aspire to that.
Quanah had the ability and the determination to distinguish himself. By 1875 he was a man of some influence among the Quahadas, the only Comanche band never to have visited the agency
headquarters, the band on whom the whites blamed many of the
Comanche attacks against settlers.

After years on the reservation had brought Quanah fame and
power, he and others portrayed his role in the presurrender years
in exaggerated terms. He became the war chief of the Quahadas,

who had led the last raids on the white settlers and buffalo hunters. According to these accounts it was under his leadership that
the Quahadas trailed into Fort Sill in 1875 to surrender. The best
evidence is that the acknowledged leader of the Quahadas at that
time was Eschiti, the medicine man who inspired the southern
plains Indians preparing for their attack on the buffalo hunters at
Adobe Walls in June 1874. Quanah, in contrast, had been a young
warrior whose opinions were beginning to carry weight, but that
is all.[4]

The shift of the Quahadas to the reservation environment
markedly accelerated Quanah's rise to prominence among the
Comanches by introducing new political conditions. The
problems inherent in administering an Indian reservation encouraged agents to foster a degree of political unity among the
Comanches previously unknown to them. Clearly it was easier to
treat with them as a single group and through only a few chiefs, or
preferably a single chief, than to deal with several autonomous
bands and their leaders.

A certain amount of self-selection entered into the emergence
of particular Comanches as those with whom the white officials
preferred to deal. A willingness not only to remain on the reservation but to use one's influence to keep others there, or to track
them down if they fled, earned good marks. Conversely, the
reputation as an inveterate raider in the prereservation days,
while still very prestigious among the Indians, might render a
warrior suspect in the eyes of the white officials. Indeed, several
Comanches had been included among the seventy-five southern
plains Indians selected for imprisonment in Florida for past
crimes. This had taken place before the Quahada surrender, or
some of their leaders might have been imprisoned as well.

In the weeks immediately following the surrender of the last
Comanches in 1875, two of them seemed particularly singled out
for leadership roles by both army officers and Indian Service personnel. One of these was Mowaway (Shaking Hand), a
Cochetethka chief who had had the sobering experience of imprisonment at Fort Leavenworth in 1869. The other was Eschiti,
who had been praised by the agency employee who arranged the
Quahada surrender.

It would also appear that Toshaway (Silver Brooch) and

Adobe Walls

Washita River **Oklahoma**

Wichita Reservation

*North Fork
of the Red River*

Anadarko

Ft. Sill

Cache

Red River

Texas

Kiowa
Comanche
Kiowa–Apache
Reservation

Esahabbe (Milky Way), Penetethka chiefs, would have had an edge in any contest for preeminence among Comanche leaders in the new environment. The Penetethkas had first settled on a reservation in Texas in 1855, subsequently to be moved north of the Red River and attached to the Wichita Agency. However, when the other Comanches came into the reservation and were administered by an adjoining but separate agency, the Penetethkas remained isolated from the principal Comanche population. Moreover, they were scorned by some Comanches for having been collaborationists so early.

Other leaders who might have been expected to have a better chance than Quanah to emerge as the principal chief of the Comanches were Howeah (Gap in the Woods) and Iron Mountain, both of them Yamparekas, and Horse Back, a Noconie. They along with Toshaway had been among the eight Comanches of sufficient stature to be signatories in 1867 of the Treaty of Medicine Lodge Creek, which provided the legal framework for their reservation life.

Several things contributed to Quanah's emergence. The most important was the interest taken in him by Indian agents and army officers when they learned he was the son of a white captive. He made this fact known to Colonel Ranald S. Mackenzie, to whom the Quahadas surrendered, and the colonel promptly sought to contact Cynthia Anne, only to learn that she was dead.[5] Two years later Mackenzie wrote one of Cynthia Anne's brothers in Texas, conveying Quanah's desire to meet his Texas relatives and his request for a wagon to help him live like a white man.[6] His letter apparently brought no response. It was not until Quanah became a celebrity that his white relatives were interested in acknowledging their relationship to a former Comanche raider.

P. B. Hunt, who served from 1878 to 1885, was just one of the Comanche agents who took a personal interest in the mixed-blood. Agent Hunt heard that the Texas legislature had granted Cynthia Anne a large tract of land as compensation for the suffering she had undergone as a Comanche captive. Working through a Texas attorney, he tried to establish Quanah's right to the tract as Cynthia Anne's heir. This effort to make the young Comanche a Texas landholder was blocked when the lawyer discovered that Cynthia Anne had failed to confirm her title, which then lapsed in the confusion of the Civil War.[7]

There were other, more practical ways in which an agent could promote the fortunes of an Indian in whom he took an interest. These officials could make or break chiefs by manipulating the size of bands. Government rations, on which the Indians depended heavily, were issued to what were called beef bands, the principal component of the ration being beef that was issued on the hoof. The annual issues of annuities promised by the 1867 treaty—clothing, tools, and other useful articles—were also delivered to individual bands. The band chief presided over the distribution of the rations and annuities to his people and it became in the reservation environment a major source of his power. Indian agents were well aware of this and they could whittle an obstreperous chief down to size by encouraging members of his band to break off and be recognized by the agent as a separate beef band. In this fashion a chief could see his following melt from 175 people to 50 in a very short time, and with it would go much of his power and influence.

The individual singled out by the agent to be the chief of a new beef band might be taking the first step in a career that would carry him to the top of the tribal hierarchy. Quanah certainly was not a chief when he came into the reservation in 1875, but shortly afterwards he was so designated by his agent. By 1878 he had ninety-three people in his band, which was the third largest of the thirty-two Comanche bands listed, not including the Penetethkas, assigned to the Wichita Agency.[8]

Quanah's rise had been rapid. By 1878 he would be referred to by the current Fort Sill post commander as "undoubtedly the most influential man among the Quahadoz [sic], and one of the most influential man among all the bands of the Comanches."[9] That same year he began to appear among the ranks of Comanche spokesmen at councils called by the agent or army officers. At one only five chiefs spoke—Horseback, Esahabbe, Toshaway, Tabananaka, and Quanah. Other than Quanah all had been recognized as chiefs well before 1875. Three of them, Horseback, Esahabbe, and Toshaway, would die within the next ten years.

The decade of the 1870s, during which the Comanches fought their last wars and tried to adjust to the reservation and, at times, near-starvation rations, saw a tragic decline in the tribe's population. Among those who died were other men who would have rivaled Quanah for tribal leadership. They included Asatoyet (Gray Leggings), Iron Mountain, Prairie Fire, the prominent Quahada chief Paracoom (He Bear), and Big Red Food. The last was regarded by some as the bravest of all the Comanches. Mowaway, the Cochetethka, lived into the 1890s, but took himself out of contention by abdicating his authority as a chief in 1878.

During these first few years on the reservation Quanah and his fellow Comanche leaders were in substantial agreement in the councils they held with the white officials. All, understandably, wanted rations increased. All protested the movement of agency headquarters from Fort Sill to the Washita River when the Wichita Agency was consolidated with that of the Kiowas, Comanches, and Kiowa-Apaches in 1878. The shift in location of agency headquarters would leave most Comanches about forty miles from the source of rations. When these were issued weekly they spent much of their time on the road between their camps and the agency.

As late as 1881 Quanah continued to defer to the older, more prominent chiefs. That year in a council in which only two other Comanches, Esahabbe and Howeah, spoke, Quanah referred to himself as both white and Indian. He added, "For that reason I will not do anything bad, but looking forward for the good road, a suppliant for the red people, so when Washington hears he will help us." Although he spoke the longest of the Comanche chiefs, he observed humbly, "I am young and almost a boy, talking for assistance for my people."[10] Quanah, if the situation demanded it, could adopt the role of the obsequious subordinate in dealing with white officials. Basically, however, he was a man of considerable pride and self-assurance.

At the council in 1881 the chiefs of the Comanches, Kiowas, and Kiowa-Apaches were unanimous in denouncing the practice of Dodge City–bound Texas cattlemen driving their herds across the reservation. The joint elimination of the Indian menace and the southern plains buffalo herds in the late 1870s had led to a rapid expansion of the cattle industry into the area west of Fort Worth and south of the Red River. For cattlemen like S. B. Burnett and Daniel Waggoner, one of the shortest routes to a cattle market was across the Kiowa, Comanche, and Kiowa-Apache

Reservation. There were no Indians living in the western part of the reservation traversed by the north-bound herds, and a few steers judiciously distributed usually quieted any protesters.

The drive to Dodge City acquainted the cattlemen with the fine grazing to be found on the reservation. As early as the fall of 1878 some were suspected of holding their herds along its borders to permit them to cross the line to eat Indian grass. Intruding cattle would be a problem for a long time. In 1880 it began to be serious. The total population of the reservation's three tribes was less than three thousand and they cultivated little more than one thousand of their three hundred thousand acres. There were areas in the south and west of the reservation where thousands of cattle could graze for months without interference. The recently organized Indian police force did not have the resources to handle all of the intruders, and the agent frequently had to call on the commanding officer of Fort Sill for a detail of cavalry to help. If rounded up and driven south of the Red River, the cattle might drift back onto the reservation within days, the absence of any fences making it impossible to keep them off without the cooperation of their owners. A bad drought in North Texas in 1881 encouraged more cattlemen to leave the overgrazed land south of the Red River for the underutilized Indian pastures north of that stream.[11]

Quanah was one of the first Comanche chiefs to protest these intrusions. His tribe had a greater stake in it than the Kiowas or Kiowa-Apaches because the Comanches were between the camps of those two tribes and Texas. However, the cattlemen learned how to appease Quanah and other Comanche chiefs and headmen. Quanah soon appeared on the payroll of the Texans, as did Eschiti and Permansu (Comanche Jack). Primarily they were being paid for their influence. They rode the range with white cowboys, guaranteeing that other Indians did not poach on the herds, and helping the white men reclaim cattle that had become mixed with Indian stock.

Naturally, other Indians resented Quanah, Eschiti, and Permansu deriving income from grazing land that belonged to all. A solution would be to lease land to the cattlemen formally, thus permitting all members of the three tribes to share in the income. However, even this was opposed by some, and by the mid-1880s leasing and antileasing factions appeared among the three tribes.

Presumably the cattlemen saw Quanah as their most able Indian advocate of leasing, and he seemed happy to play the role. The Texans got an articulate Comanche ally and expressed their gratitude in financial terms to a young Indian trying to live like a white man. Quanah wanted to build a house and furnish it, and he needed the money the cattlemen were happy to pay him. Together with a few other Comanches, Quanah was beginning to fulfill the government's hope that the Indians would build herds of their own. To the stock cattle he received from the agent, he added animals obtained from his friends the Texas cattlemen. Even Charles Goodnight, the legendary West Texas rancher, provided Quanah "a good Durham Bull" and a few cows to go with it.[12] Goodnight did not run cattle on the Kiowa, Comanche, and Kiowa-Apache Reservation. He apparently was just another white man intrigued by this mixed-blood chief who exhibited such an interest in traveling the white man's road.

Inevitably there were charges by other Indians that Quanah had sold out to the cattlemen, particularly since he emerged as the principal spokesman for the faction advocating leasing. In one communication on the subject, Tabananaka (Hears the Sun), a Yampareka chief, and White Wolf, a Noconie, denounced the Quahadas as a band, and Quanah in particular, for supporting leasing. On another occasion his critics used the term *half-breed* in referring to him when denouncing Quanah and Permansu for their proleasing stance.[13]

It was in 1884 that Quanah made the first of his numerous trips to Washington. This one, like many of those to follow, enabled him to present the arguments for leasing directly to officials in Washington, and he was accompanied by a cattleman. Usually these trips were financed from Indian Service funds. However, if official authorization were denied him, the Comanche would pass the hat among the Texans. He became a well-known figure to a succession of commissioners of Indian affairs and to members of the House and Senate Indian committees. Representative J. W. Throckmorton, whose constituents included many of the Texans leasing Indian grass, described Quanah in 1885 as "the most intelligent Indian I know of among the wild tribes."[14] Although Quanah had to have his letters written for him and spoke English poorly, there was no question of his role as the principal

Comanche spokesman by the late 1880s. There also could be no question about the importance of the cattlemen in his rise. They had given him a cause, exposure in official circles, and substantial income by Comanche standards.

In 1886 a Court of Indian Offenses was organized for what was now referred to as the Kiowa, Comanche, and Wichita Agency. It included both the Kiowa, Comanche, and Kiowa-Apache Reservation, and the Wichita Reservation adjoining it, the home of several other tribes. Quanah was awarded one of the three judgeships on the court, reflecting his stature among the Comanches as well as his reputation for cooperating with government policy. To be effective, a judge had to command respect from his fellow Indians, but nevertheless be willing to try to enforce the white man's conception of law. It was a difficult assignment that paid poorly, only ten dollars a month. However, the status and power inherent in the position appealed to Quanah's ambition to excel, and he cherished the honor.

In 1898 Quanah finally was dismissed from the court on the ground that it was improper for a polygamist—he at the time had five wives—to sit on a court established to, among other things, curtail polygamy. The current agent protested vigorously his removal from the court, but the commissioner of Indian affairs, who at the moment was backing an Indian faction opposed to Quanah, refused to relent.

The mixed-blood's concern for titles showed up in other ways. By the late 1880s he was being described by the agent as the principal chief of the Comanches, and before long he had had stationery printed with that in the letterhead.[15] The Indian Office, however, issued its own certificates of chieftainship and the way these were worded caused trouble among the Comanches in 1899. Quanah complained that his efforts to cope with the Eschiti faction were handicapped by Eschiti's holding a chief's certificate designating him "a Principal Chief," whereas Quanah's own certificate, issued at another time, carried a less impressive designation. Several months of haggling ensued before the agent was able to persuade the Indian Office to issue two new certificates, one establishing Quanah as "The Chief" of the Comanches, with Eschiti clearly in second place.[16]

It is indicative of the absence of any real Comanche tribal autonomy that this was a decision that ultimately rested with the commissioner of Indian affairs. The officially recognized tribal political body at any given time might be called an arbitration committee or business committee. Although the agent, and sometimes his superiors in the Indian Office, retained the right of veto over membership in these bodies, they were assumed to be capable of representing tribal desires whenever the agent saw fit to consult with them.

Councils of chiefs and headmen requiring the presence of perhaps fifteen or twenty Indians were occasionally summoned by the agent or a visiting inspector. Infrequently, councils of all adult male Comanches would convene. Even these were not considered official unless summoned by the agent. The latter could refuse to receive petitions submitted by large councils simply on the ground that he, the agent, had authorized no such council.

In such a system an Indian who aspired to leadership and the perquisites of office quickly learned the efficacy of the formula "go along to get along." No small part of Quanah's preeminence in this period was his willingness to go along with every one of the fourteen white men who served as agent between 1878 and Quanah's death in 1911. One of the rare things the fourteen had in common was that each preferred him to any of the other Comanches who headed opposing factions, men like Eschiti, Big Looking Glass, and White Wolf.

There is not, however, persuasive evidence that at any time his rivals really enjoyed more popularity than Quanah among their fellow tribesmen. They might accuse him of selling out to the cattlemen, and make disparaging remarks about his mixed-blood ancestry, but Quanah's stock remained high with most of his fellow tribesmen. Perhaps they recognized him as the one Comanche at that time who had a unique blood relationship with the whites. And they must have been impressed with his success in acquiring titles, honors, and worldly goods. Quanah built a house adorned with white stars on the roof and complete with a two-story porch, a dwelling any white man in the area would have been happy to occupy. He made nearly twenty trips to Washington and participated in President Theodore Roosevelt's inauguration. When President Roosevelt traveled through Oklahoma, he singled out the Comanche chief for recognition.

Distinguished travelers through the area, including the British ambassador, Lord Bryce, made a point of calling on him. An uneducated Comanche could appreciate this, and he also knew that a word from Quanah to the agent might help him secure the wagon he wanted or permission to visit his children at the Carlisle Indian Industrial School in Pennsylvania.

Quanah satisfied the agents by cooperating with policies designed to move the Indians toward self-support and get their children educated. With his own herd of several hundred cattle and over a hundred acres under cultivation, he was an example an agent could point to. In cultural matters Quanah was less progressive, and that undoubtedly helped maintain a bond between him and the common Indians. He refused to cut his hair, despite his conversion from the blanket and moccasins to sedate black suits, white shirts, and black shoes. He was a polygamist to the end of his days and probably introduced the Comanches to peyote; certainly he was a leader in the peyote cult.

The most important decision that faced the Comanches in the 1890s related to the opening of the reservation. In 1892 the Jerome Commission conferred with the three tribes to secure their consent to an agreement by which they would accept allotments of land in severalty. The land remaining after the Indians had received their allotments would then be purchased from them and thrown open for white settlement. According to the Treaty of Medicine Lodge Creek, any such agreement would require the approval of three-fourths of the adult males of the three tribes.

The majority of the Indians opposed such an agreement. They had adjusted, after a fashion, to reservation life. With a combination of their annuities, government rations, and income from leased pastures and farms tilled by white tenants, they were able to live in modest comfort. The treaty provision for annuities was due to expire in 1898, and if the reservation were allotted and the surplus land sold, the grass money from the Texas cattlemen would cease. An Indian, like Quanah, who had fenced several thousand acres as his own private pasture and pocketed the proceeds from its rental stood to lose even more.

Nevertheless, the commissioners, after a hectic round of negotiations, managed to obtain the signatures of three-fourths

of the Kiowa, Comanche, and Kiowa-Apachemen. As might have
been expected, Quanah was a leading figure in the deliberations.
He did not flatly refuse to negotiate an agreement. Had he done
so and used his influence with his fellow tribesmen, the Jerome
Commission could not have prevailed. Apparently he concluded
that the government would have its way, and the best strategy was
to get as good a deal as possible. As a result he sought to extract a
higher price per acre than the commissioners offered, tried to increase the size of the allotments, and attempted to postpone as
long as possible the implementation of the agreement. Given the
set policy of the government to push allotment and open up more
land to white settlement, perhaps Quanah was right. The commissioners did threaten to open the reservation under the less
favorable terms of the 1887 Dawes Land in Severalty Act if the Indians refused to arrive at other terms with the Jerome Commission.[17]

Ratification of the Jerome agreement, modified to make it
somewhat more palatable to the Indians, did not occur until 1900.
Allotment and opening of the reservation followed quickly. In
the years between the negotiation and the ratification of the
agreement, life had gone along as usual for the Comanches. They
continued to quarrel among themselves over leasing and a number of other issues. Quanah's leadership and motives were challenged, but he continued to be the favorite of the Indian agents
and the Texas cattlemen.

His reservation was the prey of a variety of white special-inter-
est groups, each striving for advantage, usually at the expense of
the Indians. Intermarried whites, or squaw men as they were
known, and licensed traders were two of the more difficult problems facing any Indian agent trying to protect his charges. The
squaw men and traders had contacts and influence among the Indians that were extensive and of many years' duration. The
agents, whose tenure averaged no more than two or three years
and who generally arrived at their position ignorant of Indians
and reservation problems, usually did not challenge the special-
interest groups. One agent who did was Captain Frank O. Baldwin, an army officer detailed to this special duty from late in 1894
to the spring of 1898.

Captain Baldwin soon found himself opposed by an active faction of squaw men, traders, and conservative Indians like Big Looking Glass of the Comanches and Lone Wolf of the Kiowas. However, he had the support of a progressive faction headed by Quanah, and Baldwin was a fighter. His opponents struck at him through Quanah, and it was during this period that Quanah lost his seat on the Court of Indian Offenses. His opponents also managed to deprive his son-in-law Emmett Cox, a white man, of the trader's license he had obtained through Quanah's influence. And while the agent was able to reduce the size of the pastures held by other squaw men, his opponents evened the score by striking back at Quanah after the Spanish-American War drew Baldwin back on regular duty. For years Quanah had held a twenty-three-thousand-acre pasture exclusively for his own use, and this meant that he regularly rented most of it to cattlemen, pocketing the proceeds. An Indian Service official who had been aligned with Baldwin's opponents forced Quanah to begin paying rent into the tribal treasury for land he held in excess of that available to other Comanches. The official referred to his action as "the best thing I have done since I came here . . . it brings Quanah to a level with other people and makes him divide with the people the big estate over which he has held kingly sway."[18]

Although Quanah opposed the opening of the reservation, he accepted the advice of his current agent that further resistance was useless after Congress finally enacted the Jerome agreement into law. Conservatives led by Lone Wolf, a Kiowa, with the support of Eschiti and a few other Comanches, made a futile last-ditch legal fight, supported by the Indian Rights Association, to block the opening of the reservation.

Even after the opening, for a few years the Indians still held a block of land in common and it precipitated the usual factionalism over its use. When this block was broken up in 1906, the Comanches no longer had property in common over which to quarrel. Issues that had divided them since the 1870s no longer existed. Other issues would develop, but they were not as important monetarily as the pasture leases and the opening of the reservation had been.

Quanah's last years saw the elderly Comanche finding it difficult to maintain the life-style to which he had become accustomed. He no longer profited from a special relationship with the cattlemen. Nor did he have the twenty-three-thousand-acre private pasture from which to derive income. The agent did put him on the payroll as an assistant farmer to partially compensate him for the administrative help he continued to provide the agent.[19] That also was the justification for the government's installing a telephone in Quanah's home, and when he was summoned to agency headquarters on business the Comanche applied for per diem like any Indian Service bureaucrat.

Quanah continued to use his influence in behalf of friends and relatives. With his help, a son-in-law secured a position on the government payroll as farmer and a daughter obtained a job at the Comanche boarding school as assistant matron. He also was able to promote Comanche adoption, with its financial benefits, for a son-in-law and daughter-in-law and a long-time white tenant of his farm.

The Comanches had become wards of the federal government, and the influence Quanah enjoyed was in the context of the network of government regulations and services in which the Comanches had become enmeshed. The only triumphs now open to a man who in his youth had ridden with war parties that dominated the southern plains were minor feats of one-upmanship over agency clerks. As he learned when he tried to draw on funds from the sale of an allotment he had inherited, Indian Service personnel had to approve even minor expenditures.[20] Wardship brought security of a sort, but it was a powerless state.

At the time of his death in 1911, Quanah still held the title of principal chief of the Comanches, but it was largely honorific and no successor was appointed by the government. Had the Comanches continued to lead their nomadic life on the plains, Quanah would never have had the title principal chief of the Comanches, but he undoubtedly would have become a prominent band chief. He had the ability and the desire to excel. As a white man sent to investigate the charges and countercharges generated by reservation factionalism had reported after a thorough examination in 1903, "Quanah would have been a leader and governor in any circle where fate might have cast him—it is in his blood."[21]

Notes

1. For an account of his funeral, see the *Daily Oklahoman* (Oklahoma City), February 25, 1911, p. 2; and the *Cache Register,* March 3, 1911, p. 1.

2. This is based on E. Adamson Hoebel, "The Political Organization and Law-Ways of the Comanche Indians," *Memoirs of the American Anthropological Association* 54 (1940): 18–36.

3. This is indicated in a brief autobiographical sketch in the possession of the Fort Sill Museum, Fort Sill, Oklahoma.

4. The best evidence for this is in the reports and journal of the employee, J. J. Sturm. The journal is in Letters Received, Department of the Missouri (221–5–1875), Record Group 98, National Archives.

5. Colonel W. H. Wood to unknown, June 11, 1875, in Fort Sill Register of Letters Received, Fort Sill Museum.

6. Mackenzie to Isaac Parker, September 5, 1877, in Fort Sill Letter Book, Fort Sill Museum.

7. T. H. Miller to Hunt, June 4, 1881, in Kiowa Agency Files: Quanah Parker, Oklahoma Historical Society, Oklahoma City.

8. Agent Hunt's response to Civilization Circular no. 21, December 31, 1878, in Letters Received, Office of Indian Affairs, microfilm M234, roll 384:646.

9. Lieutenant Colonel J. W. Davidson to Assistant Adjutant General, October 29, 1878, in Letters Received, Office of Indian Affairs, National Archives, microfilm M234, roll 384:444.

10. Council of June 10, 1881, Letters Received, Office of Indian Affairs, (10933–1881), National Archives.

11. For a more thorough discussion of this topic, see William T. Hagan, "Kiowas, Comanches, and Cattlemen, 1867–1906:" A Case Study of the Failure of U.S. Reservation Policy, *Pacific Historical Review* 40 (August 1971): 333–55.

12. Goodnight to P. B. Hunt, Kiowa Agency Files: Quanah Parker, Oklahoma Historical Society.

13. Paris H. Folsom to Commissioner of Indian Affairs, August 1, 1884, in Congressional Serial Set, 2362:667.

14. J. W. Throckmorton to Commissioner of Indian Affairs, October 17, 1885, Letters Received, Office of Indian Affairs (24723–1885), National Archives.

15. For a sample, see Quanah to his agent, October 27, 1891, in Kiowa Agency Files: Quanah Parker, Oklahoma Historical Society.

16. Commissioner of Indian Affairs to Agent Randlett, September 23, 1899, Letter Book (Land), Office of Indian Affairs, 209:241, National Archives.

17. "Commissioner's Journal," *Senate Document 77,* 55th Cong., 3d sess. (1899), pp. 51–52.

18. Gilbert Pray to Commissioner of Indian Affairs, August 30, 1898 (40390–1898), in Special Cases, No. 191, National Archives.

19. Agent Randlett to Commissioner of Indian Affairs, February 1, 1904, in Letters Received, Office of Indian Affairs (8733–1904), National Archives.

20. Acting Commissioner of Indian Affairs to Kiowa Agent, December 19, 1905, in Kiowa Agency Files: Quanah Parker, Oklahoma Historical Society.

21. *Senate Document 26*, 58th Cong., 2d sess. (1903) (serial 4646), p. 468.

Dennis Bushyhead

H. Craig Miner

DENNIS WOLFE BUSHYHEAD was not the Irish Catholic Indian chief some imagined when they heaped invective upon the "tanned Yankees" who, it was claimed, used tribal citizenship in Indian Territory for selfish ends. Neither, however, was this chief—in blood, background, or philosophy—the sort one might expect to have existed in earlier times. There is every reason to believe that Bushyhead was a tribal patriot but also a necessity for understanding that during his tenure as principal chief of the Cherokees, 1879–87, a war whoop was not what was required. Bushyhead faced the problem of salvaging such tribal powers and culture as remained after more than three centuries of pressure from outsiders and fifty years of bitter interfactional and inter-tribal quarreling. He was a man living in two worlds who attempted to ensure that as the new world arose, much of the old, including the sovereignty of his tribe, would be preserved.

Bushyhead's family name originated when John Stuart, a British officer who later became Indian superintendent, was captured by the Cherokees in August 1760. Among the Indians, Stuart was known as Oo-na-du-ti, or Bushyhead, because of his heavy blond hair. He married Susannah Emory of the Cherokee Nation, and their offspring took the surname Bushyhead. Dennis, born in about 1826, was Stuart's great grandson, and the son of Jesse Bushyhead, who was a Baptist minister and leader of one of the parties traversing the Trail of Tears to Indian Territory in 1839. Young Dennis attended the Candys Creek Mission school in Tennessee before the removal, then the Park Hill school in Indian Territory. In 1841, he left his western home to travel to Washington with a Cherokee delegation and then attended school at Lawrenceville, New Jersey. While in Washington he witnessed the inauguration of President William Henry Harrison. By 1844 he had entered Princeton University, but on the death of his father he returned home to enter the mercantile business. He first served in the Cherokee government, as clerk to the legislature, in 1847, but abandoned the post when news came of gold strikes in California. In the spring of 1849 Dennis left Indian Territory and went by way of Fort Scott in present-day Kansas; Westport, Missouri; and the Platte River route to California, arriving at the Sacremento River in September. He stayed on in California long after the gold fever ended, as did his brother Edward, who became a newspaper editor in San Diego. Dennis did not return to Indian Territory until 1868, after a long journey through the Isthmus of Panama. When he arrived at Fort Gibson, Indian Territory, he found that his tribe, formerly secure in its isolation, had been devastated by the Civil War. Bushyhead also realized that his people now were threatened by the white man's railroads and by white concepts of landownership that differed markedly from their own.

In a sense Bushyhead was an ideal leader for these times. His experience in the mercantile business had yielded him a wide reputation as a first-class financial administrator. The tangled economic affairs of the Cherokees, who had a large but uncertain amount of money held in trust in Washington and much more to arrive as the result of treaty provisions, required the kind of touch he was prepared to lend. Moreover, having been away so long, Bushyhead was not directly involved in the internal disputes that kept the tribe paralyzed in their attempts to meet external problems. He returned briefly to his store and then, in 1871, was elected tribal treasurer. He gained stature in his eight years at that post, and was elected principal chief in 1879 and again in 1883.[1]

The new chief brought some changes in the nature of Cherokee leadership. In contrast to the opposition party, which bore the name of former Cherokee chief Lewis Downing, Bushyhead's party, known as the National party, held some promise of freeing tribal politics from the interpersonal power plays of strongmen and their cliques that had often been typical in the past. Also, Bushyhead was less eager to dominate the government and more willing to submit to the checks and balances of the Cherokee legis-

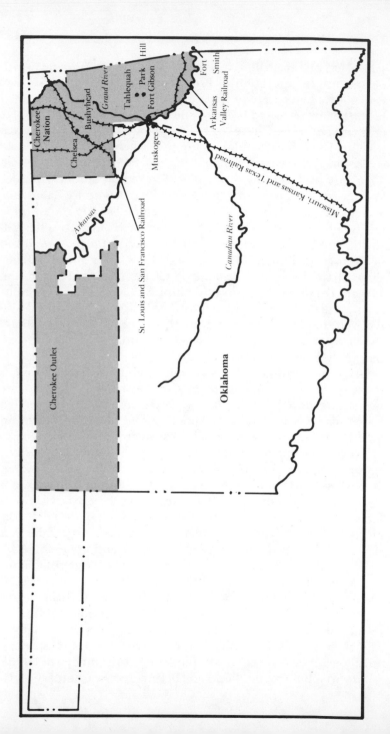

lature and courts. These institutions, especially the courts, were under attack from outsiders. If they failed, Cherokee sovereignty would be endangered. Therefore, if the chief contributed to their vulnerability by using them for personal ends, he would endanger the nation. Bushyhead often emphasized in letters to other branches of the tribal government that he, as executive, was giving "suggestions" and not "instructions," since the constitution did require of him "a certain oversight over all the Subordinate Branches of the Govt." He promoted education among the Cherokees partly because he believed that intelligent public opinion was the best guide to government leaders, and he regularly expressed the view that such leaders should be held responsible if the nation should "fall, stumble or go astray." These leaders might "fairly expect honorable mention," he thought, only if something they had done advanced the people as a whole, and not for their personal charisma.[2]

Among those issues Bushyhead faced that involved the future of his people, three stand out as critical in any evaluation of his success: railroads, cattle leasing, and citizenship.

In the treaty of 1866, the Cherokees had granted two railroad rights of way across the Cherokee Nation. The question in 1879 therefore, was not whether there would be railroads, but how far the existing railroads would intrude upon Cherokee land and the privileges of tribal government. Bushyhead's predecessor, former chief Charles Thompson, had outlined a policy which Bushyhead endorsed. Thompson had said that the railroads themselves were not evil, but that the Indians must insist that the land surrounding the tracks belonged to the tribes. The U.S. courts should have authority over railroad employees, but the Cherokee courts must control Cherokees, even if they committed crimes on the railroad right of way. Thompson stated that his opinion of railroads was of a "mixed character," and Bushyhead's seems to have been so, too. He opposed the railroads' claims for land grants and criticized them for pushing territorial legislation "in a manner abusive of our rights." At the same time, he advised his people that they needed the railroads, which would replace the wagon just as the wagon had replaced the pack horse. "With these changes," he wrote in his message of 1884, "the wants, and habits and necessities of our people have changed also. . . . It is

. . . certain that the more readily we adapt ourselves to the progress of our neighbors . . . the stronger will be our position and the more secure our rights."[3]

Because he saw the complexity of the railroad issues, Bushyhead sometimes appeared to be a mere opportunist bending with the political wind. For example, his personal letters show that he pursued a consistent policy of encouraging certain railroads that he felt would respect Cherokee controls. He did this in order to avoid a situation in which Congress, on the grounds the Cherokees were holding back "progress," would force more railroads on the Indians—railroads that the tribe could not regulate. At the same time, when Bushyhead felt that a railroad's requests were unjustified or threatening to Cherokee rights, he could be intransigent. Such was the case in 1881, when the M. K. & T. Railroad attempted to build a new line to Fort Smith, Arkansas. In this instance he wrote to railroad attorney David Keiso that the Cherokees were always "willing to accord to the United States and to her citizens as a whole the credit of being accuated by the same honorable feelings and motives" as was the tribe. But, he said, in running a survey from Muskogee to Fort Smith without the consent of the Cherokees, the M. K. & T. had "unwittingly gone beyond both treaty and law." His letter was polite but firm. Bushyhead, perhaps because of an instinct that the clandestine survey boded no good for future relations with the line, was adamant about it and at last forced the U.S. government to require that the several miles of track laid on this branch be torn up. In contrast, five years later the chief was severely criticized for vetoing a bill in which the Cherokee National Council had refused to accept a damage allowance set by Congress for the Kansas and Arkansas Valley Railroad. In 1886, while chief, he accepted a position in the pay of the U.S. government as commissioner to appraise damages by a railroad running through Indian lands. Some thought his action high treason.[4]

The best analysis is that Bushyhead favored controlled railroad development and tried through any means to prevent it from damaging tribal rights. He also knew a fait accompli when he saw one and was not prone to useless gestures. As with other issues of his time, he was playing for high stakes with powerful forces. "Gigantic corporations and federations of corporations have spread out and menaced the power of great states," he told the National Council, "and even make their powers felt in Congress, and their menaces are not without significance to the Cherokee Nation." But, he said in 1885, "everything depends upon the way they are regarded and treated, whether their great power is used for or against—to aid or to injure."[5]

The pattern of Bushyhead's policy was much the same when it came to the question of leasing the western portion of the Chero-kee Outlet. His political enemies cited the lease of the Outlet in 1883 to the Cherokee Strip Live Stock Association as an example of the chief's inconsistency. He had worked hard for that lease, they pointed out, thus welcoming one class of intruders, while on the other hand working equally hard to tighten the permit and mineral laws in order to make other kinds of white intrusion more difficult.

Again some knowledge of the complexities of the situation re-veal that Bushyhead was more subtle than such charges suggest. The Cherokees had been having a difficult time collecting a tax from the small operators who were grazing cattle in the Outlet. Bushyhead reasoned that through judicious leasing he might be able to tie the interest of an influential American cattle corpora-tion to the continued sovereignty of the tribe. Actually, the diffi-culty turned out to be that the Live Stock Association was not powerful enough, and in the end asked the Cherokees for protec-tion of its rights rather than, as Bushyhead hoped, defending those of the tribe.[6]

Throughout the Cherokee cattle leasing era, which ended with the transfer of the Outlet to the federal government in 1891, Bushyhead demonstrated his pragmatic approach. Shortly after taking office in 1879, he recommended to the National Council that it lower the tax on cattle which it had approved in 1873. His argument was that it was better to be able to collect a reasonable tax than to legislate some ideal of what the grass was worth and have it universally ignored. Even fifty cents a head, he thought, would yield considerable revenue if actually collected on the fifty thousand head of cattle then grazing in the Outlet. Shortly there-after he suggested a system of intelligence that would allow the Cherokees to inform themselves of the number of cattle in their domain and the length of time of the stay. If it could be reduced to a system, the chief advised, it would be "on a safe and predictable footing . . . so as to have it run smoothly and profitably hereafter." In regard to leasing the Outlet, Bushyhead again took what at first seemed an ambivalent position. He testified before Congress that he hoped the Indians would create their own stock industry, as it would be one of the best guarantees of their sovereignty, yet he vetoed several bills from the National Council that would have leased parts of the Outlet to Cherokee citizens. Sometimes he argued that the company making the offer was financially unable to stock the land and would become the cats-paw for outside interests. At other times he argued that the proposed bill gave the federal government too much control over what should be an internal matter. Always there was a concern not so much with the surface appearance of things as with how they would affect the tribal government in the end. Some outside observers saw method in Bushyhead's strategy. The *New York Herald* noted that the lease to the Live Stock Association set an important precedent for Cherokee sovereignty, since usually any lease made by an Indian tribe was illegal. Bushyhead had always argued that the Cherokees had a fee simple title to their lands and were not occupants at will, as some courts had determined other tribes to be. The lease backed his point. The *Herald* also pointed out that the lease left the Cherokees with only one group of whites to control on their western land. The New York editor was not blind to the fact, too, that the lease temporarily prevented the federal government, which had the right to buy the Outlet by treaty, from settling other tribes or whites upon it. In addition, the lease tended to increase the value of the lands and would doubtless cause them eventually to bring a higher price from the government than they would otherwise bring. The *Herald* called the cattle lease "as impudent a fraud as though he [Bushyhead] should undertake to lease to somebody any empty house he might find on a New York street." Impudent, perhaps, but not simplistic.[7]

There is a parallel to Bushyhead's cattle policy in his approach to oil leasing. The chief at first rejected applications for oil franchises within the Cherokee Nation. However, in 1883 he favored an amendment to the Cherokee mineral code to allow native lessees of coal and oil plots to associate with noncitizens. The next year came legislation granting a monopoly to any company that would begin exploiting Cherokee oil resources. In this case Bushyhead himself was one of the incorporators of the Cherokee Petroleum Company, which acted as a front for subleasing to outsiders, and there is evidence that he used his position as chief to give bidders inside information. Conflicts of interest were not so strictly interpreted in that day, and Bushyhead probably saw no conflict between his oil deals and the welfare of the tribe. Here, however, there begins to emerge a bit of the shallow speculator alongside the subtle policy maker. This kind of excess eventually haunted Bushyhead and prevented his getting proper credit for his more altruistically inspired actions.[8]

Even in his oil scheming, however, Bushyhead demonstrated one of his rules for the protection of the tribe. Before accepting any activity, he insisted that Cherokee law be updated upon the subject and that everything be according to some stated tribal legislation. He followed this course in the case of cattle, coal mining, the taking of timber, and literally every other issue. The Cherokees had suffered when the railroads first penetrated their territory in 1871 because of a lack of clear tribal legislation regarding the taking of natural resources, and Bushyhead did not want to see that mistake repeated. He was concerned that actions be carried out in accordance with the Cherokee constitution so that the Indian citizens might not be "confused and bewildered" and so that there should be no justifiable criticism that they were incapable of self-government.[9]

Perhaps the most complex and surely one of the most important issues that Bushyhead dealt with was tribal citizenship. The arguments over who had the right to share in Cherokee lands and what direction future increases in tribal membership should take affected both the degree to which Indians could present a united front and the attitudes of the majority of the tribe toward assimilation. Not only were there arguments among Cherokees about who deserved tribal citizenship, but there were considerations of the Cherokee black population (former slaves of the Indians), the intermarried whites, and those who, like Bushyhead himself, had some Indian blood but spoke little or no Cherokee and did not share the traditionalist world view of the fullbloods.

It was not difficult to decide what to do about genuine intruders, including potential homesteaders like David Payne, who led settlers onto Indian lands without asking permission. Bushyhead minced no words about Payne and his "hungry hoods." "We regard them as the guerillas of American society, the infamous Cortez and Pizzaro element of freebooters and robbers, as contradistinguished from the honest Anglo-Saxon race." Several of the Five Civilized Tribes united on the Payne matter and sent attorneys to his trial. On this question of the "wild white men who roam on the western frontier" cooperation was immediate. If all problems of citizenship had been so clear, there would have been little argument, factionalism, or division.[10]

They were not, however, all so simple. For example, there was the problem of the North Carolina Cherokees. At the time of the removal to Indian Territory these tribesmen had elected to stay behind in the East and take individual allotments. Many had lost their allotments in later years and now desired to rejoin the tribe which they or their ancestors had rejected fifty years earlier. Understandably there was reluctance among the Cherokees who had suffered along the Trail of Tears to accept their eastern kinsmen. Bushyhead, however, felt that all tribesmen of at least half-blood lineage among the North Carolina Cherokees should be re-admitted, or at very least that the question should be disposed of finally. The argument about who was a Cherokee did not, he thought, help the tribe in dealing with real outsiders and it complicated the distribution of funds which might come to the tribe. While the question continued to be debated after Bushyhead's term, several hundred North Carolina Cherokees did emigrate in the early 1880s and for the first time genuine attention was paid to the issue.[11]

While he favored the repatriation of Cherokees by blood, Bushyhead was less positive about the encouragement of intermarriage and the employment of noncitizens. Although he was the product of racial intermarriage, he questioned whether whites marrying Cherokees should be given full tribal citizenship, especially since many such "white Cherokees" claimed that they were also still U.S. citizens and under the jurisdiction of U.S. courts. Bushyhead recommended in 1885 that these intermarried whites not be given full citizenship with ownership shares, but only residence privileges. "The mercenary inducement to intermarriage will then no longer pollute our statute book. After all, no honorable foreigner will take exception to the fact that his alliance with an Aboriginal Tribe is not open to the suspicion that it has been bought; if exception should be taken so far as to prevent alliances with greedy men, so much the better for the Nation." Bushyhead was sometimes charged, because of such statements, with being unfriendly to Cherokee citizens with no Cherokee blood, who represented by 1890 about one-third of the population of the tribe. He did, however, veto some legislation passed by the National Council to place prohibitive fines on the employment of noncitizens. While he advocated strict control of noncitizen labor, he did not wish to eliminate it. He feared the loss would result in the Indians being characterized by their enemies as lacking in enterprise. As was often the case with Bushyhead, his support of a middle position alienated some members of both camps.[12]

Citizenship issues concerning the black freedmen and the Shawnees and Delawares who had been relocated in the Cherokee Nation, as well as the proper place of white advisers, arose prominently in connection with the most significant scandal of the Bushyhead administration—the so-called $300,000 case of 1883. In 1883, possibly because of concern that the cattle lease of that year would lead to claims by the Cherokees of permanent title to the Outlet, Congress appropriated $300,000 to be paid per capita to the Cherokees as the National Council saw fit. The government presented the sum as a payment for the Outlet, but Bushyhead and the Washington delegation claimed that the money was a bonus on payments made previously to the tribe for lands already ceded to the federal government and occupied by relocated Indian tribes. Others charged that the government was "not so appreciative of advantages gained of the red men as to have its 'bowels moved with compassion' for them" to the extent of paying guilt money on underappraised property. Bushyhead's argument, said his enemies, was a "ridiculous subterfuge" and "an insult to common intelligence." What had happened, these parties claimed, was that Bushyhead and the delegation had taken a down payment for the sale of the rest of the Outlet, now leased to the cattle company. Especially controversial was a fee of 7½ percent, or $22,500, taken by William A. Phillips, a former

Kansas congressman acting as attorney and lobbyist for the Cherokees, and thought by some to be in unholy financial alliance with the chief. The government did later use the transaction to support its claim to the region, and it did incalculable damage to Bushyhead's reputation, not to mention refueling the internal fights he had sought to calm.[13]

Since the Cherokees were left to decide on the distribution of the $300,000, the citizenship question arose. The freedmen claimed a share, and Bushyhead advised that they should have it. The National Council, however, denied payment to either the freedmen or the resettled Indians on Cherokee land, thus creating a series of court cases and several new lobbies in Congress. Eventually, all these groups were given a share by fiat of Congress, and another blow was dealt to the independence of the tribe. Bushyhead's National party lost the National Council elections that took place at the height of the scandal, and thereafter he struggled with an unfriendly legislature.[14]

By the time of the election for chief in 1887, Bushyhead had lost a great deal of his ability to turn the attention of his constituents away from personalities and internal feuds. Bushyhead himself was prevented by the constitution from running for office again, and so the National party candidate was his assistant chief, Rabbit Bunch. The assistant chief's candidacy complicated the role of the election as a referendum on Bushyhead's policy because Bunch was a full-blood who spoke no English, thus introducing the race and acculturation issues. Joel Mayes, a Downing party candidate with no more Indian blood than Bushyhead and even more "progressive" views finally won the tribal election by a narrow margin (156 votes). Mayes threw a sop to the full-blood faction by appointing Samuel Smith, a full-blood, his assistant chief. The election was fought on personalities and race, not issues. Even the infamous $300,000 scandal was scarcely mentioned.[15]

Embittered, Bushyhead refused to leave office, and the Downing party, with an army of one hundred men, attacked the capitol building at Tahlequah and removed the former chief by force. In response, the "Young Turks" of the National party, led by Bunch, threatened violence, and only the intervention of federal officials prevented a civil war. In fairness, Bushyhead's action was occasioned, according to his own statements, not by greed for power but by concern that the letter of the Cherokee constitution be followed. The votes had not been counted in the approved manner, and Bushyhead wished to ensure that the transition would be orderly and lawful. Instead of giving the impression of "civilized progress," however, the events surrounding the end of Bushyhead's term gave the outside world a comic spectacle.[16]

At first glance, the final years of Bushyhead's life seem to reinforce the impression that he was a power-hungry opportunist. He served on the Cherokee Commission that negotiated the sale of the remainder of the Outlet after the cattlemen were removed. Since the price the United States paid was lower than many Cherokees hoped for, and since the praise of various memers of Congress for Bushyhead's cooperation was so voluminous, many of his tribesmen charged that he had compromised their interests. A compromiser he surely was, but not with the evil motivations assigned him by the Indian press. He remained an Indian nationalist, still trying to find the middle ground between traditional full-bloods and white industrialists. But the support of the full-bloods slowly eroded away. During the 1890s they complained that Bushyhead was receiving tribal funds to lobby for his people in Washington but that his efforts were unproductive. Ironically, he also suffered at the hands of his white adversaries. Although the federal government awarded him a small section of land in the former Cherokee Outlet, in 1891 he was arrested by United States troopers as an "intruder" in the region.[17]

Dennis Bushyhead died of Bright's disease in February 1898 at the age of seventy-three. While the official *Cherokee Advocate* obituary described him as "one of the advanced Cherokees," other comment was less kind. "You should never name your children after the living great," wrote an Indian editor. "Wait until your ideal has played his full hand and lays mouldering in his tomb; the game is never played out until it is played out; and the man you venerate to-day may prove himself a poltroon and knave to-morrow." And so Bushyhead remained a man of contradictions: a man with many elements of greatness about him, but a man also enmeshed in many snares of pettiness. At the time of his death his most significant monument was a town on an alkalai plain twelve miles west of Chelsea, Indian Territory. It was called Bushyhead. Although it had flourished earlier, by 1898 it was deserted.[18]

NOTES

1. Biographical information is from John Bartlett Meserve, "Chief Dennis Wolfe Bushyhead," *Chronicles of Oklahoma* 14 (September 1936); 351–54; Carolyn Thomas Foreman, "Edward W. Bushyhead and John Rollin Ridge: Cherokee Editors in California," ibid., pp. 295–97; *Tahlequah Arrow*, February 5, 1898, copy in Dennis Bushyhead Papers, Western Manuscripts Collection, University of Oklahoma, Norman; transcript of Bushyhead autobiography in J. B. Meserve Papers, Indian Archives Division, Oklahoma Historical Society, Oklahoma City, (hereafter cited as I.A.D.).

2. D. W. Bushyhead to D. W. Lipe, May 26, 1880, Cherokee vol. 715b, I.A.D.; Annual Message, 1883, vol. 715f, p. 575, ibid.; *Cherokee Advocate*, November 26, 1879.

3. Charles Thompson to C. C. Lipe, August 15, 1878, vol. 715a, I.A.D.; Annual Message in *Vinita Weekly Chieftain*, November 18, 1884.

4. Dennis W. Bushyhead to David Kelso, [1881], vol. 715c, I.A.D.; Craig Miner, *The Corporation and the Indian: Tribal Sovereignty and Industrial Civilization in Indian Territory, 1865–1907* (Columbia: University of Missouri Press, 1976), pp. 102, 113; *Vinita Weekly Chieftain*, October 14, 1886.

5. Annual Message, 1881, vol. 715d, I.A.D.; *Sixth Annual Message of Hon. D. W. Bushyhead to the Senate and Council* (Tahlequah, November 4, 1885), p. 17, I.A.D.

6. Miner, *The Corporation and the Indian*, pp. 122–41; an excellent account of the whole matter is William Savage, *The Cherokee Strip Live Stock Association: Federal Regulation and the Cattlemen's Last Frontier* (Columbia: University of Missouri Press, 1973).

7. Bushyhead to National Council, November 19, 1879, vol. 715a, and Bushyhead to D. W. Lipe, May, 1880, vol. 715b, I.A.D.; Bushyhead testimony, May 21, 1885, *Senate Report 1278*, 49th Cong., 1st sess. (serial 2362), pp. 50–70 (Bushyhead here explains the lease situation from his point of view); D. W. Bushyhead to National Council, December 13, 1882, and Bushyhead to Senate, n.d., pp. 365 ff., both in vol. 715d, I.A.D.. For a careful explanation of the corporate brace to sovereignty, see Bushyhead to National Council, May 2, 1883, Cherokee Strip Tahlequah file, I.A.D.. *New York Herald*, quoted in *Oklahoma War Chief* (Caldwell, Kans.), April 15, 1886.

8. Miner, *Corporation and the Indian*, pp. 145–47.

9. D. W. Bushyhead to National Council, December 18, 1886, Bushyhead Papers, Western Manuscripts Collection, University of Oklahoma.

10. Eloise Bushyhead to J. B. Meserve, July 31, 1936, Meserve Papers, I.A.D.; Annual Message in *Indian Journal*, November 11, 1880; Bushyhead to Governor Overton of Chickasaws, September 14, 1880,

vol. 715b, I.A.D.; Annual Message in *Cherokee Advocate,* November 26, 1879.

11. Bushyhead to Cherokee delegation, May 19, 1880, vol. 715b, I.A.D.; M. Thomas Bailey, *Reconstruction in Indian Territory: A Story of Avarice, Discrimination and Opportunism* (Port Washington, N.Y.: Kennikat Press, 1972), pp. 163–65.

12. *Sixth Annual Message,* pp. 11–12; *Vinita Weekly Chieftain,* November 20, 1884.

13. Savage, *The Cherokee Strip Live Stock Association,* p. 57; *Vinita Weekly Chieftain,* March 19, March 5, and March 12, 1885.

14. *Vinita Weekly Chieftain,* June 3 and July 22, 1886; December 24, 1883.

15. The election is treated in *Vinita Weekly Chieftain,* May 27 and December 30, 1886, and January 27, February 10, June 2, and August 4, 1887.

16. *Vinita Weekly Chieftain,* December 8 and December 22, 1887; "Reminiscences of Eloise Bushyhead," Meserve Papers, I.A.D.

17. *Vinita World,* July 25, 1891; *Cherokee Telephone,* March 5, 1891, both in Bushyhead Papers, Western Manuscripts Collection, University of Oklahoma; *Cherokee Advocate,* February 12, 1898; *Guthrie Daily Leader,* August 4, 1893.

18. *Cherokee Advocate,* February 12, 1898; *Cherokee Champion,* June 5, 1895, copy in Bushyhead Papers, Western Manuscripts Collection, University of Oklahoma.

Carlos Montezuma

PETER IVERSON

CARLOS MONTEZUMA ranked as one of the most prominent Native Americans in the United States during the first decades of the twentieth century. His life read at times like an improbable Hollywood script. His career and writings tell us much about the changing world of Native Americans after the frontier had been closed and the Indian wars of the late nineteenth century had been concluded. American Indians were entering a new chapter in their long history. Montezuma symbolized those who wanted Native Americans to have equal opportunities in the America of the twentieth century. Through his journal, *Wassaja,* and through his other publications, speeches, and activities, he launched a one-man crusade to improve conditions for American Indians.

Although known throughout his adult life as an Apache, Montezuma was not an Apache at all. Rather he was a Mohave-Apache, or Yavapai. His Yavapai name was Wassaja (Signaling), a name he would later give to his newspaper and would use in corresponding with his kinsmen. Born in southern Arizona between 1865 and 1867, he lived with his people only until 1871, when the Pimas captured him at Iron Top Mountain and sold him for thirty dollars to wandering Italian-American photographer and artist, Carlos Gentile. Gentile took him east and Montezuma did not return to his homeland for many years.

This abrupt change in Wassaja's life was symbolized by a change in his name. Gentile called the boy Carlos after himself: the Montezuma represented an attempt to give his charge some proud vestige of his Indian heritage. Gentile did not raise Montezuma. The two stayed together for several years in Illinois and New York, but Gentile was ruined financially by a disasterous fire.

Then a couple named Baldwin cared for Montezuma briefly in New York. Eventually George W. Ingalls, a Baptist missionary representative, entrusted Montezuma's upbringing to W. H. Stedman, a Baptist minister in Urbana, Illinois. Ingalls wrote to the president of the YMCA at Illinois Industrial University in October 1878, expressing his desire for Montezuma to become "first a *real* Christian" and then "a Physician—and with a good education and love of Christ in his heart, to go back to his people and labor for their good as Christian or Missionary Physician."[1] Montezuma would become both a Christian—not surprisingly, a good Baptist—and a physician, and eventually labor for the good of his people, though not precisely in the manner envisioned by Ingalls.

In Urbana, Montezuma advanced rapidly in his studies. After two years of private tutoring, he entered the preparatory program for the University of Illinois. Following a year's work, he enrolled in the freshman class at the university and received a bachelor of science degree in 1884. Montezuma then returned to Chicago and found employment with a druggist, who in turn introduced him to a faculty member of the Chicago Medical College. By obtaining a partial scholarship and working part-time, Montezuma completed his medical course in 1889. He was all of twenty-three or twenty-four years old when he received the degree of doctor of medicine.

Despite the assistance and encouragement given him, the years in medical school were hard. Montezuma had to muster an enormous amount of self-discipline and determination to get his M.D. degree—an accomplishment that marked him as an unusual Indian of his era. During this period he formed an iron-clad belief, often expressed in his later writings, in the power of work and of the freedom to achieve when given the opportunity. He saw, understandably, in his own life's story a lesson about the potential of Indians everywhere to be free from the forces that, as he perceived them, held Native Americans in bondage: "As I was thrown on my own resources I was fully aware that I had to climb a mountain of discipline in order to be a man among men. I realized that I belonged to a race who were being driven at the point of a bayonet instead of by persuasion. With these thoughts I felt a rash of indignation which called on me to stand firm to the rights of that race whose blood circulates through my veins." He had no doubt that if Indians "had the same opportunity . . . were treated as men . . . treated as well as immigrants . . . they would be just the same as any other person."[2]

After a short and not very successful stint in private practice in Chicago, Montezuma joined the Indian Service. Commissioner of Indian Affairs Thomas Jefferson Morgan offered him a thousand dollars a year to serve as physician at the Fort Stevenson Industrial School in North Dakota. Nearly broke, he eagerly took the next train out of town. He remained at Fort Stevenson for one year before moving on to a similar position at the Western Shoshone Agency in Nevada. After three years in Nevada, Montezuma accepted an appointment at the Colville Agency in Washington, where he served for another year. Disheartened with conditions on the western reservations, he returned in 1894 to the east to Carlisle Indian School in Pennsylvania. His two and a half years at Carlisle marked the end of his employment in the Indian Service and the beginning of his career as a reformer.

At Carlisle, Montezuma worked under the supervision of Richard H. Pratt, with whom he had corresponded as a medical student. Pratt's personality, his dogmatic nature, and his conviction that the Indian Bureau suppressed Indians would all affect the kind of war Montezuma soon declared on the Indian Service. Montezuma saw in the Carlisle program a demonstration of what proper education could mean for American Indians in that difficult era. And Pratt's fall into disfavor with the bureau and the government's closing of Carlisle during World War I, ostensibly to aid the war effort, indicated precisely to Montezuma the evil of the bureau. How could the government "take away [the Indians'] hope and destroy that which they thought would stand forever as a great sacred memorial monument, the Indian's Gibralter?"[3] Montezuma and Pratt corresponded frequently after Wassaja left Carlisle. Pratt often praised what he termed the "red hot" speeches and articles of the doctor; Montezuma remained a fervent admirer of the general. "He and I," Montezuma once wrote, "always hit the same nail."[4]

At Carlisle, too, Montezuma met a Sioux woman named Zitkala-sa, a musician and writer who was every bit as headstrong as he. Despite her outspoken criticism of Pratt, whom she described rather uncharitably as "pigheaded," Montezuma and the woman shared many ideas. Eventually they embarked upon a stormy courtship and for a short while it seemed as though they would be married, but the engagement ended unhappily. He would not marry for another decade, and then to a non-Indian woman, Mary Keller. Zitkala-sa soon married a member of her own tribe, Raymond Bonnin and took the Anglo name Gertrude. She also would emerge as an important Native American leader, and Montezuma, with whom she eventually resumed at least a friendship, would support her work.[5]

In 1896, Montezuma again returned to Chicago, where he was offered a position at the clinic of Fenton Turck, an outstanding physician whom he had met at Carlisle. It was a stroke of good fortune: the foundation of Montezuma's medical career. He would remain a resident of Chicago for nearly the remainder of his life.

By the final years of the nineteenth century, Montezuma began to speak out candidly about contemporary Native American conditions. These early talks and writings illustrate that he had already formulated many important positions on Indian affairs. The remaining years of his life saw him embellish these ideas and gain a progressively wider audience for his views. His address to Chicago's Fortnightly Club on February 10, 1898, for example, revealed his sharp disagreement with the bureau's program for improving the Indians' circumstances. Montezuma told the story of the physician who, after calling each morning on his patient, would then pass the house of one of that patient's friends. The friend would always inquire about the prognosis for the patient and the doctor repeatedly replied that the patient was "improving." Yet the patient eventually died. When someone asked the friend what the patient had died with, the friend replied: "I guess she died with improvement." It was "high time," Montezuma said, "a red flag or some other danger signal be hung up on the present Indian policy or the Indians will all die with 'improvement.' "[6]

Montezuma saw Native Americans as being in a transitional period. "The Indians of today," he reminded his audience, "are not the Indians of the past." They lacked the advantages of their aboriginal state and had yet to profit by "civilization"; thus they were "more degraded than their forefathers ever were." Montezuma remembered the "strength, prosperity and happiness" of the people of his childhood. But that old way was gone and a new way of merit had not taken its place. White Americans had "sent in more vice than virtue" and "taken out more virtue than vice." Indians were trapped on the "fifty two dark spots of the map" called reservations.[7]

In a refrain that would become insistent, Montezuma charged that reservation life demoralized the Indians. The reservation, he contended, "is not an earthly paradise, nor a land of milk and honey where the pipe of peace is continually smoked. It is a demoralized prison; a barrier against enlightenment, a promoter of idleness, beggary, gambling, pauperism, ruin and death." Reservations discouraged competitiveness and isolated Indians from the rest of American life. Montezuma wanted Indians to take responsibility for themselves, free from the restrictions that characterized life on the reservation and indeed all of bureau policy.[8]

What would solve the Indian problem, as it was customarily labeled? In Montezuma's view, the fundamental step which had to be taken was the abolition of the Indian Bureau, that "heartless and evil system," that "political wirepulling establishment that squeezes the life-blood out of the Indians." Once the American people had thrust the bureau "into the bottomless pit whence it may have originated," once Indians were freed from the control of the "generally incompetent and brokendown white derelicts" who peopled the bureau, Native Americans would "go forth to conquer and to triumph."[9] Abolishing the Indian Bureau—a radical step that was by no means universally agreed upon by other Indians—came to be an unshakable, central element in Montezuma's position on Indian affairs. His belief in this course of action would affect all of his future positions and actions in the realm of Indian policy reform.

Montezuma had long been interested in bringing other Indian activists together to forge a pan-Indian association. As early as 1901 he had told Gertrude Bonnin of his desire to form a national Indian organization, and over the next decade he was in touch with many people who seemed to share his interests. Some, including Richard Pratt, offered little encouragement. Pratt informed Montezuma that the Indian activists were politically fragmented and that "without real Yankee activity and 'ingin'-uity' there will not be much come of it." Undeterred, Montezuma corresponded with Fayette McKenzie, a non-Indian professor from Ohio State. In 1909 the two men met in Chicago and discussed the future of the pan-Indian movement. During the next year Montezuma met with McKenzie and other activists to plan a pan-Indian conference for 1911. Rosa La Flesche, who later served as an officer in the Society of American Indians, noted that Montezuma worked "diligently" to help start the association.[10]

However, when the Indian activists met to form the Society of American Indians, Montezuma distinguished himself by his absence. Despite the pleas of McKenzie, La Flesche, Charles Daganett, and others for him to attend, Montezuma stayed away. For good measure, he resigned from the newly established association, charging that it had already become contaminated by Indian Bureau influence.[11] He did attend the second annual conference, however, and afterwards received a rebuke from an Ojibwa who shared his views on the bureau: "I am certainly surprised at your action of going over to the enemy and joining their ranks against your people . . . you whom I thought was the insurgent of the insurgents for Indian rights."[12]

The third conference of the society took place in Denver late in 1913. Once again, Montezuma stayed away, this time because of a misapprehension that the society had tacitly endorsed Indian participation in a Wild West show slated to take place in that city. Pratt strongly denounced the inherent dangers of such extravaganzas and Montezuma echoed his sentiments. In fact, the society never endorsed the show, but Montezuma still refused to attend the conference. He did, however, join the executive committee of the organization when it met in Philadelphia a few months later. There he delivered a featured address entitled "The Reservation Is Fatal to the Development of Good Citizenship." He dutifully paid his membership dues during the following spring. Rosa La Flesche promptly returned his membership card showing him to be an active member in good standing. She could not resist adding, "Good Standing—isn't that Wonderful for you? Ha! Ha!" She reminded him to bring his card to the next conference, as some might not know his current status.[13]

During 1914, Montezuma attended the annual conference, renewed his membership, and corresponded regularly with such society luminaries as Arthur C. Parker, Seneca, and the Arapaho minister Sherman Coolidge. Parker invited him to address the 1915 conference on the subject of abolition of the bureau. Montezuma held forth eloquently on the subject; even the more cautious Parker conceded he was "essentially right" in his presentation. Yet Montezuma soon returned to disparaging the nature of the society's meetings and to criticizing the journal Parker edited for the society. On the most recent gathering, he wrote: "The sky is clear and we meet only to discuss. There is nothing wrong. We meet only to discuss. It is so nice to meet and discuss. We can meet and discuss as well as the Mohonk conference. . . . Meeting and discussing are so soothing and smoothing. Sh——! Sh——! Don't whisper about the Indian Bureau."[14]

In April 1916, Montezuma began publishing a journal, *Wassaja,* which he continued to publish the rest of his life. In this publication Montezuma was at his best. During the six and a half years of its existence, *Wassaja* carried on the good fight against the bureau and for a place for Indians in the America of the twentieth century. Here Montezuma's gift for polemic, his cutting sense of humor, his dedication to the present and future of Native Americans burst forth impressively. He could act autonomously and speak out freely, writing slashing editorials and printing news of Indian affairs from around the country. A single copy of *Wassaja* cost a nickel; one hundred copies could be had for two dollars. A year's subscription set one back fifty cents. Given the desultory state of American journalism, it was a handsome bargain. Montezuma accepted no advertisements and had a difficult time finding the money to publish "his chief obsession." His financial records and *Wassaja* itself carry frequent reminders of what a struggle it involved.[15]

Abolition of the bureau served as *Wassaja's* raison d'être. The first issue declared: "This monthly signal rays is to be published only so long as the Indian Bureau exists. Its sole purpose is Freedom for the Indians through the abolishment of the Indian Bureau."[16] The first numbers carried at the top of the first page a drawing of an Indian, pinned under a huge log labeled "Indian Bureau," looking up at a ray of light, labeled "Wassaja," shining down toward him. By June 1917 readers saw a different image: Montezuma, dressed in a three-piece suit, aided by other Indians in more traditional attire, holding a log labeled "freedom's signal for the Indian," and about to break down the door of the Indian Office. This image and one of Montezuma standing by the Statue of Liberty, holding a copy of his address, "Let My People Go" (labeled rather immodestly "An Indian Classic"), could be seen until August 1921. From that point until the final issue of *Wassaja*, a grimmer image appeared, perhaps reflecting Montezuma's ultimate despair over his unsuccessful campaign: an Indian, held in stocks marked "work of the Indian Office," gazing bleakly out at a distant sunrise with "freedom's signal for the Indian" emblazoned in its rays.

Montezuma decried often the incompetency of bureau personnel. "On the Stage of Indian Affairs," published in January, 1917, is a good case in point:

THE HONORABLE COMMISSIONER of Indian Affairs addressing his employees:
"Who says 'Freedom for the Indians?' "

A BOLD GLADIATOR employee in the U.S. Indian Department . . .:
"Not I, for I work in the Indian Service. I got my job under Civil Service. Not I,—not I,—not I, my Lord!"

A VETERAN FEMALE employee in the Indian Service, testifies from her heart:
"Oh, how I love to work for the Indians. I could live and die doing what the Indians ought to do."

ONE LOYAL STAUNCH EMPLOYEE . . ."
"All these requirements of our Master we faithfully obey; we shut our mouths, see nothing and get our pay."[17]

He objected, too, to the bureau's role in killing Indian pride: "When you kill racial pride, you kill the Man; his stoic independence; his high spirit of what is right and what is wrong; his relation of man with man and his abiding faith in the Great Spirit."[18]

Nonetheless, *Wassaja* did more than criticize the bureau. It frequently looked to the future. Montezuma talked about the different world that Indians of the present lived in and the chance they had to create a better world for their children:

Fennimore [*sic*] Cooper's Indians do not exist today. We are their children's children. Things have changed and we have changed with them. We do not see things as our forefathers saw them nor do we live

as they did. Let it be known that within the breast of every Indian
there is a heart which throbs with the same yearnings that throb in all
human kind.[19]

Although the Indian commissioner, Board of Indian Commissioners, bureau employees, Indian Rights Association, and the
missionaries all believed to the contrary, Montezuma insisted,
"The Indians themselves, say they CAN TAKE CARE OF THEMSELVES.
They do not want to be babies any longer. They want the rights of
man."[20]

Wassaja also provided the medium through which Montezuma
could comment on pan-Indian activities, including those of the
Society of American Indians. He disagreed with the way in which
Arthur C. Parker ran the association's journal and he let the
world know about his displeasure. According to Montezuma, the
American Indian Magazine could "straddle any old thing that
comes along. Buffalo Bill and P. T. Barnum used the Indians.
Now is the American Indian Magazine's turn."[21] After Parker became president of the society in 1916, Montezuma criticized its
leadership in his journal's columns:

> SAI is all right but the officers are all wrong. SAI has good ideas for
> the Indians, but any good ideas can be killed by officers who have
> wrong notions of doing the best thing for the Indians.
>   WASSAJA most emphatically must say that the present officers are
> not for the best interest of the Indians, because their environment
> does not permit them to take right views on the welfare of their race.
> They have turned their ears, shut their eyes and ignored the path of
> freedom for their enslaved race.[22]

In response, Parker summarily dropped Montezuma as
contributing editor to the *American Indian Magazine*.

Montezuma's criticism was based on policy issues and not on his
personal dislike of Parker. He attacked the society because it
chose to work within the existing power structure, the Bureau of
Indian Affairs. When the society finally voted in 1918 to advocate
abolition of the bureau, Montezuma immediately encouraged
"everyone to join the Society of American Indians." He heaped
praise on all the new officers: Charles Eastman, Philip Gordon,
Henry Roe Cloud, Gertrude Bonnin, De Witt Hare and Sherman
Coolidge. "They are the most loyal of the Indian race," he said.
"Indians," he urged, "if you wish to help yourself and your race,

join the Society of American Indians." He admitted that he had criticized the society as much as anyone in the past, but added that he had tried to "direct it aright for the best interest of the Indians." "In our crude and often rude way," he said, "we tried to steer the Society in the right path."[23]

With the society on the right path, Montezuma generally supported it during his last years. He proved particularly supportive of Gertrude Bonnin, who had deposed Parker as editor of the journal. Even after Bonnin departed from the society a year later, following the unsuccessful campaign of her husband for the SAI presidency against Omaha attorney Tom Sloan, Montezuma encouraged readers of *Wassaja* to attend the organization's conferences. In 1921, for example, he commented:

> We cannot urge too much to have all Indians and friends of the Indians to attend the Conference. No Indian organization should be supported and encouraged more than the Society of American Indians. It has stood by the Indians and the Indians should encourage it by attending the Conference. . . . We are going to the Conference with our hearts full of great interest in the Indian race . . . and do something that will be vital and life-giving to the enslaved Indian people.[24]

After 1920, *Wassaja's* coverage of the society's affairs declined. Apart from reminding his readers to attend its conferences, he devoted little space to its activities. This is perhaps a commentary on the declining fortunes of the organization, but it also indicates Montezuma's renewed disillusionment with it. At the 1922 meeting he was disheartened that the society was backing off from its stand on the bureau. He was also discouraged that no new and dynamic leadership was emerging within the society. The next to last issue of *Wassaja* blasted the meager results of the conference. Montezuma, at least intermittently, had entertained real hopes for the society. It now was clear that his expectations would not be fulfilled. For Montezuma, the Society of American Indians had nearly run its course.

The same issue of *Wassaja,* in October 1922, also gave notice of Montezuma's failing health, "Dr. Montezuma Is Not Well" read the headline. "For many years," the paper stated, "he thought he was made of cast iron physically," but now he had "found out that he is mere flesh, bone and blood." He hoped in time to regain his health, but his limited finances threatened the future not only of

Wassaja but of its publisher as well. He ventured that if he could scrape together enough money, a trip back to "camp life" in Arizona "would regain him his health."[25] In truth, he was completing his life's circle: he was returning home to die.

Given Montezuma's antipathy toward reservation life, this decision seems peculiar. Yet for years Montezuma had maintained a close relationship with the McDowell community. In fact, he had been a vitally important figure in the reservation's affairs for two decades, and without his strong guidance and assistance, it would almost certainly have been abolished.

Montezuma's correspondence with fellow Yavapais preceded the creation of the Fort McDowell Reservation. Before the establishment of the reservation in 1903, Montezuma wrote fairly regularly to two cousins, Mike Burns and Charles Dickens, who at that time lived in central Arizona, at Camp Verde and San Carlos, respectively. After the reservation was established, both men moved to McDowell, where Dickens and his brother George soon emerged as leaders. Montezuma continued to correspond with Burns and the Dickens brothers, and his letters reflect a genuine concern for the well-being of the people at McDowell.

Although Montezuma hated the reservation as an institution, he believed passionately that his people were entitled to land and to a decent life. Fort McDowell was small in area, approximately fifty square miles. But even more than half a century ago outsiders coveted the reservation because it straddled the Verde River. With access to the river, the land became valuable. No sooner had the Mohave-Apaches been settled at Fort McDowell than attempts commenced to have them moved.

In the context of a period when "Americanization" was emphasized, and given his personal views, it is not startling that Montezuma saw the allotment of McDowell as a possible solution. McDowell had a relatively small population and each family would have obtained a fairly adequate acreage. But Montezuma insisted that the Mohave-Apaches accept allotment only if guaranteed water rights and adequate timber and pasture land. He realized that the allotment of McDowell would not satisfy those who wanted its occupants removed entirely. The real threat was removal to the nearby Salt River Reservation, occupied by Pimas. There the Yavapais would have had less and poorer land,

and would have had to share it with people who had once been their enemies. "Stay put," Montezuma advised in letter after letter. "Don't sign anything until I see the documents." If "you Indians," as he was wont to say, "stand together, the government cannot force you to leave."[26]

The Yavapais did stay. George Dickens wrote Montezuma: "We always do believe that you are the means of having us remain here at McDowell. And had it not been for your aid; we might have been down on the deserts; with Pimas; who are our deadly enemies."[27] Various people in the bureau, including Commissioner Cato Sells and the local superintendent, Byron Sharp, attempted to get the Yavapais to move to Salt River, but to no avail. Dickens and the rest, reinforced by Montezuma's advice and determination, strongly resisted the notion.

The fight to retain McDowell became the principal cause of Montezuma's life during his final years. He raised it at every opportunity, through the Society of American Indians, through *Wassaja,* and through his correspondence. Montezuma and his attorney published blistering criticisms of bureau practices in which they spelled out government attempts to force the people off the land. In the end, Montezuma won his fight. Today, they still remember the victory at McDowell.[28]

In 1922 the urbane doctor left Chicago for the last time. Arriving at McDowell, he refused the assistance of a Tempe physician who urged him to go to a sanitarium where he might be cured of his tuberculosis. Insisting that he wanted to die like his ancestors, Montezuma took refuge in a brush shelter built for him by the Dickens family. There he died in January 1923.

In many ways Carlos Montezuma's career illustrates the dilemmas facing Indian people during the first quarter of the twentieth century. Placed on reservations and forgotten as "vanishing red men," many Indians now realized that the different tribes shared common problems in their struggle to maintain an Indian identity. Because these problems were so immense, Montezuma and other educated Indian leaders believed that a pan-Indian approach offered the only chance for any solution. Montezuma still saw himself as a Yavapai, but his leadership reflected pan-Indian principles more than any particular tribal values.

It is not surprising that much of Montezuma's resentment was focused on the Bureau of Indian Affairs. As later investigations indicated, during this period the bureau was poorly managed and often insensitive to the Indians' problems. But Montezuma's dissatisfaction with the bureau resulted from deeper causes. Uncertain of their role in twentieth-century America, Montezuma and other Indians focused their indignation on the bureau because that agency most closely controlled their new and unhappy existence. The bureau, therefore, became the focal point for all the resentment and unhappiness they felt. Although Montezuma was generally free from bureau restrictions, when he saw his kinsmen lagging behind other Americans in terms of economic opportunity, housing, health care, and education, he too blamed the bureau for its paternalistic control over the reservation communities.

Like other "progressive" Indian leaders of his time, Montezuma accepted parts of the white value system, for example, formal education, the work ethic, and individual enterprise. Because his paper championed these virtues, it probably appealed more to educated Indians and their white sympathizers than to many members of the reservation communities. Yet Montezuma provided important leadership during these years, not only as a major proponent of the pan-Indian movement, but also as a spokesman for Indian rights who tried to make the public aware of the bad conditions on the reservations.

Ironically, during the latter part of his life, he also developed a tribal identity. Intellectually he denounced the reservation system for denying his people access to equal opportunity, but emotionally he was drawn back to the reservation community at McDowell, with its ties to the land and traditional life-style. And so, at the end, the university-trained physician even rejected the white man's medicine, dying like his fathers in a brush shelter.

NOTES

1. George W. Ingalls to YMCA President, Illinois Industrial University, October 16, 1878, Carlos Montezuma biographical file, Chicago Historical Society.

2. Carlos Montezuma, "The Indian of Yesterday," Carlos Montezuma Papers, State Historical Society of Wisconsin (hereafter cited as SHSW). This collection and another collection of Montezuma's papers at Arizona State University, both recently acquisitioned, make possible a richer, more complete portrait of Montezuma.

3. *Wassaja* 3, no. 5 (August 1918): 3, SHSW.

4. Montezuma to Rep. Charles Carter, December 14, 1912, Montezuma Papers, SHSW, box 2.

5. The SHSW collection includes a great many letters from Bonnin to Montezuma, but unfortunately contains none of the letters written by Montezuma to Bonnin during this period.

6. Montezuma, "The Indian Problem from an Indian's Standpoint," Montezuma Papers, SHSW, box 5.

7. Ibid.

8. Ibid. See also, for example, a later piece, "The Reservation Is Fatal to the Development of Good Citizenship," *Quarterly Journal of the Society of American Indians* 2, no. 1 (January–March 1914): 69–74, Arizona State University Library (hereafter cited as ASU).

9. Montezuma, "Abolish the Indian Bureau," Montezuma Papers, SHSW, box 5.

10. Richard H. Pratt to Montezuma, July 8, 1909; Fayette McKenzie to Montezuma, September 2, September 14, and October 11, 1909; Rosa La Flesche to Montezuma, August 12, 1911, Montezuma Papers, SHSW, box 2.

11. McKenzie to Montezuma, July 31, 1911; La Flesche to Montezuma, August 12, 1911; Charles Daganett to Montezuma, September 13 and September 19, 1911, Montezuma Papers, SHSW, box 2.

12. August Breuninger to Montezuma, December 17, 1912, ibid.

13. Pratt to Secretary of the Interior Franklin Lane, May 7, 1913; Pratt to Montezuma, May 7, 1913; Pratt to Daganett, May 13, 1913; Pratt to Lane, May 21, 1913; Pratt to Montezuma, June 6 and June 18, 1913; draft of Montezuma to Arthur C. Parker, n.d.; Montezuma to Parker, August 29, 1913; McKenzie to Montezuma, October 23, 1913; La Flesche to Montezuma, May 26, 1914, Montezuma Papers, SHSW, box 3.

14. *Wassaja*, no. 2 (May 1916): 3, Newberry Library, Chicago. the so-called Lake Mohonk Conferences of Friends of the Indian, initiated in 1883, were annual gatherings of persons concerned with Indian reform.

15. Elsie E. Severance interview, February 25, 1976, conducted by Charles C. Colley, ASU archivist and field collector. Severance grew up as a neighbor to the Stedmans, the family that raised Montezuma in Urbana. She also met Montezuma later in Chicago. I am indebted to Dr. Colley for the text of this interview and for his assistance generally during the course of my research.

16. *Wassaja* 1, no. 1 (April 1916): 1, ASU.

17. Ibid., no. 10 (January 1917): 1, SHSW.

18. Ibid., no. 6 (September 1916): 1, SHSW.

19. Ibid., p. 3.

20. Ibid., 5, no. 11 (February 1920): 1, SHSW.

21. Ibid. 1, no. 2 (May 1916): 3, Newberry Library.

22. Ibid., no. 10 (January 1917): 3, SHSW.

23. Ibid. 3, no. 7 (October 1918): 3, SHSW.

24. Ibid. 7, no. 9 (September 1921): 4, SHSW. The Volume numbering of *Wassaja* is incorrect by this point.

25. Ibid. 8, no. 19 (October 1922): 1–4, SHSW.

26. See both the SHSW and the ASU collections for letters from Montezuma to this effect. The only published piece that indicates Montezuma's role at McDowell is Sue Abbey Chamberlain, "The Fort McDowell Indian Reservation: Water Rights and Indian Removal, 1910–1930," *Journal of the West* 14, no. 4 (October 1975): 27–34.

27. George Dickens to Montezuma, January 18, 1916, Montezuma Papers, ASU, box 4.

28. Interview with John Smith, Fort McDowell, January 7, 1978. I wish to thank Charles Colley and particularly Carolina Butler, of Paradise Valley, Arizona, for their assistance in introducing me to members of the Fort McDowell community.

Peter MacDonald

Peter Iverson

UNLIKE THE OTHER STUDIES in this volume, this chapter is about a man who is fully a product of the twentieth century. Peter Mac-Donald, Navajo, observed his fiftieth birthday in 1978. He has gained an unprecedented third term as chairman of the Navajo Tribal Council and has emerged as a leading Native American spokesman. His political career is not over yet; thus a full assessment of his contributions as a Native American leader is not possible. Nevertheless, one may still analyze his significance.[1]

MacDonald's perspectives and his career reflect the contemporary situation of American Indians. Hence his values and his choices say a good deal about the changing yet ongoing life of Native Americans. He is a man with traditional roots who has come to terms with the demands of the modern Navajo and American world. His successes and failures as the elected head of the United States' most populous tribe illustrate the difficulties and the potential of present-day Indian politics, economics, and society. They also show that in many important respects the challenges and decisions faced by Indian leaders of any era remain relatively constant: how to deal with the values and demands of Anglo-American society, how to provide for a viable socioeconomic life for one's people, how to satisfy the needs of the present without sacrificing the well-being of one's children and grandchildren.

Peter MacDonald's life story delights advocates of the Operation Bootstrap school of enterprise. He was born December 16, 1928, on the Navajo Reservation in the small northern Arizona community of Teec Nos Pos, and his childhood was like that of most Navajo boys of his generation. He spoke Navajo as his first language and learned traditional Navajo ways. Later he enrolled in school, but before he left elementary school, World War II erupted. As it would for many other Americans, the war changed the course of Peter MacDonald's life.

World War II proved to be a watershed period in modern Indian existence. Twenty-five thousand Native Americans served in the armed forces. Thousands more left their home areas for the first time to work in war-related industries. The war provided new experiences and created new values, among them an increased awareness of the utility of Anglo-American education. Despite the inherent horror of the war, it meant for many an opportunity to achieve and to prove themselves. Not surprisingly, American Indians compiled a distinguished battle record. The Navajos recorded a well-known chapter in this story. As Code Talkers in the South Pacific, they used the Navajo language as part of a code which baffled the Japanese. To this day, the Code Talkers are honored men within Navajo society.

Peter MacDonald entered the United States Marine Corps in 1944. He served as a member of the Code Talkers and was honorably discharged as a corporal in 1946. Two years later, he entered Bacone Junior College in Muskogee, Oklahoma, in an institution which for decades has enrolled large numbers of Indian students. MacDonald enrolled in Bacone High School and graduated in one year as a Dean's List student. By 1951 he had completed the associate of arts degree at Bacone, again making the Dean's List. In 1957, he graduated from the University of Oklahoma with a B.S. degree in electrical engineering.

During the 1950s the federal government encouraged young Indians to leave their reservations and move to the city, where they could obtain training and a job. For well-educated Indians, the city represented the place where they could put their knowledge and skills to best use. Peter MacDonald followed this pattern.

On receiving his degree from Oklahoma, he moved to southern California. He worked in El Segundo for six years as a project engineer and member of the technical staff of the Hughes Aircraft company. At Hughes Aircraft he gained a position of responsibility and useful experience in such areas as contract negotiation, budget preparation, and cost estimation. During this period he also enrolled in the University of California at Los Angeles as a graduate student in management.

In 1963 the governor of New Mexico appointed MacDonald as the first Indian member of a nine-member Economic Development Advisory Board. MacDonald returned to the Navajo Reservation that year and in June became director of the tribal division of Management, Methods, and Procedures. He served in that capacity for nearly two years before assuming the position which would catapult him to the center stage of Navajo political life: director of the Office of Navajo Economic Opportunity (ONEO).[2]

ONEO represented a sharp contrast to the economic strategy of industrial promotion then being avidly pursued by the incumbent chairman of the tribal council, Raymond Nakai. Although funded primarily through federal money allocated under the Economic Opportunity Act, ONEO was designed as an internally directed, locally centered program to be run by the Navajos themselves. Bureau of Indian Affairs officers first attempted to operate the program but prompt Navajo protests permitted the tribe to gain control over its design and function. MacDonald assisted in drafting a plan which would assure the Navajos management of the project. In September 1964, the Navajo Tribal Council authorized participation in the Community Action Program under the Economic Opportunity Act. That autumn, meetings at various chapters (the local Navajo political unit) and interviews with Navajos across the reservation enabled MacDonald to draft a specific proposal for government funds. In January 1965, the Office of Economic Opportunity granted the funding request, and in April the Office of Navajo Economic Opportunity was established. Peter MacDonald became director of the agency the next month and held the post for five years, before resigning in 1970 to seek the chairmanship of the tribal council.[3]

ONEO programs expanded into many fields and had an impact on almost literally everyone living in the Navajo Nation. By its own estimate, through 1967 ONEO had directly served 23,382 people and indirectly had an impact on the lives of the other 78,000 Indians on the reservation. The programs included everything from local community development, Head Start, and migrant and agricultural placement, to recreation and physical fitness, home improvement training, alcoholism rehabilitation, and a medicare alert project. In addition, the ONEO Legal Aid and Defender Society, soon rechristened Dinebeeina Nahiilna Be Agaditaha ("Attorneys Who Contribute to the Economic Revitalization of the People"), or more popularly DNA, began under the aegis of ONEO before becoming an independent entity.

ONEO worked because it had money, involved bread-and-butter issues, encouraged local involvement, and had Navajo administrators. From fiscal year 1965 through fiscal year 1968 ONEO received slightly over twenty million dollars in federal grants. The money was put to use in tangible projects visible to individual Navajo communities. At the end of 1967, ONEO employed Navajos in thirty-four of forty administrative positions; only 46 of 2,720 persons employed by ONEO at that time were non-Indian, serving primarily as preschool teachers (26) and DNA attorneys (7).[4]

Thus by 1970 Peter MacDonald had gained an enviable position from which to try for his first elected office. He benefited from being unscarred by earlier political battles. The Nakai years had been faction-ridden and the incumbent chairman injured by the internal division. As ONEO head, MacDonald utilized a new power base within the Navajo Nation. He had become well known throughout the reservation, and ONEO programs had generally been well received. Moreover, MacDonald combined a traditional reservation upbringing with a college education and significant off-reservation work experience. And a different set of concerns dominated the 1970 campaign. The use of peyote, for example, which Nakai had capitalized on in the past, had been neutralized as an issue (both Nakai and MacDonald favored leaving members of the Native American Church alone). On the other hand, the effective application of Navajo human and natural resources would be more strongly emphasized, and MacDonald's direction of ONEO represented to Navajo voters the potential yet untapped in their midst. Finally, as a candidate from Teec Nos Pos, MacDonald could cut into the strong majorities Nakai had previously forged in the northern part of the reservation.

MacDonald did not officially announce his candidacy until June, 1970, but an endorsement by his home chapter of Teec Nos Pos on April 11 made it quite clear that he would run. Pressure mounted from the Tribal Council and the Advisory Committee for MacDonald to resign his ONEO position, as tribal and BIA employees are required to do when seeking tribal office. He finally resigned under duress in early June, and the impression given to many people that he was being forced out of office perhaps boosted his chances for election. In less than a week after his resignation became official, 11 of the 102 chapters had endorsed MacDonald for chairman: Kayenta, Chilchinbeto, Teec Nos Pos, Pinon, Navajo Mountain, Coppermine, Gap, Sanostee, Jeddito, Low Mountain, and Hard Rocks. Seven of these chapters had voted for Nakai in the previous election, several of them overwhelmingly. Jeddito councilman Ned Benally argued that MacDonald was the only candidate who had proven he could obtain financial assistance on a large scale from the federal government. A Hard Rocks chapter officer added that MacDonald differed from Nakai and another candidate, Sam Billison, in that he had visited and worked with the community people during the previous five years. Henry Zah of Low Mountain complained that nothing had been done by Nakai about ensuring Navajo claims to the Navajo-Hopi joint-use area. These three comments represented arguments that proved central to the effectiveness of MacDonald's candidacy.[5]

MacDonald, Nakai, Sam Billison, Donald Dodge, Joe Watson, Jr., and Franklin Eriacho all sought the chairmanship in 1970. Navajo election law decreed that only the two candidates with the most precinct support could be formally nominated at a central nominating convention. When the votes from the seventy-two precincts were counted, forty supported MacDonald and twenty-six backed Nakai. The other votes were scattered among the remaining candidates. The popular vote reflected a similar pattern.[6]

During the autumn campaign both men essentially repeated the main points they had stressed prior to the convention. MacDonald elected Wilson Skeet of Bread Springs, New Mexico, as his running mate. His choice made good political sense, for Skeet was well known and came from the area off the reservation whose residents traditionally complained about underrepresentation in tribal affairs. In the weeks before the election, MacDonald reemphasized his belief in local participation in tribal programs, his interest in eliminating factionalism, his intention not to interfere with the Native American Church, and his concern for preserving Navajo land resources, developing a private sector in the Navajo economy, and involving young people more fully in tribal affairs. Nakai countered by underlining the achievements of his two terms as chairman, which he said included new industry that "pays good wages to our Navajo people," improved education, increases in tribal funds and assets, purchases of off-reservation land, and freedom of religion for the Native American Church.[7]

The Navajo electorate chose Peter MacDonald as its new chairman by a substantial majority of almost 3 to 1. He thus began his administration with a solid mandate from the Navajo people. Nakai had opposed DNA; MacDonald had supported it and could count on good cooperation between the chairman's office and that agency. He could, of course, rely as well on close ties with the ONEO operation, and planned to integrate some of its features into the tribal government programs as time went on.[8]

In his inaugural address in January 1971, MacDonald called for an end to "the ways of distrust, of recrimination, of acting in the dark, of counsel with oneself" and outlined the goals of his administration: "First, what is rightfully ours, we must protect; what is rightfully due us we must claim. Second, what we depend on from others, we must replace with the labor of our own hands and the skills of our own people. Third, what we do not have, we must bring into being. We must create for ourselves." In the first area, MacDonald pledged not to "barter away the Navajo birthright for quick profit that will cheat our children and their children after them," promised to work to update the operation of the long-awaited San Juan irrigation project, and insisted his administration would act forcefully to claim funds due them as Navajos and as citizens. In the second category, he contended, Navajos must cease "to depend on others to run our schools, build our roads, administer our health programs, construct our houses, manage our industries, sell us cars, cash our checks and operate our trading posts." MacDonald promised to work to alter this situation, to throw off "the bonds of forced dependency": "We must do it better. We must do it in our own way. And we must do it now." In the third classification, MacDonald reminded Navajos they were fortunate in many respects, for they had the three classic sources of wealth: land in abundance, sources of capital—"not enough, but some"—and labor. What must be added, he said, was a Navajo-owned private sector, good jobs, trained specialists and professionals, and credit: "We must move from a wage and welfare economy to an ownership economy." Again, he noted the limits to the advantages of bringing in non-Indian industry and emphasized the need for all kinds of training: "Every time someone says how good we Navajos are with our hands, I want to ask, 'Why not give us the chance to show what we can do with our minds?' "[9]

Many people expressed skepticism about the Navajos' ability to achieve self-determination. As one seasoned BIA veteran stated: "Now, it's self-determination! They have no economy. They're utterly dependent on government. How in hell can you talk about it? Self-determination must mean being able to spend the white man's money without accounting for it."[10] Nonetheless, the Navajo national government and Navajos in general moved toward this objective throughout the first term of MacDonald's administration.

Self-determination is not achieved for a people solely by one man. In reviewing the successes and failures of MacDonald's two administrations, it would be simplistic to give all the credit or all of the blame to one person. But while MacDonald had considerable assistance in various areas, he surely set a clear tone which marked a definite departure from the past. Not all Navajos would agree on his means, but most would subscribe to his ends, as stated in his inaugural address: "Protecting what is ours, claiming what is due us, replacing what we depend on from others with what we do ourselves, creating for ourselves what we do not have and desire." The Navajos in the late 1970s had made some progress in that direction. Their political and economical position in the American Southwest and the United States had been altered. As the elected leader of the Navajo people during this period. MacDonald not only presided over this transformation; he helped to effect it. To ascertain his role, one must review some of the developments in his first term, his reelection in 1974, and some of the features of his second term.

The effectiveness and direction of administrations in Navajo tribal government have been affected centrally by the choice of legal counsel. Norman Littell, for example, served as general counsel to the tribe for nearly twenty years, from the late 1940s to the late 1960s, and cast a long shadow over the workings of the council and the actions of the chairman. In his second term, Ray-

mond Nakai finally succeeded in ousting Littell and selected
Harold Mott to replace him. Inexperienced in Indian law, Mott
proved relatively ineffective. But Mott was still influential, and
MacDonald had made him a campaign issue, charging him with
not only being inexperienced but having "too often assumed a decision making role which infringes on the powers of the Navajo
Tribal Council and the Navajo people."[11]

To replace Mott, MacDonald chose the Phoenix firm of Brown,
Vlassis, and Bain. It proved less a departure from the tradition of
an individual attorney as counsel than it might seem. The tribe, in
fact, did not utilize the services of the two dozen attorneys in the
firm, but relied principally on George Vlassis, a partner in the
firm, and Lawrence Ruzow, a young attorney from Harvard who
had worked from 1969 to 1970 as attorney for Navajo Community College. Vlassis and Rozow, as had Mott, inevitably became closely identified not only with the Navajo Tribal Council
but with MacDonald's political fortunes. They advised him on a
great many matters, helped draft some of his speeches and testimony, and provided him with legal opinions on economic development and the Navajo Nation's relationship to the states, the
Bureau of Indian Affairs, and the Hopi people, with whom the
Navajos were embroiled in a land dispute. They clearly influenced the form, if not the substance, of many of MacDonald's
public positions. Like MacDonald, Vlassis and Rozow prided
themselves in being pragmatic men, working for incremental
progress based on achievable goals.[12]

MacDonald moved early in his first term to emphasize the goal
of Navajo control of Navajo education. The Tribal Council approved the creation of the Navajo Division of Education in 1971.
The division sought to promote greater Navajo involvement at all
levels of the educational process and to ensure the preservation of
the Navajo cultural heritage while providing the kind of education needed in the contemporary world. In 1973 MacDonald
urged the establishment of a tribal educational agency "on an in-
stitutional level commensurate with and supplemental to state de-
partments of education" to "formulate the educational policy that
will affect our children," to work with other agencies for funding
purposes, and to work toward ultimate control and operation of
an autonomous Navajo school system. A reorganization of the

Navajo Division of Education marked movement toward the achievement of agency status. In addition, the division became involved in bilingual curriculum development, plans for new school facilities, and implementation of research proposals in special education and fiscal resources. The division also worked for the establishment of a demonstration program for high school dropouts and a school board training program. More significantly, it championed the inauguration of the Navajo Teacher Education Program, a project designed to increase greatly the number of Navajos teaching in the Navajo Nation. All of these programs helped to create the type of transition that MacDonald envisioned.[13]

In the area of economic development as well, MacDonald emphasized the need for Navajo control of Navajo resources and for the development of new skills and economic enterprises. He encouraged training programs, the continued growth of the tribe's Navajo Community College, and a multifaceted approach to economic development—including tribally run enterprises and individual Navajo businesses. His ten-year plan for economic development provided an overview of the direction he believed the Navajo national economy should take. BIA officials had urged Navajos to lease their resources; southwestern metropolitan areas had relied on the ready exploitation of these resources to satisfy their growing energy appetites; officers of extractive industries such as the Peabody Coal Company viewed Navajo resources as a valuable resource to their firms. But now, MacDonald reiterated, previously negotiated leases would have to be reviewed and new leases could no longer be had at bargain basement rates: "It must be clearly understood that it will no longer be accepted practice to sell the reservation off by the ton or by the barrel."[14]

MacDonald moreover looked beyond total reliance on outside companies. The Navajo Nation held its first sale of uranium in April 1971, bringing in nearly a three-million-dollar bonus. Six million dollars came to the tribe solely for exploration rights bought by Exxon in northwestern New Mexico; more significantly, the operation would be underground and not displace people or livestock, or disrupt the land in the manner of the Black Mesa operation. Most important, as MacDonald observed, the development would allow the "Navajo Nation to participate in a joint venture, [as] joint owners in the production and marketing of their resources." The knowledge gained through this undertaking, MacDonald emphasized, could help the Navajos to utilize other resources without outside assistance.[15]

In the critical area of water rights and water usage, MacDonald served notice that the Navajos would aggressively assert their rights to their share of the water. Previously, in 1968, through hope of greater employment opportunities and because of remarkably bad legal counsel, the Navajos had traded in their rights to 34,000 acre feet of upper-basin Colorado River water in exchange for guarantees that a new power plant near Page, Arizona, would be built on tribal land and would employ Navajo workmen. The agreement was based on the assumption that the Navajos, under existing circumstances, could not utilize much water from the Colorado River. Four years later, MacDonald argued along entirely different lines. He contended that Indians must claim water that they could not fully utilize at present in order to safeguard their future: "If we are to retain our culture and remain as a tribal entity on our traditional lands, we must make a rapid transition to a modern agricultural and industrial economy. And to do so, we need our share of the water."[16]

Supported by a tribal council resolution of January 1972, MacDonald forged a working alliance with the AFL-CIO to encourage the development of skilled Navajo workers and to increase the number of Navajos employed on various construction and industrial projects throughout the reservation. The resolution did not specifically mention the union, but it empowered the chairman "to do any and all things necessary, incidental or advisable to accomplish the purposes of this resolution." In actuality, the AFL-CIO set up a training program for Navajo workers. This arrangement eventually met with criticism from both within and outside the Navajo Nation, but according to tribal officials it led to the training of hundreds of Navajo workers per year and the consequent placement of them on reservation jobs, thus significantly decreasing the reservation's unemployment rate.[17]

MacDonald proved a severe critic of the Bureau of Indian Affairs and the general failure of the federal government to uphold its trust responsibilities. He advocated placing the bureau directly under the White House, rather than having it continue in the Department of Interior, where other agencies such as the Bureau of Reclamation had not only conflicting interests, but the upper hand. But even with a change in administrative structure, he doubted bureau officials' ability to alter their attitudes. MacDonald charged that they "regard Indian people and Indian governments much in the way that an overbearing parent regards a recalcitrant child. Instead of encouraging Indian people to become self-sufficient and Indian Tribes to take up new responsibilities the Bureau seems bent on frustrating innovation and stifling initiative." Bureau personnel serving in the Navajo area, he contended, should be able to speak Navajo and understand the changing nature of Navajo culture. MacDonald advocated that the director of the Navajo Area office and agency superintendents serve at the pleasure of the Navajo Tribal Council, and stressed that "the standards for matters requiring Bureau approval of Tribal actions should be both defined and narrowed."[18]

During MacDonald's first term, many Navajos expressed greater interest in county and state political affairs than ever before. MacDonald took an active part in encouraging Navajo voter registration, which soon confronted several counties with strikingly increased Navajo voting power. In Apache County, Arizona, one of three parallel, gerrymandered Arizona counties drawn nearly two hundred miles long and fifty miles wide in order to ensure off-reservation dominance to the southern portions, Navajo voters suddenly outnumbered Anglo voters. When Navajos started gaining county offices, southern residents threatened secession. MacDonald proposed a plan to obtain representation for the Navajo Nation in the Arizona state legislature by providing for an all-Indian legislative district; Navajos, in essence, would elect one state senator and two state representatives. Meanwhile, Navajos voted overwhelmingly for Democrat Raul Castro in the 1974 gubernatorial election, providing him with the margin he needed to eke out a narrow victory. This divergence from a traditional proclivity for the Republicans dismayed such GOP stalwarts as Barry Goldwater, who charged that Navajos were being bought off by the AFL-CIO. MacDonald observed that certain politicians had always taken the Navajo vote for granted and had voiced their appreciation for the Navajo way

of life just so long as the Navajos had been content to play the cen-
terfold role for *Arizona Highways*.[19]

The Navajo people had an opportunity in the 1974 tribal election to express their opinion of MacDonald's efforts to increase
Navajo self-determination. MacDonald sought reelection and
faced the opposition of Raymond Nakai as well as two other
candidates, Charles Toledo and Leo Watchman. Toledo ran as a
representative of the isolated easternmost Navajo area and as a
spokesman for the belief that the Navajo Tribal Council chairman
should be an individual with less formal education and more direct
ties to grass-roots people. Watchman stressed fiscal responsibility,
more authority for local people, and less power for the executive
branch of tribal government. Nakai argued for a return of power
"back to the people, not the Chairman or tribal council." He disagreed with recent tribal involvment in state and county politics,
with tribal efforts to reduce BIA policy-making powers, and with
the ten-year economic plan and general policy of encouraging self-
determination—all of which, he said, would force Navajos into the
Anglo system. He pledged to reduce the powers and salaries of the
council and chairman, the general counsel's salary, and the tribal
budget. MacDonald contended that in his administration the
Navajos had moved from "a state of dependence toward a state of
self-reliance and initiative"; in sum, he said, "we have transformed
our colonial status into an independent nation with greater opportunities for self-sufficiency and independence." Passage by the
tribal council of the largest tribal budget in history—$23.46 million
for fiscal year 1975—fueled the debate about the growing power
and ambition of Navajo national government.[20]

MacDonald easily defeated his challengers in the primary election. Eighty percent of the Navajo electorate turned out to vote in
November 1974 and reelected Peter MacDonald and Wilson
Skeet to a second term, although their percentage of the total vote
declined from the 62 percent achieved in 1970 to 56.5 percent.
On election night, in thanking his supporters, MacDonald offered the following interpretation of the results:

> During the campaign, my opponent argued for Navajo dependency
> on the Bureau of Indian Affairs and an outside development of
> Navajo resources. In a real sense, then, the results of this election are
> a referendum on Navajo dependence or Navajo self-sufficiency

founded upon the treaty of 1868. By your votes, you have resound-
ingly chosen self-sufficiency under the treaty of 1868 and this should
be the mandate of my administration for the next four years.[21]

His inaugural address of January 7, 1975, likewise emphasized
the growing trend of Navajo nationalism:

> The theme of this second administration will be "The Emerging
> Navajo Nation." During these next four years we will continue the
> program we have begun to fully develop the Navajo Nation as an im-
> portant economic, social and political force in the Southwest and in
> the United States. We will improve the daily lives of our people; we
> will improve the education of our young people; we will ease the bur-
> dens of our old people; we will demand, and one way or another, we
> will get, the respect of the United States Government—in particular
> its Bureau of Indian Affairs—as well as the respect of the states which
> border our lands. We will neither be patronized nor insulted. We will
> be treated as human beings, as members of the proud Navajo Tribe,
> and as citizens of the United States.[22]

Unfortunately, MacDonald's second administration fell short
of these lofty expectations, marred by the indictment and conviction of members of his administration. And it was marked by
some major disappointments, including the failure to resolve sat-
isfactorily the Navajo-Hopi land dispute, the inability to design an
acceptable plan of Navajo government reapportionment, and a
decline in certain facets of Navajo economic development.[23]

In retrospect, 1976 and 1977 proved to be long years for Peter
MacDonald and his supporters. In February 1976, Senator Barry
Goldwater demanded that an audit of the fiscal affairs of the
Navajo Tribe be made by the General Accounting Office. A week
later, news surfaced of a federal investigation of the investments
made by the Navajo Housing Authority (NHA). The NHA director, NHA board chairman, and director of the tribe's Office of
Operations were implicated in fiscal irregularities involving the
agency's funds. Two of the men were later cleared of any illegal
involvement; the third resigned and later entered a plea of guilty
to charges of conspiracy to defraud the government in a kickback
scheme involving the alleged misuse of $13.3 million in NHA
funds. Meanwhile, the Navajo Tribal Council voted narrowly in
April 1976 to hire an auditor and two months later unanimously
approved a resolution authorizing a GAO audit of the tribe.[24]

The auditors did not discover further irregularities, but other developments indicated serious divisions within the Navajo political structure. In May 1976, several hundred marchers, calling themselves "Navajo People Concerned for Their Government," assembled at the Navajo Tribal Council chambers to present recommendations for the reform of the tribal government. Opposing a proposed coal lease, other protesters occupied the council during the following August. Several months later, in January 1977, seventeen Navajos attempting to block the approval of an Exxon mining lease took their case to court.[25]

The most serious challenge to MacDonald came in late 1976 and early 1977, when a federal grand jury in Phoenix, investigating alleged financial irregularities and mishandling of federal funds on the Navajo Reservation, subpoenaed him. An eight-count indictment followed, alleging that MacDonald and a former assistant had devised a scheme to defraud the Tucson Gas and Electric Company by submitting false travel invoices while MacDonald and other tribal officials talked to groups protesting the completion of power lines across the reservation.

Rallying to his assistance, the Navajo Tribal Council appropriated seventy thousand dollars for MacDonald's legal defense and passed a formal resolution pledging their support. In addition, by mid-April 1977, 85 of the 102 chapters of the Navajo Nation had passed resolutions in support of the chairman and his legal battle against the indictment. Only one chapter, Shiprock, called for his resignation. MacDonald eventually secured the services of attorney F. Lee Bailey and the trial began on May 10, 1977. After only one week's proceedings, the presiding judge ordered acquittal. Since the jury could not reach a unanimous decision, he decided that the prosecution's evidence was insufficient to prove a guilty verdict. According to one jury member, the jury had voted 8 to 4 for acquittal before announcing itself deadlocked.[26]

MacDonald put the best possible face on the trial, calling it a test of the unity and strength of the Navajo people: "I am happy that when difficulty afflicts us, we still have the strength and determination to prevail over such difficulties." But the months surrounding the trial delayed and hampered the chairman's efforts in critical areas. Plans for the reorganization of tribal government were not implemented. Other vital programs, such as the establishment of a larger private economic sector on the reservation or the creation of a more substantial tax base, failed to make much progress. Meanwhile, a dispute between the Navajos and Hopis over reservations boundaries—a dispute that could not be fully won—also sapped energy from more productive areas. Although the number of Navajos to be relocated and the amount of acreage to be forfeited to the Hopis was significantly reduced in the final settlement, many Navajos still were scheduled to lose their home and their livelihoods.

It is not surprising that some members of MacDonald's administration feared that the chairman, beset by a multitude of problems, would fail in his bid for a third term. In the spring and summer of 1978, many challengers emerged, including the ubiquitous Ramond Nakai and Dr. Taylor McKenzie, a well-known physician. Twelve candidates eventually ran in the August primary. Two former political allies, vice-chairman Wilson Skeet and James Atcitty, entered the contest, but DNA head Peterson Zah decided not to seek office and instead supported Raymond Smith. Despite all of this opposition—or perhaps in part because the multiple candidacies splintered the support for the opponents—MacDonald captured a clear majority of the primary votes. Once again he faced Nakai in the November general election. Although Nakai picked up some support from the other candidates, MacDonald won by about a 3 to 1 margin. For the first time in history, the Navajos had returned a chairman to office for a third term.

It was an impressive achievement, for some of the problems of MacDonald's second term might have ended the career of a less able politician. But by 1977 MacDonald had assumed a position of leadership in another realm of Indian-white relations—the confrontation over natural resources—and his leadership in this crisis undoubtedly contributed to his reelection.

With the energy crisis of the 1970s, the Navajos and other Indian tribes found themselves in a strengthened bargaining position. The Navajo Reservation held substantial natural resources, including coal and uranium. MacDonald hoped to develop these sources of energy in a manner that would prove beneficial to the tribe. But as elected leader of all Navajos, he continued to be caught in the inevitable dilemma: how to work for economic change that will benefit all the people, but which may alter the situation of individual Navajos and disrupt their lives.

MacDonald summed up his position in his State of the Navajo Nation address in 1977:

> The developments in coal and uranium . . . are the first developments that we ever had in which we can truly have a sense of participation. Our laws apply to these developments, not the laws of some state, and for the first time we will receive a fair return, both for our minerals and in terms of obtaining professional employment for the many Navajos who will be able to work on these economic developments. These proposals have been carefully reviewed with respect to their environmental and cultural impacts. . . . The people who are located in the area of the proposed economic development deserve our respect—they deserve our time and attention. Their wishes must be considered and measured against the needs of our Nation as a whole. . . . We have always said in the past that the needs of all of us are greater than the wants of a few of us. I see no reason to change our custom.[27]

MacDonald's determination to assert Navajo control over the reservation's resources resulted from the tribe's unhappy experiences in the past. During the previous two decades the Navajos had been advised that nuclear power soon would make their coal resources obsolete, and they had signed leases which returned relatively little in comparison to the actual value of the mineral mined. Now many looked to the utilization of such resources as a means of reducing unemployment and promoting tribal self-determination. On this issue Peter MacDonald again emerged as a spokesman, serving as chairman of the Council of Energy Resource Tribes (CERT).

A consortium established in 1975, of more than twenty tribes, CERT is attempting to develop Native American mineral resources on terms most favorable to Indians. After the federal government balked at providing assistance to the group, MacDonald encouraged a rumor that CERT would approach OPEC nations for money and advice. Government support surfaced quickly. At the end of 1977, CERT opened its Washington office to oversee Indian energy development. One of the key elements on CERT's program has been the renegotiation of old leases which offered a miserly return. The Navajo Nation, for example, renegotiated a lease with El Paso Natural Gas Company and raised the royalty from a maximum of thirty cents per ton to a minimum of fifty-five cents. Such results augur well for CERT's future and for a fairer return for Native Americans. MacDonald put it this way: "In the past, whenever the Indians were sitting on something the country wanted, the U.S. brought out the legislative cavalry and the judicial cavalry and the bureaucratic cavalry and took it away. That will not happen again."[28]

This kind of determination has made both MacDonald and the Navajo Nation forces to be reckoned with in the American Southwest. And as MacDonald and the Navajos fully realize, it is a fateful time for both the Navajos and other Americans. In 1976 the Navajo Nation exported enough kilowatt hours to meet the energy needs of the state of Arizona for thirty-two years. The Southwest is utterly dependent on these energy resources, and as MacDonald warned a 1977 conference on "The Rise of the Southwest": "There can be no growth without more energy. And there will be no more cheap energy given away by the Indian nations who control such resources until we all can find a way of living together as neighbors with fairness and equity."[29]

Fairness and equity have not been the hallmarks of American policy toward Indians, MacDonald reminded:

> The first conference on growth in this country occurred when the Pilgrims landed in New England and invited the Indians to a conference on growth. Such conferences have been held with great regularity as the nation expanded westward. But we were not normally the luncheon speaker; more often than not, we were cooking the lunch. . . . Every time a coal gasification company like WESCO and El Paso or a uranium company like Kerr-McGee or Exxon or United Nuclear invites me to come talk about growth, I know whose growth they are talking about. And whose resources will fuel that growth.

For growth to continue, he declared, there must be "a cessation of hostilities between the States of Arizona and New Mexico on the one hand and the Navajo Nation on the other" and the acquisition of "the technical assistance, the resources, the staff and the expertise needed to chart our future." If necessary for Navajo survival, he concluded, "we will withhold future growth at any sacrifice."[30]

MacDonald's chairmanship illustrates the new direction of Indian leadership that emerged during the 1960s and '70s. Such leadership approaches traditional Indian problems with political and economic tactics geared to the twentieth century. Indians have always been forced to struggle to protect their land base, and MacDonald's defense of natural resources on the Navajo reserva-

tion lies within this tradition. But his tactics, including the threat of
outside assistance from the OPEC nations, reflects a modern
sophistication often lacking in more traditional leaders. Trained
in the corporate image, he has successfully negotiated with both
federal officials and private industry to increase economic
development on the reservation.

MacDonald's leadership also reflects his broad knowledge of
politics, both on the Navajo reservation and in the state of
Arizona. Through his association with the popular ONEO
programs, MacDonald was able to build a political base to run for
the chairmanship of the tribal council. Once in power, he has
championed a middle-of-the-road policy supported by large
numbers of politically moderate Navajos who want some
economic development of their reservation, but who also wish to
keep that development under tribal control. His administration,
therefore, has undercut both ends of the Navajo political spec-
trum: those who support an unbridled exploitation of tribal
resources and those who want no development at all.

During his three terms in office, MacDonald has extended the
political influence of the Navajo people throughout Arizona and
the greater Southwest. By encouraging his people to participate
in state and local elections, he has forced state officials to be more
receptive to the Navajos' needs. Indeed, under MacDonald's
leadership the Navajos and their reservation resemble a "state
within the states," and like many modern governors, MacDonald
seems determined to protect his "state's" resources.

In addressing a 1977 conference on "The Rise of the
Southwest," the Navajo chairman noted that some of the vast
energy resources contained on Indian lands were necessary for
the development of the region. He warned the conference that
these resources must be utilized under terms acceptable to the
tribesmen. For according to MacDonald, echoing Scott
Momaday, all the Southwest, both Indian and white lands, was
once

> A house made of dawn. It was made of pollen and of rain and the
> land was very old and everlasting. There were many colors on the
> hills, and the plain was bright with different colored clays and sands.
> Red and blue spotted horses grazed in the plain and there was a dark
> wilderness on the mountains beyond. The land was tilled and strong.
> It was beautiful all around.

Peter MacDonald admitted he did not know the fair market value of that house, but he did know "it is the house we must all live in—together."[31]

Notes

1. The safe road to take is to avoid any individual still alive. See, for example, the three-hundred brief biographies in Frederick J. Dockstader, *Great North American Indians* (New York: Van Nostrand Reinhold, 1977).

2. These biographical details of MacDonald's early career are based on material in the *Navajo Times*, the official tribal newspaper, and information provided by the chairman's office, I am indebted to Ada Bluehouse, the chairman's secretary and formerly a neighbor of mine at Navajo Community College, for copies of many of MacDonald's speeches.

3. Evan Roberts, "Early History of ONEO," paper prepared for the ONEO supervisory training workshop, Farmington, New Mexico, March 11, 1974; *Navajo Times*, October 8, 1964, p. 2; December 2, 1965, p. 2.

4. Ibid.; Office of Navajo Economic Opportunity, "A History and Report, June–November, 1967."

5. *Dine Baa-Hani*, April, 1970; *Gallup Independent*, May 5, June 2, June 17, 1970.

6. *Gallup Independent*, August 25, 1970; *Navajo Times*, August 27, 1970, p. 1.

7. *Dine Baa-Hani*, June–July, 1970; *Gallup Independent*, November 9, 1970.

8. *Gallup Independent*, January 7, 1971.

9. Peter MacDonald, inaugural address, January 5, 1971.

10. Anonymous Bureau of Indian Affairs official, personal interview, March 4, 1974.

11. *Gallup Independent*, October 30, 1970.

12. Lawrence Ruzow, taped commentary, November, 1974. I have known Ruzow since 1969. He sent the commentary in response to my request for his perspective on the role being played by his firm as general counsel.

13. Navajo Division of Education, "Strengthening Navajo Education." 1973; Peter MacDonald, "Strengthening Navajo Education," in Navajo Division of Education, "Eleven Programs for Strengthening Navajo Education," December 1973; *Navajo Times*, September 5, 1974, p. C-2.

14. Peter MacDonald, "The Navajos and the National Energy Crunch," reprinted in *Navajo Times*, February 17, 1972, p. 17.

15. *Navajo Times,* January 31, 1974, p. A-1.

16. Peter MacDonald, "Indians Need Their Share, Too," address given at the Colorado River Water Users Association meeting, December 1972.

17. *Navajo Times,* October 23, 1975, p. A-1; October 30, 1975, p. A-12; November 7, 1975, p. A-3; November 27, 1975, p. A-1; December 4, 1975, p. A-2; December 11, 1975, p. A-5; December 1, 1977, p. A-2.

18. Ibid., September 16, 1971, p. 1; January 13, 1972, p. 2; November 30, 1972, p. A-3; September 13, 1973, p. A-1; September 20, 1973, p. A-1.

19. Ibid., March 16, 1972, p. 1; Peter MacDonald interview, "Today" show, January 16, 1975.

20. *Navajo Times,* October 18, 1973, p. A-1; April 18, 1974, p. A-1; June 13, 1974, p. A-1; June 20, 1974, p. A-1; June 27, 1974, p. A-9; July 4, 1974, p. A-1; July 11, 1974, p. A-1.

21. Ibid., November 14, 1974, p. A-4.

22. Peter MacDonald, inaugural address, January 7, 1975.

23. The land dispute between the Navajos and the Hopis focused on a joint-use area that members of both tribes had utilized for nearly a century. Population growth and conflicting land claims forced settlement of the disagreement, with the inevitable result being that some Navajos would have to move elsewhere. Given the long-term associations many Navajo families had with this region and the difficulty of finding available land in another part of the Navajo Nation, the land dispute understandably became an emotional and important tribal political issue.

24. *Navajo Times,* March 4, 1976, p. A-2; April 1, 1976, p. A-1; April 8, 1976, p. A-8; April 15, 1976, p. A-1; June 3, 1976, p. A-1; November 11, 1976; March 10, 1977, pp. A-4, A-10.

25. Ibid., May 20, 1976, p. A-1; August 26, 1976, p. A-1; January 6, 1977, p. A-1.

26. Ibid., November 18, 1976, p. A-1; February 10, 1977, p. A-1; April 7, 1977, p. A-1; April 14, 1977, p. A-3; May 12, 1977, p. A-1; May 19, 1977, p. A-1.

27. Peter MacDonald, "State of the Navajo Nation," February 3, 1977.

28. *Washington Star* article, n.d., reprinted in *Navajo Times,* November 17, 1977, p. A-14; *Business Week* article, December 19, 1977, reprinted in *Navajo Times,* December 29, 1977, p. A-6.

29. Peter MacDonald, "Preconditions for Growth," address given at a conference on "The Rise of the Southwest: Promise and Problems," Phoenix, April 21, 1977.

30. Ibid.

31. Peter MacDonald, "Fair Market Value of the Indian Resources in the Nation's Economy," address given at Southwest Minerals Conference, Albuquerque, November 3, 1977.

The Contributors

R. DAVID EDMUNDS is associate professor of history at Texas Christian University. He has written *The Otoe-Missouria People* (1976) and *The Potawatomis: Keepers of the Fire* (1978), which was awarded the 1978 Francis Parkman Prize. He is currently writing a biography of the Shawnee Prophet.

MICHAEL GREEN is assistant professor of history–Native American studies at Dartmouth College. He has written *The Creeks: A Critical Bibliography* (1979) and *The Politics of Indian Removal: Creek Society in Crisis* (forthcoming). Professor Green is now writing a study of Creek politics in Indian Territory.

WILLIAM T. HAGAN is distinguished professor of history at State University College, Fredonia, New York. Among his many publications are *The Sac and Fox Indians* (1958), *American Indians* (1961), *Indian Police and Judges* (1966), and *United States–Comanche Relations* (1976). Professor Hagan is currently writing a history of the Indian Rights Association.

HERBERT T. HOOVER is professor of history at the University of South Dakota. His publications include *To Be an Indian* (1971), *The Chitimacha People* (1975), and *The Sioux: a Critical Bibliography* (1979). He is now writing a history of the western Sioux.

PETER IVERSON is assistant professor of history at the University of Wyoming. He has taught at Navajo Community College and is the author of *The Navajos: A Critical Bibliography* (1976) and *The Navajo Nation* (forthcoming). Professor Iverson is currently writing a biography of Carlos Montezuma.

CRAIG MINER is professor of history at Wichita State University. Among his publication on American Indian subjects are *The Corporation and the Indian* (1976) and *The End of Indian Kansas* (1978). He is currently writing a history of Wichita, Kansas, as a center of the early cattle trade.

GARY E. MOULTON is associate professor of history and editor of the journals of the Lewis and Clark Expedition at the University of Nebraska–Lincoln. His publications include a biography, *John Ross, Cherokee Chief* (1978) and, more recently, an edition, *The Papers of Chief John Ross* (in press). He is currently preparing a multivolume edition of the Lewis and Clark journals.

JAMES O'DONNELL is professor of history at Marietta College. Among his publications is *The Southern Indians in the American Revolution* (1973). Professor O'Donnell is now writing a history of the role of the northern Indians in the American Revolution.

DONALD WORCESTER is Lorin A. Boswell Professor of History at Texas Christian University. He has published more than a dozen books, including *Forked Tongues and Broken Treaties* (1975) and *The Apaches: Eagles of the Southwest* (1979). He is currently writing a study of the plains Indians during the height of the horse-buffalo culture.

PETER M. WRIGHT is assistant professor of history at Fort Lewis College in Durango, Colorado. He has written numerous articles for scholarly journals and is currently conducting research on the Wind River Shoshones during the reservation period.

MARTIN ZANGER is professor of history at the University of Wisconsin at La Crosse. He has published articles in several scholarly journals and serves as director of the Winnebago Archival Project. Professor Zanger is writing a history of the Winnebago tribe.

Index

Adams, John Quincy: pardons Winnebagos, 81
Adobe Walls, Battle of, 125, 177
AFL–CIO, 232; training programs for Navajos, 231
Alabama Indians, 43
Allen, Alvaren: accompanies Sitting Bull, 164
Allison, Edward, 162
Allison, William B.: attempts to buy Black Hills, 158
Alvord, H. E.: meets with Kiowas, 123
American Indian Magazine: criticized by Montezuma, 214
Amherst, Jeffrey: actions of precipitate Indian revolt, 25
Anadarko, Battle of, 126
Apache County, Arizona: Navajos politically active in, 232
Apache Indians, 206
Apple River: refugee camps on, 74
Arapahoe Indians, xiii; at Treaty of Medicine Lodge Creek, 112; raid Kansas, 116; attacked by Custer, 117; attack Shoshones, 135, 144; at Fort Laramie treaty council (1851), 139–40; at Wind River Reservation, 147–48; cede lands, 149
Arbuckle, Matthew: interferes in Cherokee politics, 98–99
Arikara Indians: trade with Kiowas, 108; at Fort Laramie treaty council (1851), 140
Aroghyiadecker (Nickus Brant), Mohawk, 22
Asatoyet (Gray Leggings), Comanche: dies, 181
Ash Hollow, Battle of, 155
Assapau, Miami: meets with British, 6–7
Assiniboin Indians: at Fort Laramie

treaty council (1851), 140
Atcitty, James, Navajo: candidate for chairmanship, 236
Atkinson, Henry, 64; meets with Sauks and Foxes, 73–74; invades Winnebago homeland, 76
Ato-tain (White Cowbird), Kiowa: receives Satanta's shield, 125
Auchiah, James: reinters Satanta's body, 129
Augur, Christopher: meets with Washakie, 143

Bailey, F. Lee: defends MacDonald, 235
Baldwin, Frank O.: supported by Quanah Parker, 187–88
Bannock Indians, 132, 146; hostile to Americans, 133
Battey, Thomas: defends Satanta, 127
Bazil, Shoshone: attempts farming, 140
Bear Face, Sioux: sells Sioux lands, 166
Bear Hunter, Shoshone: hostile to the United States, 142
Beede, Aaron: describes Sitting Bull, 166–67
Belknap, William: recommends Satanta's imprisonment, 127
Bellestre, Sieur de: attacks Pickawillany, 14
Benally, Ned, Navajo: endorses MacDonald, 226
Bent, William: warns against Indian wars, 109
Big Bow, Kiowa: with Black Kettle, 117
Big Looking Glass, Comanche: opposes Quanah Parker, 185, 188

245

Big Robber, Crow: killed by Washakie, 143

Big Tree, Kiowa, 126; raids Texas, 119; arrested, 120–21; imprisoned, 122–23; surrenders, 127

Billison, Sam, Navajo: candidate for chairmanship, 226

Blackfoot Indians: hostile to Shoshones, 135, 136; attack Flatheads, 136

Black Hawk, Sauk, 65, 82

Black Hills: invaded by whites, 158; Sioux refuse to sell, 158

Black Horse, Kiowa: gives shield to Satanta, 108

Black Kettle, Cheyenne: attacked by Custer, 117

Black Moon, Sioux: meets with De Smet, 157

Bonnin, Gertrude, Sioux, 210; courted by Montezuma, 208–9; marries, 209; praised by Montezuma, 214–15

Bonnin, Raymond, 215; marries, 209

Boudinot, Elias, Cherokee: assassinated, 98

Bowles, William Augustus: leadership of among Creeks, 58–59

Boxer, Winnebago: offers to surrender, 69

Bozeman Trail: established, 155; abandoned, 157

Brant, Catherine Croghan, Mohawk, 25

Brant, Joseph (Thayendenegea), Mohawk, x–ix; described by contemporaries, 21; early life, 22; education, 23; skill as interpreter, 25–26, 36; in England, 26–27; joins Howe's army, 27; at Fort Niagara, 27–28, 29, 32; attacks Mohawk Valley, 28; quarrel with Guy Johnson, 30; visits Ohio tribes, 30–31; attacks American convoy, 31; at Detroit, 32–33; at Grand River Reserve, 34–38; champions acculturation, 36–37; leadership analyzed, 36–38; death, 37

Brant, Margaret, Oneida, 25

Brand, Molly, Mohawk, 22, 29, 33, 36; influence of among Mohawks, 22; withdraws Joseph Brant from school, 23

Brant, Susanna, Mohawk, 25

Brewer, Willis, 41

Bright Journey, 64

British Indian policy, x, 2; treaty with Miamis, 7; refuses to arm Miamis, 16; analyzed, 18; causes Pontiac's revolt, 25; among Creeks, 42

Brotherford, D.A.: accepts Sioux surrender, 162 ·

Brown, George C.: at Treaty of Medicine Lodge Creek, 113

Brown, James S.: missionary among Shoshones, 140

Brown, Vlassis, and Bain, legal firm: appointed by MacDonald, 229

Bryce, Lord, British ambassador: visits Quanah Parker, 186

Buchanan, James: Indian policy of, 141

Budd, H.J.: describes Satanta, 114

Buisson, Marie, Sioux, 163

Bullhead, Sioux: arrests Sitting Bull, 170

Bureau of Indian Affairs, xiii, 93; Montezuma employed by, 208; criticized, 209–10, 212–14, 218, 231–32; tries to close Fort McDowell Reservation, 217; attempts to control ONEO, 223; critical of Navajo aspirations, 228

Burgoyne, John: campaign in American Revolution, 28

Burnett, S. B.: grazes cattle on Indian lands, 181

Burns, Mike, Yavapai: corresponds with Montezuma, 216

Bushyhead, Dennis, Cherokee, xii; evaluated, 192–93, 195–96, 203; early life, 192–93; elected chief, 193; policy toward railroads, 195–97; policy toward grazing leases, 197–98; policy toward oil leases, 198; policy toward tribal membership, 199–200; accepts money for Cherokee Outlet, 201, 203; loses position as chief, 202; as lobbyist, 203; death, 203

Bushyhead, Edward, Cherokee: newspaper editor, 193

Bushyhead, Jesse, Cherokee: on Trail of Tears, 192

Butte des Morts: Indian conference at, 75

Caddo Indians, 119; raided by Kiowas,

116

Caldwell, Billy, Potawatomi: supports the United States, 73

Calhoun, John C., 68; condemns Winnebagos, 67–68; negotiates with Cherokees, 91

Cameahwait, Shoshone: assists Lewis and Clark, 132

Camp Brown: established, 145; renamed Fort Washakie, 147

Candy's Creek Mission: Bushyhead at, 192

Canojohare, Mohawk town, 22, 26

Captain Pipe, Delaware: denounces British, 31–32

Carignan, John: describes Ghost Dance, 168; warns officials, 169

Carleton, James: orders attack upon Kiowas, 110–11

Carlisle Indian school: Montezuma employed at, 208–9

Carson, Kit: attacks Kiowas and Comanches, 111

Carter, R. G.: describes Satanta, 122

Cass, Lewis, 64, 74, 82; organizes defense of the frontier, 72–73; at Buttes des Morts conference, 75–76

Castro, Raul: elected governor of New Mexico, 232

Catch-the-Bear, Sioux: attempts to rescue Sitting Bull, 170

Celoron, Pierre-Joseph, 7, 11; travels to Ohio, 8; at Pickawillany, 8–10; at Detroit, 14

Center, Mohawk, 22–23

Charging Bull, Sioux: urges acculturation, 164; sells Sioux lands, 166

Chattanooga, Tennessee: antecedents, 89

Cherokee Advocate: condemns Bushyhead, 203

Cherokee Indians, xi, xii; meet with Brant, 33; allied with Creeks, 52; acculturation of, 89; establish constitution, 93; court cases, 94–95; on Trail of Tears, 96–97; in Civil War, 100–101; debate tribal citizenship, 199–200

Cherokee Light Horse, 91

Cherokee Nation v. Georgia, 94–95

Cherokee Outlet: grazing leases in, 197–98, 201; sold, 203

Cherokee Phoenix, 92

Cherokee Strip Livestock Association: leases Cherokee lands, 197–98

Cheyenne Indians, xiii; at Treaty of Medicine Lodge Creek, 112; raid Kansas, 116; attacked by Custer, 117; attack Shoshones, 135, 136, 139, 144; hostile to whites, 138; at Fort Laramie treaty council (1851), 139–40; sent to Indian Territory, 147; help defeat Custer, 159

Chicago: fears Indian attack, 74

Chicago Medical College: Montezuma enrolled at, 207

Chickhonsic (Little Buffalo), Winnebago: attacks Americans, 70–71; trial of, 80–81; pardoned, 81

Chippewa Indians: loyal to French, 2; kill French, 5; ask French for peace, 5; meet with Brant, 33; attack Sioux, 69

Choukeka Decora (Spoon Decora), Winnebago: signs treaty, 65

Clark, George Rogers: attacks Shawnee towns, 34

Clark, William: expedition to west, 131

Claus, Daniel, 21, 25, 30, 36

"Code Talkers": Navajos in World War II, 222

Cody, Buffalo Bill: Sitting Bull tours with, 164; at Standing Rock, 169

Coeur, Jean: meets with Old Briton, 11

Collins, Mary: instructs Sitting Bull, 167

Colville Agency: Montezuma employed at, 208

Comanche Indians, xii; allied with Kiowas, 108; attack Texans, 108, 109, 175; oppose Carson, 111; at Treaty of Medicine Lodge Creek, 112–15; at Battle of Anadarko, 126; exiled to Florida, 128; hostile to Utes, 175; political organization of, 175–76, 180–81, 184–85; settle on reservation, 177–78; lands invaded by cattlemen, 181–82; allotment, 186–88

Confederate States: enlist alliance with Indians, 100–101

Connor, Patrick E.: campaigns against Shoshones, 142

Cooley, Dennis, commissioner of Indian affairs: toward Cherokees, 102

Coolidge, Sherman, Arapahoe: corresponds with Montezuma, 212; praised by Montezuma, 214

Cornwallis, Charles: defeated by Americans, 32

Council of Energy Resource Tribes (C.E.R.T.): established, 237; programs, 237–38

Coweta Indians, 43

Cox, Emmett: loses trading license, 188

Crazy Horse, Sioux, ix, 129, 159; surrenders, 147

Creek Indians, xi; meet with Brant, 33; political structure of, 42–43; 45, 48–49, 50–51, 52; population (1832), 43–44, 47; clans, 42, 49, 52; allied with Cherokees, 52; attack white Americans, 52–53

Croghan, George, 6, 25; at Pickawillany, 10, 12; meets with Piankashaws and Weas, 12–13

Crook, George: campaigns against Sioux, 146–47, 159; arrests intruders in Black Hills, 158; negotiates for Sioux lands, 166

Crow Indians: associated with Kiowas, 108; hostile to Shoshones, 135; at Fort Laramie treaty council (1851), 140; make peace with Shoshones, 143; make peace with Sioux, 164

Cusseta Indians, 43; attacked by Georgians, 53

Custer, George A., 125; statement by 107; describes Satanta, 112, 122; attacks Cheyennes, 117; seizes Satanta, 117; expedition into Black Hills, 158; death, 159

Daganett, Charles: organizes Society of American Indians, 211

Damom: in Kiowa class structure, 108

Davidson, John: at Battle of Anadarko, 126

Davis, Edmund J.: commutes Satanta's sentence, 121; advocates Satanta's parole, 123–24

Delaware Indians: meet with Celoron, 8; condemn British, 31–32; meet with Brant, 32–33; among Cherokees, 201

Derleth, August, 64

De Smet, Pierre-Jean: describes Sho-

shones, 136; meets with Sioux, 156–57

Detroit, 3, 16; reinforced by French troops, 5; Iroquois at, 30; Indian councils at, 31, 32–33

Dickens, Charles, Yavapai: corresponds with Montezuma, 216–17

Dickens, George, Yavapai: corresponds with Montezuma, 216–17

Dinebeeina Nahiihna Be Agaditaha (D.N.A.), 227; established among Navajos, 223–25

Dodge, Donald, Navajo: candidate for chairmanship, 226

Dodge, Richard: expedition of to Black Hills, 158

Dodge City: center for cattle drives, 182

Dohausan, Kiowa, 108; death, 111

Doty, James D.: urges action against Winnebagos, 68; presides over trial, 80

Downing, Lewis, Cherokee: opposes Bushyhead, 193

Drum, William E.: orders Sitting Bull's arrest, 169

Drummond Island: British post at, 65

Du Quense, Ange: orders cancellation of Langlade's expedition, 15

Eagle Heart, Kiowa: raids Texas, 119

Eastman, Charles, Sioux: praised by Montezuma, 214

Edmunds, Newton: negotiates with Sioux, 155–56, 165

Edwards, Ninian: accuses Potawatomis, 73; raises volunteers, 74

El Paso Natural Gas Company: leases of with Navajos, 237

Emory, Susanne, Cherokee: marries John Stuart, 192

Eneah Mico, Creek: opposes McGillivray, 49; signs treaty with Georgia, 51–52; joins McGillivray, 53–59

Esahabbe (Milky Way), Comanche, 179, 180; at council, 181

Eschiti, Comanche: attacks Adobe Walls, 177; surrenders, 177; accepts money from Texans, 182; opposes Quanah Parker, 184, 185; opposes allotment, 188

Exxon, Incorporated: mining leases of on Navajo lands, 235

Factionalism, viii–ix, xi–xii; among Creeks, 43, 45, 48, 49, 58–59; among Cherokees, 96, 97–98, 100, 102, 193; among Comanches, 179, 182, 183, 184, 185, 188; in Society of American Indians, 212–14

Fallen Timbers, Battle of, 18

Fechet, Edmund: supports Sitting Bull's arrest, 169–70; describes Sitting Bull, 171

Fetterman, William: killed by Indians, 143, 155

Fever River Region: lead mining in, 68

Fibebountowat, Shoshone, 136

Fitzpatrick, Thomas: meets with Indians, 139

Flathead Indians: attacked by Blackfeet, 136

Forney, Jacob: meets with Washakie, 141

Forsyth, Thomas: meets with Indians, 74

Fort Armstrong: soldiers killed at, 67

Fort Bridger: agency opened at, 141

Fort Buford: attacked by Sioux, 156; Sitting Bull surrenders at, 162

Fort Cobb, 117, 118; Kiowa agency at, 116

Fort Crawford: Winnebagos surrender at, 69; abandoned, 69; Red Bird imprisoned at, 77

Fort Dodge: Kiowas at, 112

Fort Hall: established, 138

Fort Halleck: established, 142

Fort Kearny: established, 138

Fort Laramie: established, 138; treaty councils at, 139–40, 143

Fort McDowell Reservation: established, 216; Montezuma supports, 216–17

Fort Malden, 65

Fort Miami (British), 18

Fort Miamis (French), 3, 10; attacked by Miamis, 5

Fort Niagara, 26, 27, 32

Fort Randall: Sitting Bull detained at, 163

Fort Sill: Indian agency moved from, 181

Fort Snelling: Chippewas kill Sioux at, 69

Fort Stevenson Industrial School: Montezuma employed at, 208

Fort Washakie. See Camp Brown

Fort Yates: Sitting Bull at, 163

Four Horns, Sioux: meets with De Smet, 157

Four Legs, Winnebago: at Butte des Morts conference, 75–76

Fowler, David, 22

French Indian policy, x, 1, 8, 14, 15, 17–18

Frizzlehead, Kiowa: rescues Satanta, 108

Fur Traders, 1, 2; among Miamis, 3, 10–12, 17; among Delawares, 5; among Shawnees, 5, 10; among Shoshones, 135–36

Gagnier, Registre: family attacked by Winnebagos, 71

Galissonière, Marquis de la: orders Celeron expedition, 7–8

Gall, Sioux, 159; surrenders, 147, 162; urges acculturation, 164; sells Sioux lands, 166

General Allotment Act, 165; among Comanches, 186–87

Gentile, Carlos: guardian of Montezuma, 206

Georgia, xi, policy toward Creeks, 46, 51–52, 53; offers bribes to McGillivray, 53; seizes Cherokee property, 94; court cases, 94–95

German Flats, N.Y.: attacked by Indians, 28

Ghost Dance, x; among Sioux, 167–68

Gibbon, John: campaigns against Sioux, 159

Girty, Simon: assists Brant, 30–31

Gist, Christopher, 6

Goldwater, Barry: criticizes Navajo political activism, 232; demands audit of Navajo tribal funds, 234

Goodnight, Charles: gives Quanah Parker cattle, 183

Gordon, Philip: praised by Montezuma, 214

Goree, Thomas: describes Satanta, 128

Graham, Duncan, 71

Grand River Reserve, xi; established, 34

Grant, Ulysses: Indian policy of, 118, 126, 128; gifts to Washakie, 147

Graymont, Barbara, 21

"Great Beloved Man." See McGillivray,

Alexander; Creek Indians, political structure of
Great Sioux Reservation: established, 157; divided, 160
Green Bay, 72; organized for defense, 74
Gros Ventre Indians: at Fort Laramie treaty council (1851), 140

Hagan, William T., 21
Haldimand, Frederick, 36; assures Brant of British assistance, 29; assigns Iroquois lands in Canada, 33–34
Hamilton, James, 6; sends gifts to Indians, 12; warned of French expedition, 16
Hancock, Winfield Scott: meets with Kiowas, 112
Hans, Fred, 162
Hare, De Witt: praised by Montezuma, 214
Harney, William: at Treaty of Medicine Lodge Creek, 113; at Battle of Ash Hollow, 155
Hazen, W. B.: warns Kiowas, 116–17; replaced, 118
Head of Coosa: founded, 92; occupied by Georgians, 94
Heddrich, Gus, 162
Henderson, John B.: at Treaty of Medicine Lodge Creek, 113
Henihas. See Creek Indians, political structure of
Herkimer, Nicholas: meets with Brant, 28
Hicks, Charles, Cherokee, 91
Hoag, Enoch: negotiates with Kiowas, 124; urges clemency for Satanta, 127–28
Hoboithle Mico, Creek: opposes McGillivray, 49, 59; signs treaty with Georgia, 51–52; property of destroyed by McGillivray, 52
Hopi Indians: land dispute with Navajos, 226, 234, 236
Horse Back, Comanche, 180; signs Treaty of Medicine Lodge Creek, 179
Howe, William, 27
Howeah (Gap in the Woods), Comanche: signs Treaty of Medicine Lodge Creek, 179; at council, 181

Hoyt, John M.: meets with Washakie, 148
Hubbard, Gurdon S.: raises volunteers for Chicago, 74
Hughes Aircraft: MacDonald employed at, 222
Hunt, P. B., 179
Huron Indians: move to Sandusky, 2; revolt against French, 5; support British in American Revolution, 30; meet with Brant, 33

Illinois Indians: oppose French, 15
Indian Rights Association, 214; opposes allotment of Comanche reservation, 188
Ingalls, George W.: guardian of Montezuma, 207
Inkatushepoh, Shoshone, 136
Iron Mountain, Comanche: signs Treaty of Medicine Lodge Creek, 179; death, 181

Jackson, Andrew: elected president, 93; advocates Indian removal, 93–94; ignores Supreme Court, 95
Jerome Commission: urges allotment, 186–87
Jesuits: among Indians, 1
Johnson, Andrew, 102; Indian policy of, 143
Johnson, Guy, 25; appointed superintendent of British Indian affairs, 25; in England, 26–27; at Niagara, 29; accused of fraud, 30; dismissed, 32
Johnson, Sir John: appointed superintendent, 32; visits Detroit, 32
Johnson, Sir William, 32; influence of among Mohawks, 22; death, 25; idolized by Brant, 35–37
Johnston, Albert Sidney: campaign into Utah, 141
Joseph, Chief, Nez Percé, 82
Josephy, Alvin M., ix

Kaan: in Kiowa class system, 108
Kansas: Cherokee refugees in, 101
Kansas and Arkansas Railroad: builds on Cherokee lands, 196
Keiso, David, 196
Keller, Mary: marries Montezuma, 209

Kenoka Decora (Old Decora), Winnebago, 76; statement by, 64; leader in War of 1812, 65
Keokuk, Fox: meets with Atkinson, 73
Kickapoo Indians, 11
Kicking Bear, Sioux: in Ghost Dance, 167
Kicking Bird, Kiowa: advocates peace, 111, 112; death, 128
King Phillip, Wampanoag, vii, ix
Kiowa-Apache Indians: at Treaty of Medicine Lodge Creek, 112;
Kiowa Indians: raid Spanish, 107, 108; class structure among, 107–8; early history of, 108; attack Texans, 109, 116, 119, 120; oppose Carson, 111; at Treaty of Medicine Lodge Creek, 112–15; accept reservation, 116; raid Wichitas and Caddos, 116; flee Fort Cobb, 117–18; want Satanta freed, 123; exiled to Florida, 128; lands invaded by cattlemen, 181–82
Kirkland, Samuel: taught by Brant, 23
Knox, Henry: negotiates Treaty of New York, 55
Koasati Indians, 43
Konaya, Shoshone: attacks Cheyennes, 147
Kuzow, Lawrence: serves as Navajo tribal attorney, 229

La Flesche, Rosa, Omaha: helps organize Society of American Indians, 211
Lancaster, Pa.: conference at, 6–7
Lander, Frederick: establishes trail, 141
Langlade, Charles, Ottawa: attacks Pickawillany, 15–16
Lanham, S. W. T.: prosecutes Satanta, 121
La Pied Froid, Miami: warns French, 11
Leavenworth, Henry, 67
Le Comte, Wea, 11
Le Gare, Jean Louis, 162
Leonard, William Ellery, 64
Lewis, Meriwether: describes Kiowas, 108; meets Shoshones, 131
Lincoln, Abraham: Indian policy of, 101
Lipcap, Solomon: killed by Winnebagos, 71

Littel, Norman: dismissed by Navajos, 228–29
Little Tallassee, 42
Lochery, Alexander: defeated by Brant, 31
Lockwood, James, 71
Logstown, Pa., 13; visited by Celoron, 8
Lone Wolf, Kiowa, 124, 127; rescues Satanta, 108; becomes chief, 111; refuses to make peace, 111; seized by Custer, 117; released, 118; raids Texas, 125; at Battle of Anadarko, 126; opposes acculturation, 188
Long, Stephen H.: meets with Kiowas, 108

McCusker, Philip, 118
MacDonald, Peter, Navajo, xiii–xiv; evaluated, 221, 238–40; early life, 221–22; as "Code Talker," 222; formal education, 222; appointed director of ONEO, 223; resigns from ONEO, 225; elected tribal chairman, 227, 233, 236; appoints legal firm, 229; establishes educational programs, 229–30; economic programs of, 230–32, 237–38; criticizes BIA, 231–32; advocates political action, 232–33; cleared of charges, 235
McGillivray, Alexander, Creek, xi, xii; described by contemporaries, 41; early life, 42; as British agent, 42–43, 45; negotiates with Spanish, 46–47, 48; as Spanish agent, 51; negotiates with United States, 54–55; appointed brigadier general, 56; death, 60
McIntosh, William, Creek: offers bribe, 91
McKee, Alexander, 33
McKenney, Thomas, 74, 80, 82; statement by, 64; at Butte des Morts conference, 75–76; at Red Bird's surrender, 77; negotiates with Cherokees, 91
McKenzie, Fayette: helps organize Society of American Indians, 211
Mackenzie, Ranald S.: trails Indians, 120; attacks Cheyennes, 147; contacts Parker family, 179
McKenzie, Taylor, Navajo: candidate for chairmanship, 236

McLaughlin, James, 163, 171; appointed agent at Standing Rock, 163; urges acculturation, 165–66; opposes Ghost Dance, 168–70; orders Sitting Bull's arrest, 170

Mad Bear, Sioux: urges acculturation, 164

Mahnaatapakah, Winnebago: indicted for murder, 69; released, 81

Mamante, Kiowa, 127; visions, 119, 128

Mandan Indians: trade with Kiowas, 108; Lewis and Clark among, 131

Mandeville, "Saucy Jack": fights Winnebagos, 72

Mannypenny, George: meets with Sioux, 159–60

Marsh, John: meets with Indians, 72

Marshall, John, 95

Mascouten Indians, 11

Mayes, Joel, Cherokee: elected chief, 202

Menominee Indians: support government against Winnebagos, 72, 75

Methode family: murder of, 68, 69

Miami Indians, x; conspire against French, 2; protect French prisoners, 5; sign treaty with British, 7; attacked by Langlade, 16; abandon Pickawillany, 17. See also Old Briton

Michilimackinac, 3, 5

Micos. See Creeks, political structure of

Miles, Nelson: campaigns against Sioux, 159; meets with Sitting Bull, 160

Mingo Indians: meet with Brant, 33

Miro, Estevan, 48

Missouri, Kansas and Texas Railroad: builds on Cherokee lands, 196

Mixed-bloods, xi, 41; among Cherokees, 88, 199–201; among Comanches, 176, 181, 183

Mohave-Apache Indians. See Yavapai Indians

Mohawk Indians, x, 22; flee homes, 28; assist British, 28; move to Canada, 34. See also Brant, Joseph

Mohican Indians: meet with Celoron, 8

Montezuma, Carlos, Yavapai, xiii; evaluated, 206, 217–18; early life, 206–7; resigns from BIA, 208; friendship with Pratt, 208–9; criticizes BIA, 209–10, 212–14, 218; organizes Society of American Indians, 210–11; criticizes Arthur Parker, 214; illness, 215–16, 217; defends Fort McDowell Reservation, 216–17; death, 217

Montour, Andrew, Seneca: serves as interpreter, 6

Moor's Charity School, 22

Morgan, Thomas Jefferson, 208

Morgan, Willoughby: accepts Winnebago prisoners, 69

Mormons: establish Salt Lake City, 138; missionaries among Shoshones, 140–41; forced to accept government hegemony, 141

Mott, Harold: serves as Navajo tribal attorney, 229

Mowaway (Shaking Hand), Comanche: imprisoned, 177; abdicates leadership, 181

Mowoomhah, Shoshone: death, 136

Nakai, Raymond, Navajo: candidate for office, 225–27, 233, 236; appoints tribal attorney, 229

Native American Church. See Peyote

Navajo Community College, 229–30

Navajo Division of Education: established, 229, programs, 229–30

Navajo Housing Authority: fiscal irregularities in, 234

Navajo Indians, xiii–xiv; in World War II, 222; economic development among, 223, 230–32; political structure of, 223, 225–27; educational programs, 229–30; in state politics, 232–33; land dispute with Hopis, 226, 234–36

Navajo Teacher Education Program: established, 230

Nawkaw Caramani, Winnebago: at Red Bird's surrender, 77

Negyes, Mohawk, 22–23

Neill, Thomas: ordered to arrest Satanta, 126–27

New Echota: Cherokee capital established at, 92

New York Herald: reports on grazing leases, 198

Nicolas, Huron: revolts against French, 3–4; revolt fails, 5

No Neck, Sioux: meets with De Smet, 157

Nootka Sound crisis, 57

Occum, Samson: visits Mohawks, 22
Oconee River Region, 59; ceded by Creeks, 56
Odegupa: in Kiowa class structure, 108
Office of Navajo Economic Opportunity (ONEO), 239; MacDonald appointed director of, 223; programs, 223–25
O. H. Perry (keelboat): attacked by Winnebagos, 71–72
Ojibway Indians. *See* Chippewa Indians
Okefenokee Swamp: ceded to the United States, 56
Old Briton (La Demoiselle), x; conspires against French, 2–3, 7, 11, 15; attacks Fort Miamis, 5; moves to Pickawillany, 5; meets with Celoron, 8–10; meets with Jean Coeur, 11; denounces Ottawas, 13; killed by Langlade, 17; leadership analyzed, 17–18
Old Settlers (Western Cherokees), 89; oppose Cherokee emigrants, 97–100
Ondes: in Kiowa class structure, 107–8
Oneida Indians, 25; at Detroit, 32
Onondaga Indians, 23, 25
Osage Indians: conspire against French, 15
Oswego, 32; British traders at, 16
Ottawa Indians: loyal to French, 2; at Pickawillany, 12–13, 16–17; refuse to join French expedition, 14; join Langlade, 16; meet with Brant, 33

Padashawaunda, Shoshone: death, 136
Page, John H.: visits Satanta, 112
Paiute Indians, 132
Panton, Leslie and Company, 51, 57; established, 48; competes with William Bowles, 58; store raided by Bowles, 59
Panton, William, 57
Paracoom (He Bear), Comanche: death, 181
Parker, Arthur C., Seneca: corresponds with Montezuma, 212; quarrels with Montezuma, 214
Parker, Cynthia Ann, 175; recaptured, 176; death, 179; awarded land, 179

Parker, Quanah, Comanche, xii; funeral, 175; early life, 176; emerges as chief, 177–80; accepts money from Texans, 182; visits Washington, 183, 185; appointed judge, 184; appointed chief, 184; cooperates with government, 185; builds house, 185; meets Theodore Roosevelt, 185; leader in peyote cult, 186; removed from bench, 188; influence declines, 189; death, 189; evaluated, 189
Park Hill Academy, 192
Pasego, Shoshone: death, 136
Pashego, Bannock: hostile to the United States, 142
Pathkiller, Cherokee, 91
Patriarch Crow, Sioux: surrenders, 162
Patriot Chiefs, The, ix
Payne, David: intrudes upon Cherokee lands, 200
Peabody Coal Company: leases with Navajos, 230
Permansu (Comanche Jack), Comanche: accepts money from Texans, 182; denounced by other Comanches, 183
Peta Nocona, Comanche, 175
Peyote: among Comanches, 186; among Navajos, 225, 226, 227
Phillips, William A.: attorney for Cherokees, 201–2
Piankashaw Indians, 2; at Pickawillany, 11, 12; suffer epidemic, 11; sign treaty with British, 13; attack French, 15; treaty rejected by British, 16
Pickawillany: established in 1747, 5; Celoron at, 8–10; Croghan at, 10–11; attacked by French, 14, 16; abandoned by Miamis, 17
Pike, Albert: advocates Confederate alliance, 100–101
Pima Indians: capture Montezuma, 206; at Salt River Reservation, 216
Pocahantas, vii
Polk, James: policy toward Cherokees, 100
Pontiac, Ottawa, ix, 23, 25, 171
Pope, John: orders Satanta's arrest, 127
Potawatomi Indians, 11, 15; at Pickawillany, 11, 16–17; refuse to join

French expedition, 14; join Lang-lade, 16; meet with Brant, 33; ac-cused of attacks, 73; support United States, 73

Prairie du Chien: Winnebagos sur-render at, 68; Indians attack, 70–71, 72; organized for defense, 74; treaty at, 81

Prairie Fire, Comanche: death, 181

Pratt, Richard: quarrels with BIA, 208; discourages Indian organizations, 210–11

Quakers (Society of Friends): influ-ence British Indian policy, 16

Rabbit Bunch, Cherokee: defeated in Cherokee election, 202

Red Bird, Winnebago, xiv; attacks white Americans, 70–72, surren-ders, 76–77; imprisoned at Fort Crawford, 77–78; death, 80; lead-ership analyzed, 82

Red Cloud, Sioux, 129

Red Food, Comanche: at Battle of Anadarko, 126; dies, 181

Red Tipi, Kiowa, 107; pleads for Sa-tanta's release, 124

Red Tomahawk, Sioux: arrests Sitting Bull, 170

Ridge, John, Cherokee: advocates removal, 96; assassinated, 98

Ridge, Major, Cherokee: advocates removal, 96; assassinated, 98

Rock Landing, Ga.: American trading post at, 58

Roe Cloud, Henry: praised by Mon-tezuma, 214

Romney, George: paints Brant's por-trait, 26

Ross, Daniel, 89

Ross, John, Cherokee, xi; early life, 88–89; negotiates treaty, 91; elected president of National Council, 91; elected principal chief, 93; flees Georgia, 94; opposes Treaty of New Echota, 96–97; organizes removal, 97; joins Confederacy, 101; pro-Union, 101; negotiates peace treaty, 102–3; death, 103; leadership an-alyzed, 103–4

Russell, Osborne: describes Washakie, 136

Sagayeeanquarashtow, Mohawk, 22

Salt River Reservation, 216–17

Saragaunt, Shoshone: attacks Chey-ennes, 147

Sasterassee, Huron: meets with Brit-ish, 30

Satank, Kiowa: refuses to make peace, 111; arrested, 120–21; death, 121

Satanta (White Bear), Kiowa, ix–x; raids Mexico, 108; becomes chief, 108; raids Texas, 109, 111, 112, 119, 120; at Fort Larned, 109, 112, 113; opposes Carson, 111; refuses to make peace, 111; at Fort Dodge, 112; at Treaty of Medicine Lodge Creek, 112–15; captured by Custer, 117; released, 118; meets with commissioners, 119; arrested, 120–21; imprisoned, 122–23; re-leased, 124; surrenders, 127; death, 129

Sauk and Fox Indians: meet with Cass, 73; meet with Atkinson, 73–74; confer with Forsyth, 74

Schermerhorn, John: removes Cher-okees, 95–96

Scott, Winfield: removes Cherokees, 96–97

Sells, Cato, commissioner of Indian affairs: attempts to close Fort Mc-Dowell Reservation, 217

Seneca Indians: urge Hurons to revolt, 3; intercede with British for Miamis, 6

Shabbona, Potawatomi: spies for Americans, 73

Sharp, Byron: attempts to move Yavapais to Salt River, 217

Sharp Nose, Arapaho: cedes lands, 149

Shavehead, Sioux: arrests Sitting Bull, 170

Shawnee Indians, 5, 10; intercede with British for Miamis, 6; meet with Celeron, 8; plan war against French, 15; attacked by Clark, 31; meet with Brant, 33; among Cherokees, 201

Shawnee Prophet, xiv; Winnebagos follow, 65

Sheridan, Phillip H.: campaigns against Indians, 116–17; seizes Sa-tanta, 117; wants buffalo extermi-nated, 125; recommends Satanta's arrest, 127

Sherman, William T., 115, 117, 122, 163; at Fort Sill, 119–21; orders Kiowas arrested, 121; wants Indians restricted, 125

Short Bull, Sioux: participates in Ghost Dance, 167

Shoshoko Indians, 135

Shoshone Indians, xii–xiii; meet Lewis, 131; traditional culture, 132–35; at rendezvous, 135–36; at Fort Laramie treaty council (1851), 139–40; hostile to United States, 142; make peace with Crows, 143; move to Wind River, 145; attack Sioux, 146–47; campaign with Crook, 147; cede lands, 145, 149

Sibley, Henry Hastings: campaigns against Sioux, 155

Simcoe, John Graves, 36

Sioux Indians, x, xiii; attacked by Chippewas, 69; agitate Winnebagos, 70; refuse to join Red Bird, 72; hostile to Kiowas, 108; war with Shoshones, 135, 136, 144; hostile to whites, 138, 143, 154–55, 159; at Fort Laramie treaty council (1851), 139–40; at Fort Laramie treaty council (1868), 143; refuse to sell Black Hills, 158; defeat Custer, 159; in Canada, 160–62; acculturating, 164–65; cede lands, 165; participate in Ghost Dance, 168

Sitting Bull, Sioux, ix–x; flees to Canada, 147, 160–62; early life, 152–53; attacks Fort Buford, 156; defeats Custer, 159; at Slim Buttes, 159–60; refuses surrender, 160; surrenders, 162–63; at Fort Randall, 163; tours the United States and Canada, 164; meets with Crows, 164; opposes acculturation, 165–66; accepts Ghost Dance, 167; death, 170

Skeet, Wilson, Navajo: candidate for office, 226, 233, 236

Skenandon, Oneida, 25

Sloan, Tom, Omaha: elected president of Society of American Indians, 215

Smith, Edward: negotiates with Kiowas, 124; urges clemency for Satanta, 127

Smith, Samuel, Cherokee: appointed assistant chief, 202

Snelling, Josiah: seizes Winnebago

hostages, 74

Society of American Indians: established, 211; conventions, 212–13; factions in, 212; advocates abolition of BIA, 214

Soward, Charles: tries Satanta, 121

Spanish Indian policy, ix; toward Creeks, 46, 48, 53

Springfield, N.Y.: attacked by Indians, 28

Standing Rock Agency, x; Sitting Bull at, 163–70

Stanley, Henry: at Treaty of Medicine Lodge Creek, 113

Stokes, Montfort, 98–99

Stone, William, 21

Street, Joseph, 80

Strike-the-Kettle, Sioux: tries to rescue Sitting Bull, 170

Strong Hearts: led by Sitting Bull, 153–54; attack whites, 156

Stuart, John, 37; captured by Cherokees, 192

Stumbling Bear, Kiowa: advocates peace, 111, 112

Sullivan, John: attacks Iroquois homeland, 29

Sully, Alfred: campaign against Sioux, 155

Tabanaka (Hears the Sun), Comanche, 180; denounces Quanah Parker, 183

Tahlequah, Oklahoma: Cherokee capital at, 101, 202

Tatum, Lawrie: appointed Indian agent, 118; questions Satanta, 120

Tecumseh, Shawnee, ix, 18, 82, 171; Winnebagos follow, 65

Ten Bears, Comanche: at Treaty of Medicine Lodge Creek, 114

Tennessee: attacked by Indians, 52; attempts to bribe McGillivray, 53

Terry, Alfred: campaigns against Sioux, 146–47, 159; meets with Sitting Bull, 161

Texas, xii; citizens invade Indian lands, 109; raided by Indians, 109, 116, 119, 120

Thames, Battle of: Winnebagos at, 65

Thompson, Charles, Cherokee: policy toward railroads, 195

Thompson, David, 164

Throckmorton, J.W.: describes Quanah Parker, 183

Tice, Gilbert, 26, 27

Tilghman, Tench, 22

Toledo, Charles, Navajo: candidate for chairmanship, 233

Toshaway (Silver Brooch), Comanche, 177, 180; at Treaty of Medicine Lodge Creek, 179

"Trail of Tears": Cherokees on, 96–97

Treaty of Fort Bridger, 144

Treaty of Fort Laramie: 1851, 139–40; 1868, 143, 157

Treaty of Medicine Lodge Creek, 112–15, evaluated, 115; and allotment, 186

Treaty of New Echota: signed, 96; opposed by Cherokees, 96–97

Treaty of New York, 55–57

Treaty of Pensacola, 47–48, 55

Treaty of Paris, 45

Tribal structure, vii–ix. See also individual tribes

Tuckabatchee Indians, 43

Tucson Gas and Electric Company, 235

Turck, Fenton: employs Montezuma, 209

Tyler, John: policy of toward Cherokees, 99–100; appoints Brigham Young Indian agent, 140

University of Illinois: Montezuma enrolled at, 207

Utah: organized as territory, 140

Ute Indians, 132, 146; trade with Mormons, 138; at Fort Laramie treaty council (1851), 139–40

Vestal, Stanley: describes Sitting Bull, 152

Village chiefs, viii; among Comanches, 176

Vlassis, George: serves as Navajo tribal attorney, 229

Wabalah, Fox: meets with Atkinson, 73

Wabasha, Sioux: opposes Sioux militancy, 70

Wabokieshek (Winnebago Prophet), Winnebago: meets with Forsyth, 74

Waggoner, Daniel: grazes cattle on Indian lands, 181

War chiefs, viii–ix; among Comanches, 176. See also individual tribes, political structure

Washakie, Shoshone, xii–xiii; early life, 136–37; becomes chief, 136–37; befriends white Americans, 138; fights with Cheyennes, 139, 146; at Fort Laramie treaty council (1851), 139–40; ties with Mormons, 140–41; signs peace treaty, 142; kills Crow chief, 143; signs Treaty of Fort Bridger, 144; moves to Wind River, 145; attacks Sioux, 146; attacks Arapahoes, 146; protests government policies, 148; cedes lands, 149; analysis of leadership, 150; death, 150

Washington, George: orders campaign against Iroquois, 29; negotiates with Creeks, 55

Wassaja; xiii; founded by Montezuma, 212; critical of BIA, 212–14; critical of Society of American Indians, 215

Watchman, Leo, Navajo: candidate for chairmanship, 233

Watie, Stand, Cherokee: opposes Ross, 99; joins Confederacy, 100; negotiates peace agreement, 102–3

Watson, Joe, Navajo: candidate for chairmanship, 226

Waukookah, Winnebago: indicted for murder, 69; released, 81

Wea Indians: insulted by French, 11; at Pickawillany, 11, 12; sign treaty with British, 13; refuse French demands, 15; treaty rejected by British, 16

Wekau (The Sun), Winnebago: attacks white Americans, 70–71; surrenders, 76–77; trial of, 80–81; pardoned, 81

West, Benjamin, 26

Western Shoshone Agency, 208

Wheelock, Eleazar, 21; at Moor's Charity School, 22

White Wolf, Comanche: denounces Quanah Parker, 183, 185

Wichita Indians, 119; raided by Kiowas, 116

Winnebago Indians, xiv; in War of 1812, 65; visit British, 65; kill soldiers near Fort Armstrong, 67; conception of justice, 67, 76, 77–79,

81–82; accused of Methode murders, 68; abused by whites, 70, 79; attack settlements, 70–71; attack keelboats, 71–72; at Butte des Morts conference, 75–76; agree to white occupancy of lands, 77; unrest among, 79; sign treaty, 81

Winnebago Prophet. *See* Wabokieshek

Wirt, William: sympathetic to Cherokees, 94

Worcester v. *Georgia,* 95

Wounded Knee: massacre at, 171

Wovoka, Paiute, xiv, 167

Yarnall, Nelson: describes Washakie, 138

Yavapai Indians, xiii, 206; at Fort McDowell Reservation, 215 18; refuse to move to Salt River, 218

Young, Brigham, 138; policy of toward Shoshones, 140–41

Zah, Henry, Navajo, 226

Zit-Kala-Sa. *See* Bonnin, Gertrude